The Dead Sea Psalms Scroll

Cave 11 at Qumran. In this cave the Dead Sea Psalms Scroll was found. The photograph, taken from inside the cave looking east, shows the north end of the Dead Sea in the background. (Copyright by the Palestine Archaeological Museum, Jerusalem, Jordan; reproduced by permission.)

The
Dead Sea Psalms
Scroll

by J. A. SANDERS

Professor of Old Testament
Union Theological Seminary

Adjunct Professor of Religion
Columbia University

Cornell University Press

ITHACA, NEW YORK

Copyright © 1967 by Cornell University

Cornell University Press

First published 1967

The Hebrew text of Part II and the translations of the apocrypha of Part III are copyrighted 1965 by Oxford University Press. The scripture quotations from the *Revised Standard Version of the Bible* are copyrighted 1946 and 1952 by the Division of Christian Education of the National Council of Churches and used by permission.

Library of Congress Catalog Card Number: 66–15765

PRINTED AND BOUND IN THE UNITED STATES OF AMERICA
BY THE MAPLE PRESS COMPANY

For Dora

" She came to me in her beauty. . . . "
(11QPs[a] Sirach 2)

PREFACE

THE Elizabeth Hay Bechtel Psalms Scroll from Qumran Cave 11 is the handsomest and best preserved of all the Dead Sea Scrolls discovered since the large scrolls of Cave 1 were unearthed nearly twenty years ago. Because of its radical departure from any recension of the biblical Psalter heretofore known, it is perhaps the most interesting and intriguing ancient biblical scroll ever discovered.

This edition of the scroll is designed to make available to all students of the Psalter the treasures of this fabulous find. Part I tells the story of the scroll both since its discovery in modern times and before it was last rolled up in antiquity, and also discusses the excitingly odd order, contents, and variants of the scroll. Part II presents the scroll text and English translation on facing pages, line by line and column by column, just as the Hebrew appears on the ancient leather. Part III clarifies and explains the eight apocryphal compositions in the scroll and includes all the varying translations to date of the most intriguing of them, Psalm 151. Appendix I offers new translations, from medieval Syriac, of the apocryphal Psalms 152 and 153, which are not in the extant scroll but may nonetheless have been known at Qumran, since Psalms 151, 154, and 155 are in the scroll. Appendix II lists all the most ancient Hebrew manuscripts of the Psalter with their contents catalogued and indexed. Appendix III provides an up-to-date bibliography on the earliest Hebrew Psalter texts. And in order to provide even the youngest or most cursory readers with valid impressions, a foldout facsimile of the Psalms Scroll is attached.

This book appears one year after the critical edition of the scroll, *Discoveries in the Judaean Desert of Jordan*, Volume IV, published by Clarendon Press, of Oxford. The Oxford edition contains collotype plates of full-size infrared photographs of each column of the scroll, as well as orthographic and palaeographic essays, a critical apparatus to the text, text-critical notes to the apocryphal compositions, and an exhaustive index to the Hebrew text. The present edition, which is intended for laymen and students, is based on the more technical Oxford volume, which was expressly prepared for scholars. The critical notes in the two editions differ accordingly.

In the preface to the Oxford edition I attempted to mention the names of all those who had a part, no matter how important or how remote it might have been, in the process of bringing that volume to light. By all rights they should all be signaled here as well, for without any one of them this volume might also have been impossible. But among them I am delighted and pleased to single out Monsignor Patrick W. Skehan, of the Catholic University of America, who is editing all the psalms fragments from Cave 4, who read this typescript in the making and offered invaluable suggestions; and Professor Frank M. Cross, Jr., of Harvard University, who as mentor, friend, and colleague has constantly made himself available for critical help and encouragement. Whatever herein is of good issue is surely due to their wisdom and generosity; whatever is tenuous or erroneous is my responsibility alone.

The idea of this edition of the Psalms Scroll is a result of the vision, imagination, and interest of Elizabeth Hay Bechtel, for whom the scroll is named and to whom all students of the Psalter and of the Dead Sea Scroll literature owe an enduring debt of gratitude. Mrs. Bechtel, who provided the funds necessary for purchase and study of the scroll, has since the beginning of her interest in it urged that there be "a popular, American edition" of the scroll, to be designed for all readers rather than for scholars only. Mrs. Bechtel's wish in this regard has been a command that it has been an inspiration to attempt to fulfill.

New York
November 1965

J. A. S

Postscriptum

SOMETIME after this manuscript had gone to the publisher a fifth fragment belonging to the Psalms Scroll came to light under unusual circumstances. It was immediately apparent that every effort should be expended to include it in this volume since it is, of necessity, lacking in the Oxford edition. Hence, the full story and text of Fragment E are told in the "Postscriptum" which precedes the general index at the end of the book.

July 1966   J. A. S.

CONTENTS

Indexes

ILLUSTRATIONS

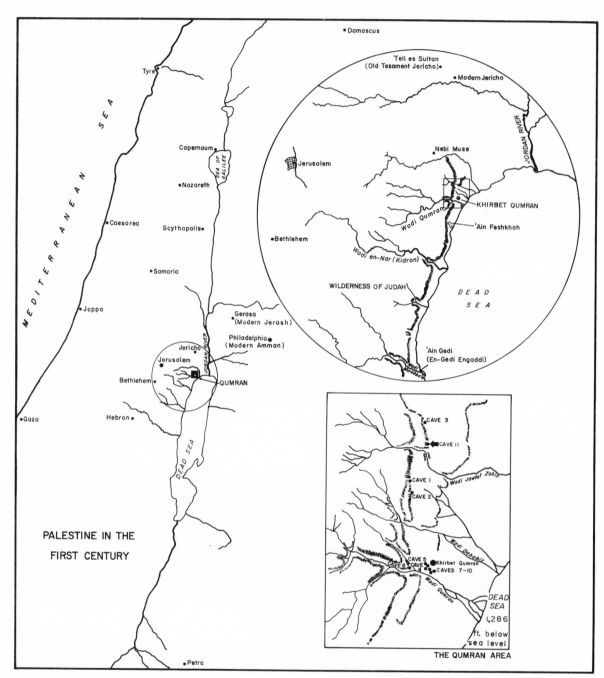

Map of the Dead Sea area. The Dead Sea Scrolls owe their name to the fact that they were found in caves along the northwest shore of the Dead Sea. The aridity of this region made possible the preservation of the scrolls and other organic material such as papyrus and linen. This barren and inhospitable region, known in biblical times as "the wilderness of Judah," has never been heavily populated and is now inhabited only by Bedouin.

PART I

The Scroll

THE STORY

Discovery and Unrolling

THE Psalms Scroll was discovered ten years ago in early February 1956 by Arab Bedouin of the same tribe that almost a decade earlier, in the spring of 1947, had discovered the first of the Dead Sea Scrolls. Cave 11, in which the Psalms Scroll was found, is located a short walk north of Cave 1, where the first discovery had been made. Cave 11, which also contained other manuscripts and materials, is so far the last of the caves near the Wadi Qumran—along the northwest shore wastes of the Dead Sea—to be found secluding ancient texts.[1]

The eleven caves in the area are believed by most scholars to be related to the complex of buildings excavated near the Wadi in five archaeological campaigns between December 1951 and March 1956.[2] Although no manuscripts were found in the buildings uncovered, there can be little doubt that the scrolls in the nearby caves had once formed a part of the library of the sect that occupied the buildings.[3] Ancient plaster materials, which probably were part of scribal furniture,[4] and ceramic and metallic inkwells found among the hellenistic-period ruins of the building clearly speak of the ancient scribal activity therein. That the scrolls in the nearby caves, or at least many of these scrolls, were actually copied by scribes at those desks in the buildings can be assumed with confidence.

The original building at Qumran was probably constructed by King Uzziah of Judah (781–740 B.C.—II Chron. 26:10).[5] And we may suppose that it was still habitable in the second century B.C., when, archaeologists tell us, occupation of the site, after the long hiatus, was resumed. Settlement of the area increased gradually until, in the middle of the first century B.C., building activity became quite dramatic, indicating a significant influx of inhabitants after the Romans had in 63 B.C. assumed hegemony over Palestine and had taken up residence in Jerusalem. Occupation probably ceased abruptly, however, in 31 B.C., when a massive earthquake shook the area and disgorged the Qumran settlers. On the death of Herod, and after the War of Varus (4 B.C.), settlement was resumed[6] but probably did not at that time reach the density attained after the middle of the first century B.C., when as many as two hundred persons, it is estimated, may have lived there. Occupation was continuous until June of A.D. 68, when, at the height of the First Jewish Revolt, Roman troops of the Tenth Legion Fretensis destroyed the area and slaughtered or dispersed the inhabitants. The buildings left standing were used to a limited extent after the year 68 both by the occupying Roman troops up to about A.D. 72 and sixty years later by Jewish insurgents in the Second Jewish Revolt (A.D. 132–135).[7]

Who were the people that took over Uzziah's old fortress, in such a deserted and secluded part

---

[1] *Wadi* is Arabic for gully or dry stream bed. Information on Cave 11 is given in *Revue biblique*, LXIII (1956), pp. 573–574, and in Millar Burrows, *More Light on the Dead Sea Scrolls* (1958), p. 14.

[2] Roland de Vaux, *L'Archéologie et les manuscrits de la Mer Morte* (1961), pp. 73ff.

[3] Frank Moore Cross, Jr., *The Ancient Library of Qumran* (1961), pp. 53ff.

[4] Kenneth W. Clark, "The Posture of the Ancient Scribe," *The Biblical Archaeologist*, XXVI (1963), pp. 63ff.

[5] De Vaux, *op. cit.*, p. 73. Cross suggested the possibility of the ninth-century construction of the original building in an article in the *Bulletin of the American Schools of Oriental Research*, No. 142 (1956), pp. 5–17; he seems to continue to hold that view in *The Ancient Library of Qumran*, p. 64.

[6] De Vaux, *op. cit.*, pp. 28–33. It is quite possible that occupation did not cease entirely but continued on a greatly reduced scale between 31 and 4 B.C.

[7] *Ibid.*, pp. 35–36.

of Palestine? A few scholars still debate the matter, but the great majority agree with the very early judgments of A. Dupont-Sommer and W. F. Albright that they were the second-century B.C. precursors of the Essenes whom we call the Hasidim. These same pietistic Hasidim, gravely concerned in their time over the growing hellenization of Judaism, and anxious to obey the whole law of Moses, were probably the precursors as well of the Pharisees.[8] But at Qumran, where such Hasidim came to settle around 165–150 B.C., they were those whom Jewish and Roman writers, such as Philo, Josephus, Pliny the Elder, and Hippolytus, later called Essenes. Not all the Essenes lived at Qumran, however, for the Essene movement in the first century B.C. and the first century A.D. was quite widespread and had within it more than one branch or denomination. In Egypt ascetics similar to the Essenes were called Therapeutae.[9] Throughout Palestine quite a few Essenes lived normal lives in villages in addition to the ascetic and (partially) celibate group at Qumran. Some scholars believe that Essenes may have lived in Syria near Damascus.[10]

The library of the particular denomination of Essenes who lived at Qumran was remarkably extensive, containing some five hundred volumes.[11] All the books of the Old Testament except Esther were there, and many other works such as the Jewish apocryphal writings already known to us and preserved by some branches of the Christian Church, as well as Jewish sectarian works of the period totally unknown heretofore.[12] Most of the latter may have been peculiarly Essene.

The Old Testament books most highly regarded at Qumran were the very ones that were important

to the earliest Christians, as indicated in the New Testament: Isaiah, of which two nearly complete copies were found in Cave 1; Deuteronomy, of which twenty-five fragmentary copies are available; and the Psalter, of which thirty fragmentary copies have been counted from the eleven caves (see Appendix II).

Cave 1 yielded seven very well-preserved scrolls. But, except for the copper scroll from Cave 3, Caves 2 through 10 yielded no large well-preserved scroll, but only innumerable fragments. Cave 4 contained tens of thousands of fragments, indicating an original cache of over four hundred scrolls, for the publication of which eight quarto-size volumes will be required. Cave 11, the last of the caves, has yielded, aside from the very handsomely preserved, though partially damaged, Psalms Scroll, a considerably damaged scroll of Job in Aramaic, a completely ossified scroll of Ezekiel, which it was impossible to unroll, large fragments of the Apocalypse of the New Jerusalem (also found in Caves 1, 2, and 4), and fragments of Leviticus written in palaeo-Hebrew script.[13]

Although the materials from Cave 11 had been discovered and brought from Qumran to the Palestine Archaeological Museum in Jerusalem, Jordan, in February 1956, the Psalms Scroll was not unrolled until November 1961. It had lain securely stored in the museum those five and a half years, awaiting the successful completion of the negotiations necessary, financial and otherwise, for bringing it out into the scrollery so that work could begin. It is due to the vision and generosity of Elizabeth Hay Bechtel, of San Francisco, that the scroll was made available for opening, study, and publication. The museum had,

---

[8] Werner Foerster, *From the Exile to Christ* (1964), pp. 35–37.

[9] See the tractates by Philo of Alexandria entitled "Every Good Man Is Free" and "On the Contemplative Life" translated by F. H. Colson in *Philo*, IX (1940), in the Loeb Classical Series.

[10] The best overview of the Essenes is in J. T. Milik's *Ten Years of Discovery in the Wilderness of Judaea* (1959), pp. 83–98. De Vaux and others have thought of Damascus literally and suggested that the Essenes of Qumran journeyed and lived there during the reign of Herod; but see his latest discussion in *op. cit.*, pp. 87–89. Frank Cross and others are inclined to view Damascus as a pseudonym, after prophetic usage, for Qumran itself (*Ancient Library*, pp. 81–83, n. 46).

[11] Cross, *Ancient Library*, pp. 30–47.

[12] See Milik, *op. cit.*, pp. 20–43, and the list in Burrows, *op. cit.*, pp. 407–409. Known apocryphal writings found at Qumran include portions of Tobit, Sirach, Epistle of Jeremiah, Enoch, Jubilees, Testaments of the Twelve Patriarchs, and the Prayer of Nabonidus.

[13] The same archaic script used in the Psalms Scroll wherever the divine name (YHWH) appears. For available information to date on other scrolls from Cave 11 see J. van der Ploeg, *Le Targum de Job de la Grotte 11 de Qumran (11QtgJob)* (1962); A. S. van der Woude, "Das Hiobtargum aus Qumran Höhle XI," *Vetus Testamentum*, Suppl. IX (1962), pp. 322–331; and William H. Brownlee, "The Scroll of Ezekiel from the Eleventh Qumran Cave," *Revue de Qumrân*, No. 13 (1963), pp. 3–28.

through the dedication and foresight of its Board of Trustees, especially of its President, Father Roland de Vaux, and of its Curator, Yusef Saad, by use of some of its precious endowment, secured the Cave 11 materials for safe storage until funds could be raised.

On the morning of November 10, 1961, Father de Vaux, Mr. Saad, Dr. Paul W. Lapp, Director of the Jerusalem School of the American Schools of Oriental Research, and I gathered at the museum for the occasion of bringing the Psalms Scroll out of the vault into the scrollery.[14] After some thirty minutes of consultation on the necessary procedure for opening the scroll, I began the tedious and delicate task of attempting to coax the document to yield to being unrolled just one more time in its long history. I am not ashamed to admit that I was nervous and apprehensive. I had done my homework: I had read all the available reports of the experiences of others who had had similar assignments, and I had talked with a few of them, trying to glean all I could of their expertise. The fraternity of scroll openers is, I suppose, rather limited in membership, but on the morning of November 10, 1961, all I could seem to remember was that the others had arrived and I was only just beginning.

The amount of time spent thereafter in unrolling was far less than our most optimistic estimates, for the actual time consumed was six rather short working days. Owing to the appearance of the scroll—caked mud, bat dung, and black mucous matter of its own decomposition covered one side, and the black, ossified matter of advanced stages of decomposition marked one end—estimates had run as high as two or more months. The scroll behaved itself so beautifully, and I experienced daily such waves of relief from my initial apprehensions, that (I hesitate now to tell it) even the odor of the desiccated bat dung became a pleasant association. I shall never forget my first visit soon thereafter to Cave 11 at Qumran, when I stepped into its dark recesses and experienced the sharpening of my senses to the familiar and welcome odor. It was an abnormality

in which I rejoiced because of the association.

Careful use of a camel's-hair brush, the museum humidifier, and a small penknife reduced fragmentation and chipping to a minimum. The few pieces that did come loose from the main body of the scroll were immediately put in individual boxes and labeled as to their provenance and exact locus of separation. These pieces were then carefully replaced as the scroll was put under glass for photography. When on November 17 the last hard-core section of the scroll had been reached, where the blackened end of it gave the appearance of a tight unyielding knot, I invited Father de Vaux and Mr. Saad in for a conference. Father de Vaux suggested that I cut away a bit of the black substance and that Mr. Saad turn the room off the scrollery, where I was working, into a sort of humidifier itself. On November 20, when I was able to return to work following the Jordanian census of that year, we set a kettle of water on an oil burner, closed all the vents and windows and the door, and let the steam work its wonders. By early that afternoon the final section of the scroll yielded, and the job was done.

Later, soon after the announcement of the feat had been officially released by the government in Amman and by the museum in Jerusalem, Dana Adams Schmidt of the *New York Times* came down from Beirut for an interview. Schmidt asked the inevitable question about what it took to unroll an ancient scroll. I explained as well as I could, stressing how humble I had felt that morning sitting in front of the scroll, wondering if instead of succeeding I would by some inadvertent gesture be the agent of the scroll's destruction and of my own undoing. Would I through my lack of skill forever conceal its message, instead of revealing it as I had been charged to do? In my desire to convey to him my feelings of unworthiness and the accompanying apprehension, I used the wrong word, and, of course, it was printed in his article. I had in mind the Yiddish word *ḥuṣpah*. *Ḥuṣpah* means a lot of things, but in English it at least means "nerve" or perhaps "gall." But instead of using one of those words I

---

[14] The next several paragraphs are taken, partially, from my article, "The Scroll of Psalms (11QPss) from Cave 11; A Preliminary Report," *Bulletin of the American Schools of Oriental Research*, No. 165 (1962), pp. 11–15. See also J. A. Sanders, *The Psalms Scroll of Qumran Cave 11* (*Discoveries in the Judaean Desert of Jordan*, Vol. IV [1965]), pp. 3–5.

used another, and his article at that point read, "All it required was a penknife and guts, plus a humidifier."[15] "Guts" is what I said; "gall" is what I meant.

On November 20, Father de Vaux came again to the scrollery to see the scroll completely under glass. On that occasion he asked Mr. Saad to bring in the loose fragments from Cave 11, some of which had been purchased with the scroll and some of which had been recovered when the archaeologists subsequently excavated the cave. Four of them belong to the scroll and are designated as fragments A to D.*

The scroll was last rolled up, in antiquity, in a rather hasty manner, as one might quickly roll a map, so that its clean or undamaged end was not even but curved gently out and then in toward the center or last columns of the scroll. This is the principal reason for the varying width of the scroll, or from another perspective, the varying length of the columns. Because of gradual decomposition and decay through the centuries the four outer layers of the roll were not continuous but were left only as four separable leaves increasing in size until at the fifth layer the leather was continuous thereafter, sewn together in five sheets of varying length, to almost thirteen feet; all told, edge to edge, disregarding lacunae, there are about thirteen and a half feet of leather in the five sheets, four leaves, and four fragments. Every column, including the last one, which is blank, is ruled or lined by stylus in the manner of the other scrolls from Qumran. Each column contains from 14 to 17 lines of text according to the length of column preserved; originally, however, the columns ran 21 to 23 lines. The scroll in its present condition is six to seven inches wide, whereas it originally was nine to ten inches wide; thus six to seven lines of invaluable text are lacking at the bottom of each column. There is no way of guessing how long the scroll was in its initial state. Since the original width was nearly that of the completely preserved large Isaiah scroll from Cave 1, it is possible that its original length was

comparable to its companion from Cave 1—about 24 feet. If so, it could easily have contained seventy-five psalms, half the number in the traditional Psalter; but there is simply no way of knowing.

The skin of the scroll is somewhat less than a millimeter thick, about .03 of an inch. It is the thickest of any in the scrollery, or so I am told, and it is not impossible that instead of being goatskin, as almost all the rest are, it may be calfskin. As on all the others, the writing is on the hair side of the skin, which may have been tanned and prepared, like the others, in the ancient workrooms that have been excavated a mile and a half south of Qumran near 'Ain Feshka. The ink is carbon black and contrasts well with the deep yellow-to-brown of the skin itself. The reader should be apprised of the fact that the photographs of the columns are done with the infrared process, which means that the blackness of the ink in the photos is true but not the color of the skin around it, which in actuality is considerably darker.

The scribe's handwriting is precise, the letters being carefully drawn in the formal book-hand style of the Herodian period. Palaeographic analysis indicates that the date of the scroll should be set between A.D. 30 and 50.[16]

The scroll contains all or parts of forty-one canonical psalms, including the psalm which in the Bible appears in II Sam. 23:1–7. In addition it includes eight apocryphal compositions, seven of which are nonbiblical psalms and one of which is a statement about David in prose. (One of the apocryphal psalms, Psalm 151, appears in the scroll in two parts, 151A and 151B, and could be counted as two psalms.) The prose insert, in column XXVII, states that David composed 4,050 psalms and songs! But the Hebrew (and Protestant) Bible includes only 150 psalms in its Psalter (and the Greek and Old Latin only 151). Granting that the figure 4,050 may be considered as but a demonstration of exaggerated affection for David, the scroll itself, with its apocryphal

* For Fragment E, see the "Postscriptum," pp. 155–165.
[15] The *New York Times*, March 8, 1962, p. 10.
[16] This is the date I suggested to the reporter, which is given in the *Times* article mentioned above. Within three weeks of my return to the United States, in September of

1962, I took photographs of the columns of the scroll to Harvard for inspection by Professor Cross; Cross immediately confirmed my findings. See the palaeographic analysis, which was in effect co-authored by Cross, in *Discoveries in the Judaean Desert of Jordan*, Vol. IV, pp. 6–9.

psalms scattered among the canonical, clearly indicates that the figure 150 (or even 151) must now be considered as quite limited and perhaps even arbitrary.

Interesting in this regard is a letter written in the eighth century A.D. by the Nestorian Patriarch Timotheus I to a friend in Damascus. In it he tells of the discovery of scrolls in the vicinity of Jericho; among them were books containing the Old Testament, and other works, in Hebrew script. But most interesting for our purposes is the following sentence from the letter: "My Hebrew informant told me, 'We found among those books more than 200 Psalms of David!'"[17] All such figures, whether 150, 200, or 4,050, it must be clearly understood, come from the first century, and later; and the estimates, pious or otherwise, of that time as to how many psalms should be attributed to David cannot be taken at face value. The historical value of such estimates is limited to our appreciation of what was believed about David in the first century and does not extend back to any reconstruction of the activities of the tenth-century B.C. King David: their value there is minimal at best. Nontheless, no matter how exaggerated the figure 4,050 may appear, it clearly shows, along with the scroll itself, that some branches of Judaism in the mid-first century had not yet limited the canon of the Psalter to the Masoretic, or traditional, scope.[18]

Although the Psalms Scroll cannot be taken as typical either of general Judaism or of Essene Judaism in the first century, it nonetheless admits us to a view of how the Psalter could be arranged and used by some Jews of the time; and though they may not have been orthodox by Pharisaic or later Masoretic standards, we may assume they were nonetheless equally as pious as the "orthodox" sects, and certainly men of as deep faith as they. Conformity is not a measure of faith. The conformity which prevailed in Judaism after the destruction of Jerusalem in A.D. 69–70, and the survival thereafter of Pharisaism alone of all the sects that had existed formerly, simply was not available earlier. And while the Psalms Scroll may appear a bit "maverick" to our modern eyes, we are constrained to remember that it has survived nearly two millennia of Pharasaic-Rabbinic conformity in a Qumran cave, lying there for centuries among distinctly Essene writings, and deserves as prominent a place in the ancient library of Qumran, now slowly being reconstructed, as any other document therein, biblical or sectarian. It was just as Jewish in its first-century setting as the

---

[17] The following is part of the account given by Timotheus I of the discovery of Hebrew manuscripts in the region of Jericho about A.D. 786:

"We have learnt from certain Jews who are worthy of belief, and who have recently received instruction in Christianity, that ten years ago books were discovered in the vicinity of Jericho. It is said that the dog of an Arab who was out hunting went into a cave after a certain animal, and failed to come out. So his master went in after him and found a small cave in the middle of the mountain with many books in it. The hunter went to Jerusalem and made the matter known to the Jews, who came from Jerusalem in numbers and found books containing the Old Testament, and other works, in Hebrew script. Because my informant was a man of letters, I asked him about several passages which are cited in our New Testament as from the Old but of which there is no mention in the Old Testament itself, neither as we Christians have it nor as it is known among the Jews. He said to me that these passages exist and are found in the books dicovered there . . . ."

In a letter to Metropolitan Subhalerahman of Damascus, Timotheus wrote, "It is written in the *Miserere* 'Sprinkle me with the Hyssop of the blood of thy Cross and purify me': this is not found in the Septuagint, nor in the other versions, nor in the Hebrew. But my Hebrew informant told me, 'We found among these books more than 200 psalms of David.'"

The Syriac text may be found in Oskar Braun, "Ein Brief des Katholikos Timotheos I über biblische Studien des 9 Jahrhunderts," *Oriens Christianus*, I (1901), pp. 299–313, esp. pp. 304–307; the German translation there and in Otto Eissfeldt's article in *Theologische Literaturzeitung*, LXXIV (1949), col. 598. The date 786 for the discovery is that of Raphael J. Bidawid, *Les lettres du Patriarche nestorien, Timothée I (Studi e Testi*, CLXXXVII [1956]), p. 71. John Strugnell, "Notes on the Text and Transmission of the Apocryphal Psalms 151, 154 and 155," forthcoming in the *Harvard Theological Review*, provides the English translation on which the quotations are largely based.

As explained in Part III below, Syrian Christians at one time had 155 psalms in their biblical Psalter, and three of them are represented among the eight apocryphal compositions in the Psalms Scroll. Other apocryphal psalms have also been attributed to David. For the loci of a few see note 1 on page 60 of *Discoveries in the Judaean Desert of Jordan*, Vol. IV; Professor Strugnell has recently been studying the ones noted there and it is to him that I owe the references.

[18] The 4Q psalms materials are not as rigidly traditional or Masoretic as those which have been discovered dating to the First and Second Jewish Revolts both in the Nahal Hever and at Masada (Appendix II). The scale, from heterodox to orthodox, for Psalter materials recently recovered would appear thus:

11Q—4Q—Masada—MT.

For more recent information on 4Q and 11Q psalms, see the "Postscriptum," pp. 155–165.

psalters, more like the Masoretic in appearance, of Masada and Nahal Hever. Its value in reconstructing the varieties of expression of Jewish faith in Palestine during the first century cannot be exaggerated.[19] With the many other documents of the period which have recently been recovered,[20] and with the many "apocryphal" Jewish writings preserved through the centuries by the Church, as well as with the Pharisaic Tannaitic literature, it is a welcome primary source of information on Judaism in the intertestamental or general New Testament period.

[19] Who is to say that the Apostle Paul exhibits a "basic misunderstanding" of Torah? See Hans-Joachim Schoeps, *Paul* (1961), p. 200.

[20] Discoveries continue apace. Aside from those found in 1960 in the Nahal Hever and in 1964–1965 at Masada (mentioned below in Appendix II), there are the very valuable early fourth-century B.C. Aramaic papyri recovered from the Wadi ed-Daliyeh in 1962 (Frank Moore Cross, Jr., "The Discovery of the Samaria Papyri," *The Biblical Archaeologist*, XXVI [1963], pp. 110–121).

The Wadi Qumran looking east toward the Dead Sea. Cave 11 was discovered in 1956 about one and a half miles north of the ancient Essene community buildings, the ruins of which are here shown in the process (1952) of excavation. (Copyright by the Palestine Archaeological Museum, Jerusalem, Jordan; reproduced by permission.)

The Dead Sea Psalms Scroll before unrolling. The scroll, as it looked when it was found, was photographed November 10, 1961. (Copyright by the Palestine Archaeological Museum, Jerusalem, Jordan; reproduced by permission.)

THE SCROLL

*Ancient Manuscripts**

FROM early in the sixteenth century until 1937, the standard printed Hebrew text of the Old Testament was that of the Second Rabbinic Bible, edited by Jacob ben Chayyim and published in Venice by Daniel Bomberg in 1524–1525. Since 1937, with the publication of the third edition of Rudolf Kittel's *Biblia Hebraica*, the Aaron ben Moses ben Asher text, dated A.D. 1008, has been used. Professor Paul Kahle had discovered the older text in the Russian Public Library in Leningrad in 1926 and later persuaded Kittel, who had used the Ben Chayyim text in the first two editions of *Biblia Hebraica*, of the superiority of the older Ben Asher Codex. Since 1937, Kahle's Leningrad–Ben Asher Codex (B19^A or L) has been the basic standard Old Testament text. It antedates the Ben Chayyim text by about half a millenium.[1]

The Ben Asher text in Leningrad, which contains the whole of the biblical Psalter, had been brought there in the third quarter of the nineteenth century by Abraham Firkowitch from the Old Cairo Ezra Synagogue Geniza. Many fragments of biblical manuscripts, some of which date from the fifth to the ninth centuries A.D., were recovered from the same Geniza again after 1890, when the synagogue underwent extensive repairs.

The Aleppo (Syria) Ben Asher Codex, which is now reportedly in Israel, dates from the first half of the tenth century A.D.; it contains all but ten (Pss. 15:1–25:2) of the biblical psalms.

One of the oldest Bible fragments emanating from Egypt, but not from the Geniza, was acquired there in 1902 by W. L. Nash. The "Nash papyrus" contains a variant form of the Ten Commandments and Deut. 6:4–5. Paul Kahle dates it in the first century A.D. and W. F. Albright in the second century B.C.

The Qumran texts, discovered in Palestine near the Dead Sea during the nine years 1947–1956, provide the oldest biblical manuscripts to date, and antedate the current standard Old Testament manuscripts from Cairo by about a millennium. They also antedate the earliest manuscripts of the Greek and other versions of the Old Testament heretofore known. The Qumran manuscripts, along with the Nash papyrus and very recent finds in Israel, are the oldest biblical textual witnesses discovered to date. The Qumran library has not yielded a complete Old Testament text in the sense of the Ben Asher Codex in Leningrad, but it has yielded, at least in fragments, sizable portions of every Old Testament book with the single exception of Esther. Some Old Testament books have been found in several copies, in different scribal hands. In Cave 1 two copies of the book of Isaiah were found, and in the large Cave 4, where over four hundred scrolls were discovered in the form of tens of thousands of fragments, two and three quite different recensions of the same biblical book were found.[2]

Fragments of the biblical psalms have been found in Caves 1, 2, 3, 4, 5, 6, 8, and 11—and from Cave 11 the large Psalms Scroll as well. There were undoubtedly more copies of psalms in the Qumran library than of any other biblical writings, thirty accounted for to date. By and

---

* A portion of the material in this and the following section has appeared in an article in the *Harvard Theological Review*, LIX (1966), pp. 83–94; copyright 1966 by the President and Fellows of Harvard College, used by permission.

[1] Paul Kahle, *The Cairo Geniza*, (1959), pp. 3–17, 132–141.
[2] See Frank Moore Cross, Jr., "The History of the Biblical Text in the Light of Discoveries in the Judaean Desert," *Harvard Theological Review*, LVII (1964), pp. 281–299, esp. pp. 281–287.

large, the biblical psalms recovered thus far from Qumran are in very close textual agreement with the psalms of the early medieval Ben Asher manuscripts from Cairo and Aleppo (the *textus receptus*). In fact, all witnesses to the texts of the biblical psalms, whether in Hebrew or in early Greek, Latin, Aramaic, or Syriac translations, are in broad general agreement, that is, are of one basic recension—an observation that made it possible in a comparatively short time in 1961–1962 to construct a supporting critical apparatus for the scientific edition of the Psalms Scroll. The texts of the forty-one biblical psalms in the Psalms Scroll are, with some very interesting exceptions, the texts we have always known; the order of the psalms and the presence among them of nonbiblical psalms, however, are surprising.

Fortunately, the date of the Psalms Scroll is ascertainable through the science of palaeography, and by this means alone it is clear that the scroll dates from about the second quarter or the middle of the first century A.D. These dates are generally corroborated by archaeological data. (Contrary to popular opinion, the radiocarbon test is not greatly useful, since it requires a two-to-four century margin of error.)[3]

Father Roland de Vaux, who has been responsible since the beginning for the archaeological work at Qumran, suggests that some of the scroll caves were inhabited by members of the Qumran community (5Q, 7Q, 8Q, 9Q, and 11Q) and that the manuscripts in those caves may have been simply abandoned in the last moments of occupation.[4] By contrast, Caves 1 and 4 may have been used intentionally as places of hiding for the principal library. Very few members of the Qumran community seem to have had lodgings in the community center near the caves; and the manuscripts from 11Q, including the Psalms Scroll, may have been left quite hurriedly by those members of the community who had been living in 11Q. One might think of Caves 1 and 4 as used by the community members expressly for hiding the library, and of the nine other caves as places where manuscripts were abandoned during June and July of A.D. 68, when a contingent of Vespasian's troops, part of the Roman Tenth Legion Fretensis, under Trajan père, ransacked the area south of Jericho.

(For the convenience of the student of the Hebraic Psalter a catalogue of and an index to all extant pre-Masoretic Psalter texts are provided below in Appendix II.)

Content and Order

If one would be precise in his use of the word *variorum* for the Psalms Scroll, he should list not only the variants to the canonical psalms (*variae lectiones*) but also the larger-unit variants to the Psalter itself, namely, the compositions in the scroll which are not found in the biblical book of the Psalms.

Perhaps the first such that should be mentioned is the psalm (and it is a psalm!) which in the Bible is located in II Sam. 23:1–7, but which in the scroll is included as a "Davidic" psalm among psalms. The superscription to it in the biblical book of II Samuel states that it contains the "last words of David." Be that as it may, it is clearly just as "Davidic" as the psalm which precedes it in II Samuel 22, which is also Psalm 18! There can be

no doubt that the full Qumran Psalter contained Psalm 18, for there are fragments including Psalm 18 from one of the small Qumran caves (8Q2). And if Psalm 18 was present in the Qumran Psalter, why not II Samuel 23? In the Psalms Scroll it plays a part in the literary (colophonic) conceit which extends over the last columns of the scroll. Following the "Last Words of David," which are located at the (lost) bottom of column XXVI and the top line of column XXVII, is the prose composition of column XXVII, which claims that David "spoke through prophecy" 4,050 compositions. And then in the last column, XXVIII, are found the two poems which make up Psalm 151, which tells how the shepherd-musician David was elevated by God, and Samuel, to be king of Israel. These

---

[3] A physicochemical analysis recently conducted on uninscribed pieces of scroll leather at the University of Leeds also requires considerable tolerance, but, like the radiocarbon tests, confirms the findings of archaeology

and palaeography: Roland de Vaux, *L'Archéologie et les manuscrits de la Mer Morte* (1961), pp. 76–77.

[4] *Discoveries in the Judaean Desert of Jordan*, Vol. III (1962), pp. 32–36.

last columns of the scroll clearly demonstrate the belief that David composed, or "spoke," not only all the psalms in this scroll but many, many others as well. It is only fitting, therefore, that II Samuel 23 figure in such a claim. One should remember, as well, that the Samuels, Isaiah, and the Psalms contain the great bulk of the "Davidic" literature of the Old Testament, and those are the books which, along with Deuteronomy, were the most meaningful to the faithful at Qumran (and to the New Testament writers as well).

But II Samuel 23 is by no means apocryphal. It is in the Bible, whether as a psalm in the Psalter or not. To have a paragraph displaced within the Bible is at variance to the biblical order of things, but to have nonbiblical material within what was manifestly a bona fide Psalter scroll at Qumran is not only a "variant" but also, from our viewpoint, apocryphal. And although the ancient poem in II Samuel is biblical, there are eight compositions in the scroll which, whatever their age, are not biblical. The eight are as follows:

Psalm 151A, B	xxviii 3–14
Psalm 154	xviii
Psalm 155	xxiv 3–17
Sirach 51:13ff.	xxi 11–17
	xxii 1
Plea for Deliverance	xix
Apostrophe to Zion	xxii 1–15
Hymn to the Creator	xxvi 9–15
David's Compositions	xxvii 2–11

Those in the first group were known heretofore in ancient translations (especially Greek, Latin, Syriac, and even medieval Hebrew), and we now have, in the scroll, the original-language Hebrew texts for them all. That is not to say that we have the originals as they left the author's hand, but we may have something very close to the autographs in what is now available. All four of them had been known, by specialists at least, in ancient Syriac versions, the first and fourth also in Greek and Latin, and the Sirach piece also in a medieval Hebrew text from Cairo, based mostly on the Syriac version.

Those in the second group are "new" old compositions, unknown in any form before the Psalms Scroll was unrolled. Whereas those in the first

group are exciting because we now have the original (and in two cases quite surprising) Hebrew texts for them, those in the second group are all the more exciting, perhaps, because of their freshness. Students and laymen who have kept up a bit with the Qumran discoveries (Dead Sea Scrolls) in the past eighteen years realize that this newly recovered, heretofore unknown literature forms but a part of a rather sizable catalogue of such material which has in that period emanated from the Judaean caves near the sea. A scroll of psalm-type hymns was recovered from the first cave discovered in 1947 and identified in 1948: we call them Thanksgiving Hymns (1QH). Good English translations of them can be found in Theodor Gaster's *The Dead Sea Scriptures* (1964), pages 134 and following, in Geza Vermes' *The Dead Sea Scrolls in English* (1962), pages 149 and following, and in A. Dupont-Sommer's *The Essene Writings from Qumran* (1962), beginning at page 202. The remarkable difference between the Cave 1 hymns and our apocryphal psalms, aside from some question of style, is that the latter are contained in a scroll of biblical psalms. And this must not be lost sight of. The Psalms Scroll was believed, by its scribe and by those who read and appreciated it, supposedly the sectarians at Qumran, to have been Davidic in original authorship. No such claim is made for the Thanksgiving Hymns: on the contrary, there is some basis for thinking that they were composed by the leader of the Qumran sect, who was called the Teacher of Righteousness.

The apocryphal psalms located at Qumran in manuscripts of the biblical Psalter "want to be," themselves, biblical psalms. Within the various Psalms manuscripts where they are found, they are in no way externally distinguished from the psalms already familiar to us; even their poetry and their contents are biblical, or "biblicizing." One should not presume in any a priori way that they are Essene in origin or even that they are very late in date: there are reasons to think, for instance, that the "Apostrophe to Zion" and Psalm 155 may date from the fourth or third century B.C. These apocryphal psalms must be treated independently of the Cave 1 Thanksgiving Hymns.

Such apocryphal psalms, located in biblical manuscripts, have been found in Caves 4 and 11. The catalogue of ancient Psalter manuscripts in

Appendix II, below, presents a Psalms profile for both caves. So far, only three manuscripts, one from 4Q and two from 11Q, appear to include both biblical and apocryphal psalms. One must say "so far" because a discovery was made in the summer of 1965 which was unexpected and may signal other such phenomena: It was learned at that time that manuscript 4QPs^{f} contained, in addition to the three biblical psalms already identified, three apocryphal psalms, one of which is the "Apostrophe to Zion" of 11QPs^{a}. Between 1953 and 1955 the tens of thousands of manuscript fragments from Cave 4 were assigned to an international team of scholars on the basis of their contents: Monsignor Patrick W. Skehan received all the Hebrew Psalter as well as other biblical materials for study and eventual publication, while Abbé Jean Starcky received nonbiblical materials in Aramaic and Hebrew. In the summer of 1965, because Professor John Strugnell had seen both Skehan's manuscripts and mine, he was able to tell Starcky two things: his fragments containing three apocryphal psalms not only belonged, according to the script and the leather, to Skehan's 4QPs^{f}, but one of the psalms was another copy of the "Apostrophe to Zion" of 11QPs^{a}. How many other such identifications are yet to be made one cannot say: however, one should not expect more than one or two more at the most.

A cursory study of Appendix II permits the following observations. Manuscripts 4QPs^{f}, 11QPs^{a}, 11QPs^{d}, and 11QPsAp^{a} contain both biblical and apocryphal psalms. All other Psalter manuscripts from Qumran seem to have contained only biblical psalms: most of them are so fragmentary, however, that the observation is of necessity preliminary until all materials have been published. The biblical psalms from Cave 11 include some very interesting variants. While 11QPs^{b} and 11QPs^{c} contain only biblical psalms, Father J. van der Ploeg, who is editing them for the Royal Dutch Academy, informs me that in two other scribal hands he has apocryphal psalm material: in one case he has Psalm 118 with a nonbiblical refrain in the manner, one supposes, of Psalm 145 in the Psalms Scroll. The significant variants and addenda in the Psalms Scroll begin, aside from the enigma of column II, in column XVI. It is there that Psalms 136 and 145 appear with their peculiarities. The apocryphal compositions are then found in columns XVIII, XIX, XXIV, XXVI, XXVII, and XXVIII. Up to that point most of the leather of the scroll is covered by Psalms 121 to 132 of "The Songs of Ascents," and the long Psalm 119. From that point biblical and apocryphal psalms are intermixed in such a way that permits no distinction among them. Why Cave 11 should have in it material so much at odds with the traditional order and contents of psalm materials is difficult to say. The order or sequence of biblical psalms is fairly stable in the manuscripts from the other caves. So far as we know, the order was completely traditional in the psalms documents in the small caves (2, 3, 5, 6, 8). Even in the material from Cave 4, except for 4QPs^{f}, noted above, the profile is essentially, though not totally, proto-Masoretic. Psalm 32 is omitted or displaced in 4QPs^{a} as well as in 4QPs^{q}[5]; Psalms 104 to 111 are omitted or displaced in 4QPs^{b}; and Psalm 104 follows immediately on Psalm 147 in 4QPs^{d}. Psalm 32 is omitted in 4QPs^{a} and 4QPs^{q} and, indeed, is so far lacking at Qumran.[6] The omission of Psalms 104–111 in 4QPs^{b} should not be overemphasized since Psalm 104 does appear in at least four manuscripts (2Q14, 4QPs^{d,e,l}), and in one of them (4QPs^{e}) immediately precedes Psalm 105; and Psalm 107 does appear in 4QPs^{f}. The order in 4QPs^{a} of Psalm 71 immediately after Psalm 38 is possibly explained by the great similarity that exists between Psalms 38 and 70, so that the scribe had in mind the sequence, Psalms 70–71.[7]

Although one cannot, and must not, say that the canon of the Psalter was rigidly fixed by the early first century, there is no basis from the thirty manuscripts of psalms from Caves 1 through 11, no matter how fragmentary they may be, to think that the Psalter had in the Qumran and early Christian periods no shape or comeliness at all. The evidence points toward a general proto-Masoretic profile of the psalms materials. The growing belief of the time in the Davidic authorship of certain psalms, indeed of 4,050 psalms and songs as 11QPs^{a} clearly demonstrates, was un-

---

[5] See *Biblica*, XXXVIII (1957), pp. 245–255.

[6] Contrast P. W. Skehan's article in *Vetus Testamentum*, Suppl. IV (1957), p. 155. See Appendix II, below.

[7] *Ibid.*, p. 154.

doubtedly a factor in the stabilization of Psalter materials. Whether David composed a single psalm is beside the point: the belief that collections of psalms were of Davidic origin was unquestionably a stabilizing force in the diverse collections and compilations abroad in the Jewish world (at least thirty copies of which were present at Qumran). What is now very clear is that attribution of Davidic authorship did not come after the Psalter was fixed, but was applied to a smaller collection of psalms and to individual psalms over a long period of time.

Monsignor Skehan rightly thinks that 4QPs^a, which dates perhaps from the second century B.C., shows a certain fixity of order and content for the Psalter through Book II, or at least through Psalm 69, for as early as the second century B.C. (Book II ends with Psalm 72, which has the subscription, "The prayers of David, the son of Jesse, are ended.") Professor Frank Cross, who studied 4QPs^a for well over a year, has written, "A second-century B.C. copy of the canonical Psalter (4QPs^a), though fragmentary, indicates that the collection of canonical psalms was fixed by Maccabean times, bearing out the current tendency to date the latest canonical psalms in the Persian period."[8] Certainly Books I and II, Psalms 1–72, may have been fixed (except for Psalm 32's wandering about a bit perhaps) at a quite early date, but it is now clear that Books III to V were quite fluid in some textual traditions.*

All the Psalter material in the Psalms Scroll comes from Books IV and V, and while it is certainly not in the traditional order, its fluidity is amenable to more than one explanation. Four manuscripts from Cave 4 (b, e, m, o), though fragmentary to be sure, indicate the traditional sequence of the later psalms with few exceptions, and they should not be overlooked in any scientific discussion of manuscript evidence of psalm order in the later books. One may look at the fluidity of order in the Psalms Scroll in one of two ways: either as unique (*nonpareil*) and at variance with a generally accepted order; or as a "local text" representing a limited but valid Psalter tradition. The latter is clearly the more fruitful way of proceeding, since variance from an accep-

ted order, for Books IV and V, would require an explanation involving sound reasons for the variance, that is, in the case of a Qumran scroll, sectarian theological reasons, or at least sectarian liturgical reasons; and these are not present in the scroll to any convincing degree.

Psalm 145 in columns XVI and XVII is followed in column XVIII by apocryphal Psalm 154, which has largely the same theme; and that theme, praising God for his mighty acts, would undoubtedly have had great appeal to the Qumran sect. *But* the theme is certainly not exclusively Essenian or Qumranian; it is, on the contrary, quite "biblical." The prose composition in column XXVII is the most attractive candidate for a Qumranian provenance, since it is based, in its liturgical aspects, on the same calendar used by the sect at Qumran. But the same calendar was perhaps in use in other sects, as its reflection in long-known works such as Jubilees and Enoch would indicate. The fact that fragments of Jubilees and Enoch have been found in Cave 4 at Qumran does not prove a Qumranian origin for those works: it but indicates Qumranian adherence to elements found in them and an Essenian, apocalyptic tradition at best.[9] Even if the prose paragraph in our column XXVII should have been composed afresh at Qumran, or by the Essenes, that would not help particularly in determining who composed either Psalm 145 or Psalm 154.

All in all, it seems best for the time being, until all the materials from Caves 4 and 11 have been published, to think of the Psalms Scroll not as a deviation from a rigidly fixed canon of the latter third of the Psalter but rather as a signpost in the multi-faceted history of the canonization of the Psalter. Without the invaluable Qumran cave literature we should not have thought, probably, in terms of the Psalter's becoming fixed by sections progressively from front to back. And we should undoubtedly not think even now in any firm or rigid way about what the process was. That would be perilous. Some scholars have suggested that Psalm 1 was added last of all as a sort of introduction to the whole Psalter, since Psalm 2, a very Davidic psalm, had probably been a primary or primitive introduction in an earlier

* For an updated view see "Postscriptum," pp. 158–160.
[8] *The Ancient Library of Qumran* (1961), p. 165. See also

Cross, "History of the Biblical Text," pp. 286, 295–299.
[9] Cross, *Ancient Library*, pp. 198–200.

recension. Some Western Greek texts at Acts 13:33 in the New Testament call Psalm 2 the "First Psalm." But whatever may be the reason for that, and whatever may have been the first psalm in some primitive collection of psalms, those problems should probably be dealt with and solved independently of what we are here suggesting. A document from the fourth cave, which Professor John Allegro has called 4Q Florilegium, is a midrash or commentary on portions of II Sam. 7:10–14, followed by Psalms 1 and 2, in that order. The midrash is highly Davidic in theology, and Psalm 1 is in its traditional place.[10] Professor Frank Cross's early judgment that the collection of canonical psalms was fixed by late Persian or early Maccabean times needs probably to be limited to the first two books of the Psalter until all the evidence is in. Cross was basing his judgment almost totally on 4QPs[a], which is lacking beyond Book II. Of equal significance with Cross's view is the support he receives from Monsignor Skehan, who is editing the sixteen fragmentary manuscripts of psalms from Cave 4. In private correspondence, Skehan has clearly indicated his support of the general position that Cross advanced. Cave 11 fails to support Cross and Skehan only in Books IV and V of the Psalter, and even there one senses that crystallization of the collection is lurking close beneath, or perhaps close behind, the emerging order evident in the Psalms Scroll. Since the material in the Psalms Scroll lacks any clearly theological or even liturgical bias, but on the contrary wants above all, and perhaps despite all, to be "Davidic" in its cadences, it seems wise to view the Psalms Scroll as evidence of a Psalter tradition distinct from the "canonical" (Masoretic) that was accepted by the Rabbis after the First Jewish Revolt in the last quarter of the first century A.D.[11]

Discovery at Masada, in December 1964, of a fragment containing Ps. 150:1–6, with a blank column following the psalm, indicating that it was the last psalm of the psalter scroll from which the fragment had come, reveals that the Psalter used by the Zealots in the third quarter of the first century A.D. was probably very close, perhaps identical, to the Masoretic, or canonical, Psalter in order and content.[12]

If the Qumran sect did not commit itself to consistently transmitting a standardized form of text for any biblical book, as Monsignor Skehan has rightly pointed out,[13] it was perhaps due, in part at least, to the lack of the rigid standardization characteristic of the work of the Masoretes after the end of the first century A.D. It is difficult to conceive of the "sons of Zadok," as we know them in the scrolls, being any less "orthodox" in regard to a standardized text than any other group in the Judaism of their time. They were clearly not as orthodox in this regard as the followers of Nahum of Gamzu or of the Rabbis at Jamnia, who lived at a later time, but there is no secure evidence that they were not pious toward the various texts they received in the degree to which those texts were viewed as authentic. Professor Chaim Rabin's principle of "limited variability" is, of necessity, a relative matter, relative to whatever clear standard existed.[14] If one says that the Psalms Scroll was a non-Masoretic vulgate of its time, a "vulgar" text as Professor Paul Kahle would say, it does *not* mean that it was ill treated or thought of as "unofficial" by those who used it. Various biblical texts were clearly available in the late period of the Second Temple, just as various modern translations of the Bible are available (in most Western countries) to the most pious Jews and Christians today: the difference is that we stand this side of the various determinative councils and movements (Jamnia, Trent, *et al.*), and they the other side.[15]

---

[10] *Journal of Bible Literature*, LXXVIII (1959), pp. 343–346; Geza Vermes, *The Dead Sea Scrolls in English* (1962), pp. 243–244; and P. W. Skehan in the *Catholic Biblical Quarterly*, XXV (1963), p. 121.

[11] See Cross, "History of the Biblical Text," p. 286: "If the so-called 11QPs[a] is indeed a Psalter, despite its bizarre order and non-canonical compositions, mostly of the Hellenistic era, then we must argue that one Psalms collection closed at the end of the Persian period (the canonical collection), and that another remained open well

into the Greek period (11Q), but was rejected by the Rabbis."

[12] *Jerusalem* (Israel) *Post*, Dec. 20, 1964.

[13] *Vetus Testamentum*, Suppl. IV, 153.

[14] *Journal of Theological Studies*, VI (1955), pp. 174–182.

[15] See the excellent study by Shemaryahu Talmon, "Aspects of the Textual Transmission of the Bible in the Light of the Qumran Manuscripts," *Textus*, IV (1964), pp. 95–132, esp. pp. 97–98.

Variants

In the translation which follows, the words and phrases in the scroll that are different from the traditional text of the psalms appear in italics. The matter is more complicated than that, however, as is explained in the introductory section to the translations, but what is important here is to draw attention to those differences, or variants, that might hold some interest for the general reader.

The variants, *sensu stricto*, are numerous, indeed. But most of them are orthographic and important only to those scholars who are interested in clues to the pronunciation of Hebrew in antiquity, and such matters. The idea of "variants" can arise only when there is a generally accepted text, differences from which are then called variants. Some variants commend themselves immediately as improvements of the text, especially those that offer a clearer Hebrew text but make little or no difference in translation or interpretation. Those are properly matters for technicians and need not detain us at all.

Not all variants can be considered as improvements of the text, even in a manuscript, such as this, which is some nine hundred years older than the generally accepted (Leningradensis) Hebrew text of the early eleventh century A.D.: some variants do not commend themselves at all. While the Psalms Scroll is considerably older than the medieval Leningrad text, it contains some errors, recognizable as such without debate. The fact that it affords us a copy of some of the psalms much older than any we had heretofore does not mean that every reading in it is always to be preferred to those in younger manuscripts.

"Nothing is spurious to the scholar," but not everything is interesting or even meaningful to the layman. With the assurance, however, that properly qualified men will study every "jot and tittle" in the scroll in the years to come, the layman is rightly interested in and justifiably demands to know what the obvious and important differences are. In order to attempt to meet that demand I have drawn up a list of some of the interesting variants. The list is by no means exhaustive, nor is it the only such list that might be made. Another student of the text might well want to include other passages than those here noted, but certainly none noted here should be excluded. Nor have I consciously omitted any variant from the list for any reason whatever other than that of reasonable interest to the lay reader.

Variae Lectiones

Psalm	*Column and line*
93:1	xxii 16
104:29	(frag.) E II 8
105:1	(frag.) E III 8
105:3	(frag.) E III 11
105:37	i 10
118	xvi 1–6
118:27	(frag.) E I 3
119:2	vi 12
119:17	vii 3
119:37	viii 1
119:48	viii 12
119:71	ix 13
119:83	x 2
119:119	xi 15
119:130	xii 3
119:152	xiii 3
119:171	xiv 1
122:4	iii 9–10
125:5	iv 7:8
129:3	v 5
134:2	xxviii 2
135:1–2	xiv 7–9
135:6	xiv 13–14
135:21	xv 4
137:1	xx 7
138:1	xxi 2
139:11	xx 2–3
139:14	xx 5–6
139:15	xx 6
141:6	xxiii 2–3
142:4	xxv 1
143:3	xxv 9
144:15	xxiv 1
145	xvi 7–xvii 17
145:1	xvi 7
145:2	xvi 9
145:5	xvi 13
145:6	xvi 15
145:13f.	xvii 2–3
145:18	xvii 10–12
145:20	xvii 14
145:21	xvii 16
145:21f.	xvii 17

Psalm	Column and line
146:9–10	ii 2–4
147:20	(frag.) E III 7
149:9	xxvi 3
150:1	xxvi 4
II Sam. 23:7	xxvii 1

Psalm 145

By far the most intriguing variant in the whole scroll, among the biblical or canonical psalms, is that of the constant refrain to every verse of Psalm 145. "Blessed be the Lord and blessed be his name for ever and ever" pursues, like a chorus, every verse of the psalm. This feature of the psalm as it appears in the scroll is all the more fascinating in that the last four words (in English, two in the Hebrew) of the psalm in the traditional recension—"for ever and ever,"—are lacking in the last refrain of the scroll. One suggestion ready at hand, of course, is that those words exist at the end of the last verse in the later manuscripts as a sort of "historical memory" of the refrain which had somehow got lost. Another suggestion is that when the refrain was added by whatever groups would have, like that at Qumran presumably, used it, the superfluous and similar words at the end of verse 21 were excised just before the last refrain. Scientifically both suggestions are plausible even though the former is clearly the more attractive.

But Psalm 145 in the scroll offers one further marvel. It had a subscription: that is, a sort of program note followed it. The note began, "This [psalm] is for a memorial...." But unfortunately this is all of the subscription that remains; the rest is lost, probably forever, in the missing, decomposed lower third of column XVII. These few words are sufficient, however, as one might imagine, to incite all sorts of imaginative theses. It is the only genuine subscription of the sort known for the Psalter. The phrase that is numbered as verse 20 of Psalm 72 is probably a subscription to Book II of the Psalter: "The prayers of David, the son of Jesse, are ended." It does not pertain to Psalm 72. The doxologies at the ends of Books I, II, III, and IV are not, properly speaking, subscriptions at all. The subscription to Psalm 145 in the scroll seems to have been of the same order as the many superscriptions to the biblical psalms, that is, sort of program notes, to those who could make sense of them, indicating the cultic use of the psalm in the temple services in antiquity. Not all psalms have superscriptions, and this is the only such subscription available for any psalm in any biblical manuscript. A "memorial" would have been a special use of the psalm.

The psalm frequently mentions God's mighty acts and wondrous deeds, as a variant in verse 6 superfluously emphasizes. Professor Brevard Childs of Yale has made a study of the word "memorial" as it occurs in the Old Testament.[16] The stones set up in the Jordan at the crossing into Canaan were a memorial to God's mighty act of fulfilling his promise of the land (Josh. 4:7). The Torah, or the law itself, in a certain specific reference, is called a "memorial" (Ex. 13:9). And the Passover festival is a memorial (Ex. 12:14). By such memorials God is put in remembrance of his purpose with his people, and Israel is reminded of the covenant of which she is a part. The Apostrophe to Zion in column XXII is a "memorial" psalm for Jerusalem, though not labeled as such. In the memorial act Israel participates in the original events, the might acts, which gave birth to the covenant order: by the memorial act she experiences redemption anew. The Hebrew word is *zikkaron* and the Greek *anamnesis*, and they both lie back of the "in remembrance of me" idea of the Christian holy communion or eucharist. Psalm 145 nowhere mentions a specific "mighty act" which God might have executed on his people's behalf: in verses 14–20 it mentions the doctrine of divine providence only in general terms. But its frequent reference to God's marvelous and wondrous deeds makes it a hymn of praise most worthy to introduce a recital of those specific acts of God which brought Israel into being and sustained her. The apocryphal Psalm 145, which follows in column XVIII, continues the major theme of Psalm 145, of declaring and proclaiming God's might acts; and the apocryphal psalm "Plea for Deliverance" in column XIX also stresses God's mighty and victorious acts—which only weakly suggests a liturgical arrangement of the hymns at this point in the scroll. A "memorial" psalm such as Psalm 145 would appear to be primarily one in which God's

---

[16] *Memory and Tradition in Israel* (1962).

wondrous deeds are brought to mind in proclamation and recital.

The Hebraic poetic principle of *parallelismus membrorum* is supported in the scroll at verse 5, where the phrase "they will speak" appears at the end of the first colon (first half) of the verse:

> Of the glorious splendor of thy majesty
> *they will speak*,
> and of thy wondrous works I will meditate.
> [145:5]

The verbal phrases at the end of each colon are in parallel construction to each other.

Finally, Psalm 145 in the scroll contains a verse lacking in most other Hebrew manuscripts of the psalms but found in some ancient Psalter translations. It is the one that is left unnumbered between verses 13 and 14. The Revised Standard Version of the Bible had correctly included it on the basis of the ancient Psalter versions. In the scroll it reads, "God is faithful in his words, and gracious in all his deeds."

Psalm 139

Verse 16 of Psalm 139, which has always been difficult, remains as much an enigma as ever. The scroll at that point is less than helpful.

Verse 11, on the other hand, which few people have ever thought of as difficult at all, receives quite a new meaning. The RSV quite correctly, on the basis of all other manuscripts, reads:

> If I say, " Let only darkness cover me,
> and the light about me be night . . . ." [139:11]

Verse 12 is then understood to complete the thought, "even darkness is not dark to thee," and so on. It should be noted, however, that this is already an interpretive translation since the word "If" does not actually occur in the text. The scroll, in place of the noun "light" in the second colon of verse 11, has the verb "girded" or "emprisoned": so that the Hebrew poetic principle of *parallelismus membrorum*, mentioned above, is once more served and the text now reads:

> And I said, "Surely darkness covers me,
> and night has emprisoned me." [139:11]

The difference, in Hebrew, between the noun "light" and the verb "girded" ("emprisoned") is considerable when pronounced, but slight indeed when written. The same might be said of another variant in the psalm which occurs at the beginning of verse 15. The RSV reads, "My frame was not hidden from thee" and the scroll reads, "My pain is not hidden from thee." In Hebrew, in both cases, the written forms of the words are more similar to each other than their oral forms. But the verdict on which is the original or better reading in the two cases, verses 11 and 15, should probably not be the same. The scroll reading of verse 11 is probably right, whereas the traditional reading of verse 15 is preferable.

Trivia Theologica

Certainly one of the most popular psalms at Qumran was the one hundred and nineteenth. It occupies some eight columns in this scroll (11QPs^a) and it has been found as well in four manuscripts from Caves 1, 4, and 5 (1Q10, 4QPs^g, 4QPs^h, and 5Q5; see Appendix II). Only scattered verses are preserved in the other four, and the variants in them do not appear to hold great interest. There are about a dozen points of interest in the scores of minor variants to Psalm 119 in the Psalms Scroll, but only a few command attention.

In two verses in Psalm 119 verbs are read as active where in other manuscripts they are passive:

> It is good for me that *I was afflicted*,
> that I might learn thy statutes. [119:71—RSV]

> It is good for me that *thou didst afflict me*,
> that I might learn thy statutes.
> [119:71—11QPs^a]

> For *I have become* like a wineskin in the smoke,
> yet I have not forgotten thy *statutes*.
> [119:83—RSV]

> For *thou hast made me* like a wineskin in the
> smoke,
> yet I have not forgotten thy *steadfast love*.
> [119:83—11QPs^a]

In both instances God is seen, in the scroll's readings, as the active agent of the psalmist's condition. Theologically the variants are very interesting in the light of the expectations of most Jewish sects in the first century, Essene, Christian, Pharisaic and others, that God was the cause of the afflictions which were seen as prelude to the dramatic events of salvation soon to be supernaturally introduced into history. It is perhaps the same light in which a further variant should be read:

> *The unfolding of thy words gives light;*
> *it* imparts understanding to the simple.
> [119:130—RSV]

> *Unfold thy words, and enlighten him*
> *who* imparts understanding to the simple.
> [119:130—11QPs^a]

These look like purposive changes in the text made perhaps by someone, not necessarily Essene, whose teachings and sufferings were viewed under a strong belief in divine sovereignty. Some students of the Qumran literature will immediately think of the Teacher of Righteousness and similar ideas attributed to him in the Qumran Thanksgiving Hymns (1QH cols. v and IX). Others will rightly insist on how ancient and biblical the doctrines of divine providence and intervention are; and some will even entertain the possibility of the scroll readings in Psalm 119 as original and preferable.

The tendency to find the peculiar ideas and beliefs of the Qumran sect in the variants and in the apocryphal compositions in the scroll should not be permitted to get out of hand; for it must always be held in mind that the whole scroll is strongly " Davidic" in interest: it is safe to assume that the scribe who compiled and copied the scroll believed in the Davidic authorship of what he was writing. If that is the case he could hardly have had the Teacher of Righteousness, the sect's supposed leader, in mind as author. Interesting in this regard is 119:152.

> Long have I known from *thy testimonies*
> that thou hast founded *them* for ever.
> [119:152—RSV]

> Long have I known from *knowledge of thee*
> that thou hast founded *me* for ever.
> [119:152—11QPs^a]

The biblical theologian immediately thinks of God's covenant with David outlined in II Sam. 7:8–16 and frequently reflected in the Psalter, as in Psalms 2, 89, and 132. The salient feature of the Davidic covenant was God's promise to David

that his lineage and heirs would always occupy the Jerusalem kingship, which was the theological undergirding of the Davidic dynasty. Whether or not that is the reference intended in the variant above is uncertain. The most interesting aspect of the variant is that it makes good sense in the context of verses 145–152 of Psalm 119 and perhaps more than does the traditional reading. The task of establishing such a variant as the authentic reading involves considerably more, however, than " good sense."

A third case of an active form of a verb appearing instead of a passive form is in Ps. 135:21: " Blessed be the Lord from Zion . . ." reads " May the Lord bless thee from Zion . . ." in the scroll. And it has already been noted that God's " greatness" in Ps. 145:6 reads " God's might acts" in the scroll.

The transcendence of God seems to receive some emphasis in two variants. In antiquity, in biblical times, when too great a familiarity with the divine name seemed somehow to indicate lack of respect or piety, one would speak, as in Deuteronomy and elsewhere, not directly of the Lord God, but rather of the name of the Lord, particularly when it was a question of speaking of his immanence and presence. The expression " Bless the Lord" in Ps. 134:2 reads " Bless the name of the Lord" in the scroll. From another stance God's awesomeness is equally stressed in Ps. 145:20, where the familiar " The Lord preserves all who love him" appears in the scroll as " The Lord preserves all who fear him."

God's transcendence, however, does not mean that God is so distant as to be unreliable or beyond supplication, and twice the scroll has readings that stress his loving-kindness (Pss. 119:83 and 144:2).

Psalm 118 is one of the most important from the standpoint of Jewish and Christian usage through the ages, but in the scroll at column XVI it is mutilated almost beyond recognition. Only six verses of it appear, and they are tacked on to the end of Psalm 136.* It is a poor showing indeed for so fine a psalm. One might surmise that the psalm is so treated because of its being clearly a " Jerusalem" psalm, one used in biblical times during the great autumn Festival of Booths or

---

* But see now " Postscriptum," pp. 155–161.

Tabernacles in celebration of the giving of the Law on Mt. Sinai. But certainly one could not establish any anti-Jerusalem attitude in the scroll on the basis of Ps. 135:2, which has a phrase, lacking in all other manuscripts, emphasizing Jerusalem:

> *And exalt the Lord,*
> you that stand in the house of the Lord,
> in the courts of the house of our God,
> *and in your midst, O Jerusalem!*
>
> [Ps. 135:2—11QPs^a]

One might interpret the addenda as a kind of homily directed at those who in Jerusalem are not quite praising and exalting the Lord as they should, but not in any sense as anti-Jerusalemite in sentiment or theology. The Apostrophe to Zion, in column XXII, exalts the Holy City in such a way as to indicate the same centrality of Jerusalem in the faith of those who used the scroll as elsewhere in Judaism. Neither the addenda to Ps. 135:2 nor the Apostrophe to Zion needs to have originated among the Essenes in order to have been very meaningful to them—no more than any of the " Davidic" literature in the Psalter and in Isaiah, which they so clearly loved.

Addenda

Significant addenda are found in five canonical psalms: 105, 118, 135, 146, and 149. In addition to the two phrases in Ps. 135:2, noted just above, there is an odd insertion in the middle of verse 6 of the same psalm.

> What the Lord pleases he does in heaven
> and on earth *to do he does;*
> *there is none like the Lord,*
> *there is none like the Lord,*
> *and there is none who does as the King of gods,*
> in the seas and *in* all deeps.
>
> [Ps. 135:6—11QPs^a]

The added phrases remind one of such hymnic cries as those in the Song of Hannah in I Sam. 2:2 and in the later Jewish prayers and liturgy. There is a great shout of joy which marks the completion of the Sabbath morning services in most synagogues of the West and which sounds very much like these scroll additions. The syntax of the verse is not at all clear, and the purists among grammarians will regret the intrusion; for the addenda

of the verse could be excised and perfect grammar restored. These incursions had best be seen as signs of the joy of faith in God's pleasure and work—parenthetical shouts uttered by those, perhaps, who awaited a new mighty act of divine salvation. Many Jewish groups did such waiting in high anticipation of the eschaton, or God's climatic drama for the world, in the first century, not the least of whom were both the group at Qumran and the Christians.

Psalm 118 is so strangely used in column XVI, as a sort of coda to Psalm 136, that one cannot be sure that the next is simply an addendum. Nonetheless, between verses 9 and 29 in line 5 of column XVI an unknown verse intrudes:

> It is better to trust in the Lord than to put confidence in a thousand people.

This addition reminds one somewhat of Ps. 84:11, but only because of a word or two in each. Then at the end of line 6, column XVI, a "Hallelujah" ("Praise the Lord") is appended where it is lacking in other manuscripts; this is comparable to the "Hallelujah" prefixed to Ps. 93:1 as a superscription. That makes two Hallelujahs added in the scroll, but there are three omitted: those which in the traditional text open Psalms 148, 135, and 150 are left out in the scroll.

Comparable to the addendum written whole cloth into the text of the mutilated Psalm 118 is the intrusion of what was probably three lines of extraneous text between verses 9 and 10 of Psalm 146. Since only about half the column is preserved, vertically, it is difficult to make much sense of what was added. Immediately following verse 9 are words seemingly taken from Ps. 33:8. Following those are words that seem to reflect, according to Monsignor Skehan, who has seen this text, some of the ideas expressed in Ps. 145:10–12. The phenomenon of paraphrasing biblical passages was not at all uncommon either at Qumran or elsewhere in Jewish circles in the general New Testament period. Several passages in the apocryphal compositions in the scroll exhibit the same practice (see especially the " Hymn to the Creator" in column XXVI). Comparable is the addition to Ps. 149:9 of the phrase "for the sons of Israel, his holy people," which undoubtedly reflects Ps. 148:14. (Incidentally, the latter might better be read, like the addition to Ps. 149:9, "his holy people," than as in the RSV.) Whereas the Hallelujah prefixed to Psalm 93 might attract some support, the strange intrusions in Psalms 118, 135, and 146 are probably aberrations, attactive though some of them may indeed be. (On Ps. 105:1, see "Postscriptum," pp. 160 and 164.)

Other addenda are noted in the apparatus and in the following general list.

Psalm	Column and line
93:1	xxii 16
102:23	(frag.) C ii 6
102:28	(frag.) C ii 11
118:9f.	xvi 5
118:29	xvi 6
119:119	xi 15
119:129	xii 2
119:171	xiv 1
121:5	iii 4
125:8	iv 1
129:8	v 9
132:11	vi 3
134:2	xxviii 2
135:2	xiv 8–9
135:6	xiv 13–14
136:7	xv 11
143:4	xxv 10
145:1ff.	xvi–xvii
145:13f.	xvii 2–3
145:21f.	xvii 17
146:9f.	ii 2–4
149:9	xxvi 3

Superscriptions

Apart from the exciting subscription to Psalm 145 and the "Ḷallelujah" added to Psalm 118, discussed above, superscriptions to the canonical psalms are the same as those in the traditional text with few exceptions. While the opening "Hallelujah," as noted above, is omitted from Psalms 135, 148, and 150, and one is prefixed, unexpectedly, to Psalm 93, the "Psalm of David" designation, which appears in all other psalms where expected, is left out at the beginning of Psalm 144. But the word omitted there is added to Ps. 123:1 and to Ps. 104:1, in line 16, column iii, and in line 6 of Fragment E I, where MT lacks it—in each case, in Hebrew, the expression "for David."

The single psalm in the Psalter labeled "Psalm" (*t^{e}hillah*) in the scroll is changed to "Prayer" (*t^{e}fillah*) by the difference of a single letter, Ps. 145:1.

Memorabilia

The scribe who copied our scroll did not make many errors. Most of those he did make he either erased, or, in the case of the divine name which he could not erase, he set off with what are called scribal dots, which signal a recognized error.

Whether or not the superscription to Psalm 145, noted above, is to be regarded as an error, there is one definitely to be noted at Ps. 145:2, where the word "Blessed" (*baruk*) appears instead of the traditional "Every" (*w^{e}kol*). In Hebrew the two look somewhat alike, but, more than that, "Blessed" occurs in the psalm refrain after every verse, and it is quite understandable that even a good scribe might be thus induced to err.

A very fascinating scribal "goof" occurs in Ps. 145:18, where the expression "The Lord is near" in Hebrew looks and sounds so much like the beginning of the refrain of the psalm, "Blessed be the Lord" (the difference between *qarob* and *baruk*; see again Ps. 148:14), that the scribe, instead of copying the regular verse 18, as he should have, went on with the refrain, with the odd result:

> The Lord is near and blessed be his name for ever and ever . . . .

At that point the poor fellow caught himself, and instead of erasing or crossing out (which he never does), he tried to continue and salvage what he could of a poor beginning. The result is not really bad Hebrew, though it is not good poetry. An important thing to remark, however, is that he ends up with the exact number of words which he should have, had he copied the text correctly: there should be fourteen words in Ps. 145:18 with the special refrain, and there are fourteen words as the scribe left it.

There are several errors in the little Psalm 118 complex in column xvi, lines 3 to 5. These are not very interesting to the layman except, perhaps, for the possible evidence they exhibit of the scribe's having copied off the lines at this point in the scroll either from memory or from dictation. Other errors do not exhibit such evidence but may be assumed to have been caused by mistakes made while copying visually.

There is a rather fantastic oddity to be observed in the single line surviving of II Sam. 23:7 at the top of column XXVII. The traditional text is uncertain and not very helpful: most translations, such as that of the RSV, are what might be called brave attempts. The Psalms Scroll presents the same uncertain traditional text, with the exception of one word, which is just as much an enigma, if not more so, as the one it displaced. The sum of it is that I do not know what to make of the line, nor do I really know how to translate it. It appeared so strange to me out in Jerusalem when I first read it as I unrolled the scroll that I was reluctant to identify it as the last words of the psalm in II Samuel 23 until I showed it to Professor David Noel Freedman, who had come out on a visit. Freedman had, with Professor Frank Cross, made an intensive study of early Hebrew poetry, this psalm among others, and recognized it despite its fresh difficulties. He succeeded where I with the concordance had failed. Perhaps he and others will be able to make sense of it: let us hope so.

Similia Similibus

There are a few notable instances where it might be interesting for the layman to observe where the scroll (Q) has readings in accord with the Masoretic, or traditional, Hebrew text (MT) against the RSV, and others in accord with the RSV (for one reason or another) against the Hebrew text (MT).

Q = MT

Psalm	Column and line
104:3	(frag.) E I 9
119:88	x 7
119:158	xiii 10
139:14	xx 6
141:6	xxiii 2–3
144:2	xxiii 13–14
144:15	xxiv 1
II Sam. 23:7	xxvii 1

Q = RSV

Psalm	Column and line
104:27	(frag.) E II 7
105:9	(frag.) E III 15
119:108	xi 4
119:116	xi 12
137:9	xxi 1
138:1	xxi 2
142:4	xxv 1

(For a discussion of the variants in Fragment E, see "Postscriptum," pp. 159–160.)

PART II

The Translation

INTRODUCTION TO THE TEXT

THE contents of the Psalms Scroll are here presented as the text appears on the leather itself. On the even-numbered pages below is the Hebrew text as it is on the scroll. On the odd-numbered pages is an English translation corresponding to the Hebrew, column for column and line for line.

The Revised Standard Version of the Holy Bible provides the basic translation, for even with its numerous variants the text of the biblical psalms in the scroll is essentially the traditional Masoretic text on which the RSV is based. The line-for-line correspondence between the Hebrew and the English is amazingly high; the Hebraist will, of course, note a few instances where, because a good translation must be idiomatic and not literal or verbal, an English line does not exactly match the Hebrew.

Where the text of the scroll differs from the text indicated by the RSV, the English translation will show a corresponding difference from the RSV. To make these variants clear, *every word in the following English text which is not in the RSV translation is presented in italics.* A note is then offered at the foot of the page, in the manner used in the RSV itself, showing the unaltered RSV text, and by the use of a few sigla, offering a limited amount of pertinent information. *In the notes the unaltered RSV text (only) is presented in italics.*

In the style of the RSV the footnotes to each column are indicated by small superscript letters in italics, appearing immediately after the pertinent word or phrase in the text; only in a few instances does the footnote reference letter appear before the pertinent word or phrase in the text, such as at the beginning of the first line of a column, and at the beginning, as well as the end, of phrases referred to in the notes.

The Revised Standard Version, based on the Hebrew psalms in the medieval copies, is a good, worthy translation, and in most verses represents the reading(s) in those copies. In a few verses, however, the RSV represents readings not in the medieval Hebrew texts but in ancient Greek, Latin, Aramaic, or Syriac translations of the psalms—in those instances where the Hebrew is not clear or certain, or where the ancient versions seem to make better sense. In all such instances the following English translation represents the Hebrew of the scroll rather than the ancient versions. In other words, *the RSV is used in the following English translation only in so far as it faithfully represents the Hebrew text of the Psalms Scroll.* Where it does not—that is, either (1) where the Hebrew of the scroll differs from the medieval Hebrew texts translated by the RSV, or (2) where the RSV follows an ancient version, like Greek, and not the medieval Hebrew —then the RSV is abandoned and the scroll is translated directly (in italics). *The following English translation, therefore, is based only on the Hebrew as it is in the Psalms Scroll.*

The advantages in using the RSV as a base are twofold. First, the RSV affords the familiar, majestic English of the Psalter corrected for accuracy and clarity by a committee of distinguished, contemporary scholars. It would have been pretentious to attempt to create an improved English translation where the Hebrew text remains the same. Second, using the RSV as a base affords the great advantage of signaling the variants in the scroll text by noting them in italics in the English against a background of regular roman type where the text remains the same.

The sigla are as follows:

Q	11QPs^a—the Psalms Scroll
MT	The Masoretic (medieval) Text
Heb	Hebrew

RSV   The Revised Standard Version of
             the Holy Bible
LXX or Grk   The Septuagint (or another ancient
             Greek) version
Lat   An ancient Latin version: Psal-
             terium Romanum, Psalterium
             Iuxta Hebraeos, Vulgate
Syr   A Syriac version
Cn   Correction (col. XVIII only)

The brackets [ ] in the text indicate lacunae in the scroll. They are filled in, where indicated, with the RSV in the English text but left blank in the Hebrew. A dot over a letter in the Hebrew means the reading as given is uncertain. These occur at the bottoms of columns where the leather has decomposed and elsewhere in the text usually because of worm holes. An asterisk over or under a letter signifies a scribal-error dot that is actually in the text, placed there by the ancient scribe to signal the error he himself had made in adding or misplacing a letter or word. The small numbers in both the Hebrew and the English represent the familiar verse divisions within each psalm.

TEXT

Fragments A, B, C I

Pss. 101:1–8; 102:1–2

Line

101(1)[ ]שׁפט אשירה לכה[ ]ך̊ 𐤉𐤄𐤅𐤄 אזמרה

(2)[ ]י תִבוא לי אתהל[ ] בתום לבבי

[(3)]עיני דבר בל̊[ ]עֹשה

[ ]י (4)לבב[ ]

[(5)]

[ ] ורחב ל[(6)]אמני

[ ]בת עמדי הֹ[ ]רתני

(7)[ ] בקרב ביתי [ ] לוֹא

[ ] עיני (8)לבקרים א[ ]תֹ

[ ]ר 𐤉𐤄𐤅𐤄 כול פֿ[ ]ל[ ]

102(1)[ ] לעני כי יעטו[ ]

(2)[ ]שׁמעה תפל[ ]

Fragments A, B, C ɪ

Pss. 101:1–8; 102:1–2

Line

[⁽¹⁾A Psalm of David]. I will sing [of loyalty and of jus]tice; to thee, [O Lo]ʀᴅ, I will sing.   Ps. 101

[⁽²⁾I will give heed to the way that is blameless. Oh wh]en wilt thou come to me? I will wal[k] with
integrity of heart

[within my house;⁽³⁾ I will not set before] my eyes anything that [is base. I hate]

[the work of those who fall away; it shall not cleave to] me. [⁽⁴⁾Perverseness of] heart [shall be far
from me;]

5   [I will know nothing of evil. ⁽⁵⁾Him who slanders his neighbor secretly, I will destroy.]

[The man of haughty looks] and arrogant he[art I will not endure. ⁽⁶⁾I will look with favor on the
fa]ithful

[in the land, that may d]well with me; he [who walks in the way that is blameless shall mi]nister to
me.

[⁽⁷⁾No man who practices deceit shall dwell] in my house; no [man who utters lies]

[shall continue in] my presence. ⁽⁸⁾Morning by morning I [will destroy all the wicked in the land,
cutting] off

10   all the ev[ildoers from the city] of the Lᴏʀᴅ.

[⁽¹⁾A prayer] of one afflicted, when he is fain[t and pours out his complaint before the Lᴏʀᴅ.]   Ps. 102

⁽²⁾Hear my pray[er, O Lᴏʀᴅ; let my cry come to thee! . . .]

Fragment C II

Pss. 102:18–29; 103:1

Line

תולעת הערער ולוא [(19)]

אחרון ועם נברא יהלל 𐤉̇[(20)]

𐤉𐤄𐤅𐤄 משמים אל האר[(21)]
[ ]תח בני תמותה (22)לספר בצ[ ]

בירושלים (23)בהקבץ עמים[ ]
𐤉𐤄𐤅𐤄 (24)כי ענה בדרך [(25)]

תעלני בחצי ימי בדור ד̇[(26)]

נוסדה ומעשי ידיכה ש̇[(27)]

וכולם כבגד יבלו וכלבוש̇[(28)]

ושנותיכה לוא יתמו (29)בני[ ]

[ ]לד̇ור
103(1)[ ]ר̊כי נפשי את 𐤉̇[ ]

Fragment C II

Pss. 102:18–29; 103:1

Line

[a]the *worm*[b] of the destitute, and will not [despise their supplication. (18)Let this be recorded for a generation] Ps. 102

to come, so that a people yet unborn may praise the Lo[RD: (19)that he looked down from his holy height,]

from heaven the LORD looked at the ear[th, (20)to hear the groans of the prisoners,]

[to set] free those who were doomed to die; (21)that men may declare in Zi[on the name of the LORD, and in Jerusalem]

his praise, (22)when peoples gather [together, and kingdoms, to worship]

the LORD. (23)*For*[c] he has broken my strength in mid-course; [he has shortened my days. (24)"O my God," I say,]

"take me not hence in the midst of my days, [thou whose years endure] throughout all generations!" [(25)Of old *the earth*]

was founded,[d] and the h[eavens are] the works of thy hands. [(26)They will perish, but thou dost endure;]

they will all wear out like a garment. *And*[e] [thou changest them] like raiment, [and they pass away; (27)but thou art the same,]

and thy years have no end. (28)The children [of thy servants shall dwell secure; their posterity shall be established before thee,]

[generation] to generation.[f]

[(1)A Psalm of David. Ble]ss the L[ORD,] O my soul [. . . . Ps. 103

---

[a] MT v. 18
[b] Only in Q. RSV(MT) *prayer*
[c] Only in Q
[d] RSV(MT) *thou didst lay the foundation of the earth*
[e] Lacking in RSV(MT). Cf. LXX, Lat, Syr
[f] Only in Q (cf. LXX, Lat)

Fragment D

Ps. 109:21–31

Line

[(21)]מכה כי טוב

[(22)]י̇ חלל בקרבי

[(23) (24)]כי כשלו מצום

[(25)]ל̇ה̊ם יראוני

[(26)]ושיעני

[(27)]א̇תה עשיתה

[(28)]כה ישמח

[(29)]ם (30)אודה

[(31)]כי עמד

Fragment D

Ps. 109:21–31

Line

[(21)But thou, O God my LORD, deal on my behalf for] thy name's sake; because [thy steadfast love] is good, Ps. 109

[deliver me! (22)For I am poor and needy, and my heart] is stricken within me.

[(23)I am gone, like a shadow at evening; I am shaken off like a locust.] (24)My knees are weak through fasting;

[my body has become gaunt. (25)I am an object of scorn] to my accusers; when they see me,

[they wag their heads. (26)Help me, O LORD my God!] Save me

[according to thy steadfast love! (27)Let them know that this is thy hand; *O LORD*,] *thou*[a] hast done it!

[(28)Let them curse, but do thou bless! Let my assailants be put to shame; may thy ser]vant be glad!

[(29)May my accusers be clothed with dishonor; may they be wrapped in their own shame as in a mantle! (30)With my mouth] I will give great thanks

[to the LORD; I will praise him in the midst of the throng.] (31)For he *has stood*[b]

---

[a] RSV(MT) *thou, O LORD,*
[b] RSV(MT) *stands*

Column I

Ps. 105:25–45

Line

[(25)]לבם לשנוא
[(26)]רון אשר בחר
[(27) (28)]ה̇ חושך
[ ]ר̇ם (29?)שם
[(30)]רצה ארצם
[(31)]נ̊ים בכול
[(32) (33)]ך גפנם
[(34)]וילק ואין
[(35)]ד̇מתם
[(36) (37)]ת עמו
[(38)]ת̇ם כי
[(39)] לילה
[(40) (41)]ור ויזובו
[(42)]א̇ברהם
[(43)] (44)ויתן
[(45)]ר̇ ישמורו

Column I

Ps. 105:25–45

Line

[$^{(25)}$He turned] their hearts to hate   Ps. 105

[his people, to deal craftily with his servants. $^{(26)}$He sent Moses his servant, and Aa]ron whom he
had chosen.

[$^{(27)}$They wrought his signs among them, and miracles in the land of Ham. $^{(28)}$He sen]t darkness,
[and made the land dark;   ]^{a} $^{(29)}$He *made*^{b}

5 [their waters into blood, and caused their fish to die.] $^{(30)}$Their land swarmed
[with frogs, even in the chambers of their kings. $^{(31)}$He spoke, and there came swarms of flies and
gna]ts throughout

[their country. $^{(32)}$He gave them hail for rain, and lightning that flashed through their land. $^{(33)}$He]
smote their vines

[and fig trees, and shattered the trees of their country. $^{(34)}$He spoke, and the locusts came,] and young
locusts without

[number; $^{(35)}$which devoured all the vegetation in their land, and ate up the fruit] of their ground.

10 [$^{(36)}$He smote all the first-born in their land, the first issue of all their strength. $^{(37)}$Then he led forth]
his people^{c}

[with silver and gold, and there was none among his tribes who stumbled. $^{(38)}$Egypt was glad when]
they de[parted,] for

[dread of them had fallen upon it. $^{(39)}$He spread a cloud for a covering, and fire to give light] by night.

[$^{(40)}$They asked, and he brought quails, and gave them bread from heaven in abundance. $^{(41)}$He
opened the r]ock, and [water] gushed forth;

[it flowed through the desert like a river. $^{(42)}$For he remembered his holy promise, and] Abraham

15 [his servant. $^{(43)}$So he led forth his people with joy, his chosen ones with singing.] $^{(44)}$And he gave
[them the lands of the nations; and they took possession of the fruit of the peoples' toil, $^{(45)}$to the
e]nd that they should keep

---

^{a} RSV *they rebelled against his words*. MT *they did not rebel at his word(s)*. The text of Q is highly uncertain; it may have
ended *their word*
^{b} RSV(MT) *turned*
^{c} Only in Q. RSV *Israel*. MT *them*

Column II

Pss. 146:9–10; 148:1–12

יתום ואלמנה יעודד ודרך[[

מ𐤉𐤄𐤅𐤄 כול הארץ ממנ[[
בהודעו לכול מעשיו ברא[[
גבורותיו [10]ימלוך 𐤉𐤄𐤅𐤄[[
ודור הללויה
148[1] הללו 𐤉𐤄𐤅𐤄 משמים הלל̇[[2] [
כול מלאכיו הללוהו כול צבא[[3] [
הללוהו כול כוכבי אור [4]הללו[[
אשר מעל לשמים [5]הללו את[[
צוה ונבראו [6]ויעמידם לע[[

יעבור [7]הללו את 𐤉𐤄𐤅𐤄 מ[[
תהומות [8]אש וברד שלג וק[[
עושה דברו [9]ההרים וכול̇[[
ארזים [10]החיה וכול בהמה [[11] [
אר̊[ ] וכול לאומים שרים ו[[12] [
]]לות זקנים עם נע[[13] [

Column II

Pss. 146:9–10; 148:1–12

Line

he upholds the widow and the fatherless; but the way [of the wicked he brings to ruin. ?] Ps. 146
[a]*fear the LORD, all the earth,* [*let all the inhabitants of the earth stand in awe*] *of hi*[*m*! . . .]
in his being known through all his works (which) he created[?]
his mighty works.[a] (10)The LORD will reign [for ever, thy God, O Zion, to all]
generations. Praise the LORD!
(1)Praise[b] the LORD from the heavens, prai[se him in the heights! (2)Praise him,] Ps. 148
all his angels, praise him, all his host! [(3)Praise him, sun and moon,]
praise him, all you shining stars! (4)Praise [him, you highest heavens, and you waters]
above the heavens! (5)*Praise*[c] [the name of the Lord! For he]
commanded and they were created. (6)And he established them for ev[er and ever; he fixed their bounds which cannot]
be passed. (7)Praise the LORD fro[m the earth, you sea monsters and all]
deeps, (8)fire and hail, snow and f[rost, stormy wind]
fulfilling his command! (9)Mountains and all [hills, fruit trees and all]
cedars! (10)Beasts and all cattle, [creeping things and flying birds! (11)Kings]
of the ea[rth] and all peoples, princes and [all rulers of the earth! (12)Young men]
[and mai]dens together, old men and chil[dren!]

[a–a] Only in Q. Cf. Ps. 33:8 and perhaps Ps. 145:10–12
[b] RSV(MT) *Praise the LORD! Praise*
[c] RSV(MT) *Let them praise*

Column III

Pss. 121:1–8; 122:1–9; 123:1–2

Line

121(1) שיר המעלות אשא עיני אל ההרים מאין יבוא [ ]

[ ](2)עזרי מעם 𐤉𐤄𐤅𐤄 עושה שמים וארץ (3)אל יתן ל[ ]

[ ]לכה ואל []נום שומרכה (4)הנה לוא ינום ולוא יישן[ ]

[ ]שראל (5)בלילה 𐤉𐤄𐤅𐤄 שומרכה צלכה על יד ימינכה (6)יומ[ ]

[ ]מש לוא יככה וירח בלילה (7)𐤉𐤄𐤅𐤄 ישומרכה מכו[ ] יש[ ]

[ ]ת נפשכה (8)ישמור צאתכה ובואכה מעתה ועד ע[ ]

122(1) שיר המעלות לדויד ש[ ]

[ ]בית 𐤉𐤄𐤅𐤄 נלך (2)עומדות היו רגלי בשעריך [ ]

[ ]ושלים (3)ירושלים הבנוה כעיר שחברה לו (4)שמה[ ]

?[עדת ישראל להודות לשם 𐤉𐤄𐤅𐤄 (5)כי ש[ ]

[ ]משפט כסא לבית דויד (6)שאלו שלום ירוש[ ]

[ ]והביך (7)יהי שלום בחילך ושלוה בארמונותיך [(8)]

[ ]רעי אדברה שלום בך (9)למען בית 𐤉𐤄𐤅𐤄 אלו[ ]

[ ]טובה לך [ ]

[123(1)]דויד למעלות[ ]ליכה נ[ש]י [ ]ני היושב בשמ[(2)]

[ ]עבדים אל[ ]יהם[ ]ע[ ]ני[ ]

Column III

Pss. 121:1–8; 122:1–9; 123:1–2

Line

(1)A Song of Ascents. I lift up my eyes to the hills. From whence does [my help] Ps. 121
come? (2)My help comes from the LORD, who made heaven and earth. (3)He will not let your [foo]t
be [moved,] *and* he who keeps you will not slumber. (4)Behold, he who k[eeps Is]rael will neither slumber nor
sleep. (5)*By night*[a] the LORD is your keeper; your[b] shade on your right hand. (6)[The s]un
shall not smite you by da[y], nor the moon by night. (7)The LORD will keep you from al[l evil]; he will k[eep]
your life. (8)He[c] will keep your going out and your coming in from this time forth and for ev[ermore].

(1)A Song of Ascents. Of David. I was g[lad when they said] Ps. 122
[to me], "Let us go to the house of the LORD!" (2)*My*[d] feet have been standing within your gates,
[O Jer]usalem! (3)Jerusalem, built as a city which is bound firmly,[e] (4)[f]*thither* [ascends[g]]
the congregation of Israel[f] to give thanks to the name of the LORD. (5)*For*[h] th[ere thrones[g]]
[for] judgment [were set[g]], the throne[i] of the house of David. (6)Pray for the peace of Jerus[alem]!
["May they prosper who l]ove you! (7)Peace be within your walls, and security within your towers!" [(8)For my brethren]
[and] companions' [sake] I will say, "Peace be within you!" (9)For the sake of the house of the LORD our G[od],
[I will seek] your good.

[(1)*A Song of*] *David of Ascents.*[j] To thee I lift up my eyes, O thou who art enthroned in the heav[ens! (2)Behold,] Ps. 123
[as the eyes] of servants look to [the hand of] their [master, as the] eyes [of a maid to the hand]

---

[a] Only in Q
[b] RSV(MT) *The LORD is your*
[c] RSV(MT) *The LORD*
[d] RSV(MT) *Our*
[e] RSV(MT) *firmly together*
[f–f] RSV(MT) *to which the tribes go up, the tribes of the LORD, as was decreed for Israel,*
[g] Conjecture
[h] Q = MT, lacking in RSV
[i] RSV(MT) *thrones*
[j] RSV(MT) *A Song of Ascents*

Column IV

Pss. 124:7–8; 125:1–5; 126:1–6; 127:1

Line

]]נ̊מלטנו (8)עוזרנו בשם 𐤉𐤄𐤅𐤄 עושה
] [
125(1)]] הבוטחים ב 𐤉𐤄𐤅𐤄 כהר ציון שלוא
]]שב (2)ירושלים הרים סביב לו 𐤉𐤄𐤅𐤄
]]ע̊תה ועד עולם (3)כי לוא ינוח שבט הרשע

]]ד̊יקים למען לוא ישלחו הצדיקים בעולתה
] (4)]ב̊ה 𐤉𐤄𐤅𐤄 לטובים ולישרים בלב (5)עקלקולות

]]𐤄 את כול פועלי און שלום על ישראל
126(1) שיר המעלות בשוב 𐤉𐤄𐤅𐤄
]]היינו כחלו̊מים (2)אז ימלא שחוק פינו ולשוננו

]]א̊מרו בגויים הגדיל 𐤉𐤄𐤅𐤄 לעשות עם
] (3)]י̊ל 𐤉𐤄𐤅𐤄 לעשות עמנו היינו שמחים
(4)]]𐤅𐤄 את שבותינו כאפיקים בנגב (5)הזורעים
]]ה̊ יקצורו (6)הלוך ילך ובכו נושאי משך הזרע
]]נ̊ה נושאי אלומותו
127(1)]]לשלומה א̊[ ]𐤄 לוא [ ]בנה[ ]ת̊ שוא

Column IV

Pss. 124:7–8; 125:1–5; 126:1–6; 127:1

Line

[is broken, and we] have escaped! [8]Our *helper*[a] is in the name of the LORD, who made   Ps. 124
[heaven and earth.]

[[1]A Song of Ascents.] Those who trust in the LORD are like Mount Zion, which cannot   Ps. 125
[be moved, but a]bides [for ever]. [2]As the mountains are round about Jerusalem, so the LORD

5   [is round about his people, from this] time forth and for evermore. [3]For the scepter of wickedness
shall not rest

[upon the land allotted to the ri]ghteous, lest the righteous put forth [their hands]

to do wrong. [4][Do go]od, O LORD, to those who are good, and to those who are upright in *heart*.[b]

[5][c] *(In) tortuous ways*

[*The LOR*]D [*will lead*] *all evildoers!*[c] Peace be in Israel!

[1]A Song of Ascents. When the LORD restored   Ps. 126

10   [the fortunes of Zion,] we were like those who dream.[d] [2]Then our mouth was filled with laughter,
and our tongue

[with shouts of joy; then] they said among the nations, "The LORD has done great things for
[them."] [3]The LORD had done great things for us; we are glad.

[4][Restore] our fortunes, O LORD, like the water-courses in the Negeb! [5]May those who sow
[in tears] reap [with shouts of jo]y! [6]He that goes forth weeping, bearing[e] the seed for sowing,

15   shall come home with shouts of joy, [f]bringing his sheaves with him.[f]

[[1]A Song of Ascents.] Of Solomon. Un[less the LOR]D builds [the hou]se . . . in vain   Ps. 127

---

[a] Only in Q. RSV(MT) *help.* Q uncertain

[b] RSV(MT) *their hearts*

[c–c] Conjecture. RSV *But those who turn aside upon their crooked ways the LORD will lead away with evildoers!* Heb uncertain

[d] Q uncertain

[e] RSV(MT). Q uncertain

[f–f] RSV. Q uncertain

Column v

Pss. 128:3–6; 129:1–8; 130:1–8; 131:1

ל֯] (4)]גבר ירא 𐤉𐤄𐤅𐤄 (5)יברככה אדוני

]]ים כול ימי חייכה (6)וראה בנים

ל֯] [

129(1) ש]]ר֯וני מנעורי יואמר נא ישראל (2)רבות

]]א֯ יכולו לי (3)על גבי חרשו רשעים

]](4)א֯דוני צדיק קצץ עבות רשעים (5)יבושו

]]נ֯אי ציון (6)יהיו כחציר גגות שקדמת שלף

יב] (7)]צ֯ר ו֯חוצנו מעמר (8)שלוא אמרו העוברים

ב֯ד]]לוהיכמ עליכם ברכנו אתכם בשם 𐤉𐤄𐤅𐤄

]] 130(1) שיר המעלות אדוני ממעמקים

] (2)]ע֯ה בקולי תהי נא אוזנכה קשובת לי

] (3)]מ֯ור יה אדוני מי יעמוד (4)כי עמכה הסליחה

] (5)]𐤄 קותה נפשי לדברו הוחלתי (6)הוחילי

]]ב֯וקר שומרים לבוקר (7)יחל ישראל

]]ה֯חסד הרב עמו פדה (8)הוא יפדה את

]]ו֯

131(1)]]𐤅֯𐤄֯[ ]ל֯[[

Column v

Pss. 128:3–6; 129:1–8; 130:1–8; 131:1

Line

around [your table. (4)Lo, thus shall the m]an [be blessed] who fears the L<small>ORD</small>. (5)The   Ps. 128
L<small>ORD</small>*ᵃ* bless you

[from Zion! May you see the prosperity of Jerusal]em all the days of your life! (6)May you see your
children's

[children! Peace be upon Israel.]

(1)A S[ong of Ascents. "Sorely have they af]flicted me from my youth," let Israel   Ps. 129
now say—(2) "Sorely*ᵇ*

5 [have they afflicted me from my youth, yet they have no]t prevailed against me. (3)*Wicked men*ᶜ
plowed upon my back;

[they made long their furrows." (4)The] L<small>ORD</small>*ᵃ* is righteous; he has cut the cords of the wicked.

(5)May [all who ha]te Zion be put to shame [and turned backward]! (6)Let them be like the grass
on the housetops, which withers before it grows

up, (7)[with which the reaper does not fill his hand] or the binder of sheaves his bosom, (8)while those
who pass by do not say,

[" The blessing of the L<small>ORD</small>] *your God*ᵈ be upon you! We bless you in the name of the L<small>ORD</small>!"

10   (1)A Ṣong of Ascents. Out of the depths [I cry to thee],   Ps. 130
O L<small>ORD</small>!*ᵃ* (2)[L<small>ORD</small>, hea]r my voice! *Let now thy ear be attentive to me,*ᵉ

[to the voice of my supplications! (3)If thou,]O L<small>ORD</small>,[shouldst] mark [iniquities,] L<small>ORD</small>, who could
stand? (4)But there is forgiveness with thee,

[that thou mayest be feared. (5)I wait for the L<small>OR</small>]D, my soul waits, in*ᶠ* his word I hope; (6)*wait,*

[*O my soul,*ᵍ for the L<small>ORD</small> more than watchmen for] the morning, more than watchmen for the
morning. (7)O Israel, hope

15 [in the L<small>ORD</small>! For with the L<small>ORD</small>] there is steadfast love, and with him is plenteous redemption.*ʰ*
(8)He*ⁱ* will redeem

[Isreal from all] his [iniquities.]

[(1)A song of Ascents. Of David. O Lo]RD, [my] he[art is not lifted up, my eyes are not   Ps. 131
raised too high;]

ᵃ The title, not the proper name as in RSV(MT)
ᵇ Or "many times"
ᶜ RSV(MT) *The plowers*
ᵈ Only in Q
ᵉ RSV *Let thy ears be attentive*
ᶠ RSV(MT) *and in*
ᵍ RSV(MT) *my soul waits*
ʰ Q uncertain
ⁱ RSV(MT) *And he*

Column VI

Pss. 132:8–18; 119:1–6

למנוחתכה אתה וא[ ]ע֯ו֯ז֯כ֯ה֯ (9)כוהניכה ילבשו צדק וחסידיכה

ירננו (10)בעבור דויד עבדכה אל תשב פני משיחכה (11)נשבע

𐤉𐤄𐤅𐤄 לדויד [ ]ל[ ] ישוב ממנה כי מפרי בטנכה אשית

על כסא לכה (12)[ ]ש֯מ֯[ ]ר֯ו בניכה בריתי ועדוותי זה
אלמדם גם בנ[ ]ם עודי עד יעלו לכסא לכה (13)כי בחר
𐤉𐤄𐤅𐤄 בציון א[ ] למושב לו (14)זואת מנוחתי עדי עד פה
אשב כי אוית[(15)] ב֯ר֯ך אברך אביוניה אשביע
לחם (16)וכוהניה א[ ]ש֯ה ישע֯ וחסידיה ירננו (17)שם אצמיח

קרן לדויד ע֯ר֯[ ]נ֯ר֯ למשיחי (18)אויביו אלביש בושת ועליו

יציץ נזר֯ו [ ]

(1)119 אשרי תמי[ ]ה֯ולכים בתורת 𐤉𐤄𐤅𐤄
(2)אשרי[ ]עת ידורשוה
(3)אף ל[ ]ו הלכו
(4)את [ ]ור מואדה
(5)אחל[ ]מתכה
(6)אז ל[ ]ל מצוותיכה

Column VI

Pss. 132:8–18; 119:1–6

Line

to thy resting place, thou and the a[rk of] thy might. (9)Let thy priests be clothed with righteousness, and let thy saints shout for joy. (10)For thy servant David's sake do not turn away the face of thy anointed one. (11)The LORD swore to David [a sure oath] from which he will n[ot] turn back: "*Surely*[a] one of the sons of your body I will set on your throne. (12)[If] your sons keep my covenant and my testimonies which I shall teach them, [th]eir sons also for ever shall *accede to*[b] your throne." (13)For the LORD has chosen Zion; he has de[sired] it for his habitation: (14)"This is my resting place for ever; here I will dwell, for I have desired [it]. (15)I will abundantly bless her [provisions]; I will satisfy her poor with bread. (16)Her priests I [will clothe] with salvation, and her saints will shout for joy.[c] (17)There I will make a horn to sprout for David; I have pre[pared] a lamp for my anointed. (18)His enemies I will clothe with shame, but upon himself his crown will shed its luster." Ps. 132

(1)Blessed are those [whose way is blame]less, who walk in the law of the LORD! Ps. 119
(2)Blessed are [those who keep his testimonies], who seek him[d] [*at all*] *times*,[e]
(3)who also [do no wrong], but walk in his [ways]!
(4)Thou [hast commanded thy precepts to be kep]t diligently.
(5)O that [my ways may be steadfast in keeping] thy *truth*![f]
(6)Then [I shall not be put to shame, having my eyes fixed on al]l thy commandments.

---

[a] Only in Q
[b] RSV(MT) *sit upon*
[c] A word lacking in Q does not alter the translation
[d] Q uncertain
[e] RSV(MT) *with their whole heart*
[f] RSV(MT) *statutes*. Q uncertain

Column VII

Ps. 119:15–28

Line

⁽¹⁵⁾בפקודיכה אשיחה ואביטה אורחותיכה

⁽¹⁶⁾בחוקיכה אשתעשע לוא אשכח דבריכה

⁽¹⁷⁾גמור על עבדכה ואחיה ואשמורה דבריכה

⁽¹⁸⁾גל עיני ואביטה   נפלאות מתורותיכה

⁽¹⁹⁾גר אנוכי בארץ אל תסתר ממני מצוותיכה   5

⁽²⁰⁾גרשה נפשי לתאבה אל משפטיכה בכול עת

⁽²¹⁾גערתה זדים ארורים השוגים ממצוותיכה

⁽²²⁾גול מעלי חרפה ובוז כי עדוותיכה נצרתי

⁽²³⁾גם ישבו שרים בי נדברו עבדכה ישיח בחוקיכה

⁽²⁴⁾גם עדוותיכה שעשׁוֹעׁיֹ] אנשי עצתי   10

⁽²⁵⁾דבקה לעפר נפׁ]   [

⁽²⁶⁾דרכי ספרתי וֹתׁ]   ה[

⁽²⁷⁾דרך פקודׁכה הׁ]   לאׁותיכה[

⁽²⁸⁾דלפה נפשי מ]   כֹה[

Column VII

Ps. 119:15–28

Line

(15)I will meditate on thy precepts, and fix my eyes on thy ways.   Ps. 119

(16)I will delight in thy statutes; I will not forget thy word*s*.

(17)*Fulfill thy purpose for*ᵃ thy servant, that I may live and observe thy word*s*.

(18)Open my eyes, that I may behold wondrous things out of thy law*s*.

5   (19)I am a sojourner on earth; hide not thy commandments from me!

(20)My soul is consumed with longing for thy ordinances at all times.

(21)Thou dost rebuke the insolent, accursed ones, who wander from thy commandments;

(22)*roll*ᵇ away from me their scorn and contempt, for I have kept thy testimonies.

(23)Even though princes sit plotting against me, thy servant will meditate on thy statutes.

10   (24)Thy testimonies are my delight, they are my counselors.

[(25)My s]oul cleaves to the dust; [revive me according to thy word!]

(26)When I told of my ways, thou [didst answer me; teach me thy statute]s!

[(27)Make me understand] the way of thy precepts, [and I will meditate on] thy won[drous works.]

(28)My soul melts away for [sorrow; strengthen me according to] thy [word!]

ᵃ RSV(MT) *Deal bountifully with*
ᵇ RSV(MT) *take*

Column VIII

Ps. 119:37–49

Line

(37)העבר עיני מראות שוא כדברכה חונני
(38)הקם לעבדכה אמרתכה אשר ליראתכה
(39)העבר חרפתי אשר יגרתי כי משפטיכה טובים
(40)הנה תאבתי לפקודיכה בצדקתכה חונני
(41)ויבואוני חסד יהוה תשועתכה כאמרתכה
(42)ואענה חורפי דבר כי בטחתי בדברכה
(43)ואל תצל מפי דבר אמת עד מואדה כי לדבריכה יחלתי
(44)ואשמורה תורתכה תמיד ועד (45)ואתהלכה ברחוביה
כי פקודיכה דרשתי
(46)ואדברה בעדוותיכ֯ה֯ [ ]ג֯ד מלכים ולוא אבוש
(47)ואשתעשעה במ[ ]ש֯ר אהבתי
(48)ואשא כפי אל מצוו[ ]ר אהבתי ואשישה בחוקיכה
(49)זכורה דבריכה[ ]ל֯[ ] יחלתני

Column VIII

Ps. 119:37–49

Line

⁽³⁷⁾Turn my eyes from looking at vanities; *be gracious to me according to thy word.*^{*a*}   Ps. 119

⁽³⁸⁾Confirm to thy servant thy promise, which is for those who fear thee.

⁽³⁹⁾Turn away the reproach which I dread; for thy ordinances are good.

⁽⁴⁰⁾Behold, I long for thy precepts; in thy righteousness *be gracious to me!*^{*b*}

5   ⁽⁴¹⁾Let steadfast love^{*c*} come to me, O LORD, thy salvation according to thy promise;

⁽⁴²⁾then shall I have an answer for those who taunt me, for I trust in thy word.

⁽⁴³⁾And take not the word of truth utterly out of my mouth, for my hope is in thy *words.*^{*d*}

⁽⁴⁴⁾I will keep thy law continually *and ever*;^{*e*} ⁽⁴⁵⁾and I shall walk *in its broadways,*^{*f*}

for I have sought thy precepts.

10   ⁽⁴⁶⁾I will also speak of thy testimonies [be]fore kings, and shall not be put to shame;

⁽⁴⁷⁾for I find my delight in [thy commandments, wh]ich I love.

⁽⁴⁸⁾I revere [thy] commandments, [whi]ch I love, and I will *rejoice in*^{*g*} thy statutes.

⁽⁴⁹⁾Remember thy word*s* t[o thy servant, in which] thou hast made me hope.

---

^{*a*} RSV(MT) *and give me life in thy ways*
^{*b*} RSV(MT) *give me life*
^{*c*} RSV(MT) *thy steadfast love*
^{*d*} RSV(MT) *ordinances*
^{*e*} RSV(MT) *for ever and ever*
^{*f*} RSV(MT) *at liberty* (or, " in the open ")
^{*g*} RSV(MT) *meditate on*

Column IX

Ps. 119:59–73

Line

(59) חשבתי דרכי ואשיבה רגלי אל עדוותיכה

(60) חשתי ולוא התמהמהתי לשמור מצוותיכה

(61) חבלי רשעים עודוני תורתכה לוא שכחתי

(62) חצות לילה אקום להודות לכה על משפטי צדקכה

(63) חבר אני לכול אשר יראוכה ולשומרי פקודיכה   5

(64) חסדכה 𐤉𐤄𐤅𐤄 מלאה הארץ חוקכה למדני

(65) טוב עשיתה עם עבדכה 𐤉𐤄𐤅𐤄 כדברכה

(66) טוב טעם ודעת למדני כי במצוותיכה האמנתי

(67) טרם אענה אני שוגג ועתה אמרתכה שמרתי

(68) טוב אתה אדוני ומטיב למדני חוקיכה   10

(69) טפלו עלי שקר זדים אני בכׄוׄל לׄ[   ] אצורה פקודיכה

(70) טפש כחלב לבם אני תורתכ[שׁׄעׄ] וׄעׄי

(71) טוב לי כי עניתני למען אלמׄ[   ]יכה

(72) טוב לי תורת פיכה מאלפׄ[י   [

(73)] כׄהׄ[15

Column ix

Ps. 119:59–73

Line

(59)When I think of *my*^a ways, I turn my feet to thy testimonies;   Ps. 119

(60)I hasten and do not delay to keep thy commandments.

(61)Though the cords of the wicked ensnare me, I do not forget thy law.

(62)At midnight I rise to praise thee, because of thy righteous ordinances.

5   (63)I am a companion of all who fear thee, of those who keep thy precepts.

(64)The earth, O Lord, is full of thy steadfast love; teach me thy statute!^b

(65)Thou hast dealt well with thy servant, O Lord, according to thy word.

(66)Teach me good judgment and knowledge, for I believe in thy commandments.

(67)Before I was afflicted I went astray; but now I keep thy word.

10   (68)Thou art good, *O Lord,*^c and doest good: teach me thy statutes.

(69)The godless besmear me with lies, but with my whole hea[rt] I keep thy precepts;

(70)their heart is gross like fat, but thy *law is my de[li]ght.*^d

(71)It is good for me that *thou didst afflict me,*^e that I might lea[rn] thy [statute]s.

(72)The law of thy mouth is better to me than thousands [of gold and silver pieces.]

15   [(73)Thy hands have made and fashioned me; give me understanding that I may learn] thy
[commandments.]

---

^a RSV(LXX) *thy*. Q = MT
^b RSV(MT) *statutes*
^c Lacking in RSV(MT). Q = LXX
^d RSV(MT) *I delight in thy law*
^e RSV(MT) *I was afflicted*

Column x

Ps. 119:82–96

(82)כלתה עיני לאמרתכה לאמור מתי תנחמני
(83)כי עשיתני כנאוד בקיטור חסדכה לוא שכחתי
(84)כמה ימי עבדכה מתי תעשה ברודפי משפט
(85)כרו לי זידים שחת אשר לוא כתורתכה
(86)כול מצוותיכה אמונה שקר רדפוני עוזרני
(87)כמעט כלוני מארץ ואני לוא עזבתי פקודיכה
(88)כחסדכה חונני ואשמורה עדוות פיכה
(89)לעולם 𐤉𐤄𐤅𐤄 דברכה נצב בשמים
(90)לדור ודור אמונתכה כוננתה ארץ ותעמד
(91)למשפטיכה עמדו היום כי הכול עבדי̊כה
(92)לולי תורתכה שעשועי אז אבדתי בעווני
(93)לעולם לוא אשכח פקודיכה כי במה חייתני
(94)לכה אני הושיעני כי פקודיכה דרשתי
(95)לי קוו רשעים לאבדני עדוותיכה אתבונן
(96)לכול תכלה ראיתי קץ רחבה מצותכ[ ] מואדה

Column x

Ps. 119:82–96

Line

(82)My *eye fails*[a] with watching for thy promise; I ask, "When wilt thou comfort me?" Ps. 119
(83)For *thou hast made me*[b] like a wineskin in the smoke, yet I have not forgotten thy *steadfast love.*[c]
(84)How long must thy servant endure? When wilt thou judge those who persecute me?
(85)Godless men have dug *a pit*[d] for me, men who do not conform to thy law.
(86)All thy commandments are sure; they persecute me with falsehood; help me!
(87)They have almost made an end of me *from*[e] earth; but I have not forsaken thy precepts.
(88)*According to*[f] thy steadfast love *be gracious to me*[g] that I may keep the testimonies of thy mouth.
(89)For ever, O LORD, thy word is firmly fixed in the heavens.
(90)Thy faithfulness endures to all generations; thou hast established the earth, and it stands fast.
(91)By thy appointment they stand this day; for all things are thy servants.
(92)If thy law had not been my delight, I should have perished in my *iniquity.*[h]
(93)I will never forget thy precepts; for by them thou hast given me life.
(94)I am thine, save me; for I have sought thy precepts.
(95)The wicked lie in wait to destroy me; but I consider thy testimonies.
(96)I have seen a limit to all perfection, but thy commandment is exceedingly broad.

---

[a] RSV(MT) *eyes fail*
[b] RSV(MT) *I have become*
[c] RSV(MT) *statutes*
[d] RSV(MT) *pitfalls*
[e] RSV(MT) *on*
[f] RSV *In*. Q = MT
[g] RSV(MT) *spare my life*
[h] RSV(MT) *affliction*

Column XI

Ps. 119:105–120

Line

(105) נר לרגלי דבריכה אור לנתיבותי

(106) נשבעתי ואקימה לעשות משפט צדקכה

(107) נעויתי עד מואדה יהוה כאמרתכה חונני

(108) נדבות פי רצה יהוה ממשפטיכה למדני

(109) נפשי בכפי תמיד תורתכה לוא שכחתי   5

(110) נתנו רשעים פח לי אני פקודיכה לוא תעיתי

(111) נחלתי עדוותיכה לעולם   ששון לבי המה

(112) נטיתי לבי לעשות חוקיכה לעולם עקב

(113) סעפים שנאתי תורתכה אהבתי

(114) סתרי ומגני אתה לדבריכה יחלתי   10

(115) סורו ממני מרעים ואצורה מצות אלוהי

(116) סמכני כאמרתכה ואחיה ואל תבישני ממשברי

(117) סעדני ואושעה ואשא חוקיכה תמיד

(118) סליתה כול שוגים מחוקיכה כי שקר תרמיתם

(119) סיגים חשבתי כול רשעי ארץ על כן אהבתי כול עדוותיכה   15

(120) סמר מפחד[   ]בשרי וממשפטיכה יראתי

Column XI

Ps. 119:105–120

Line

(105)Thy *words are*^a a lamp to my feet, a^b light to my path*s*.   Ps. 119

(106)I have sworn an oath and confirmed it, *to do*^c thy righteous ordinance.^d

(107)I am sorely *distraught*;^e *be gracious to me*,^f O LORD, according to thy *promise*!^g

(108)Accept^h my offerings of praise, O LORD, and teach me fromⁱ thy ordinances.

5   (109)I hold my life in my hand continually, I^j do not forget thy law.

(110)The wicked have laid a snare for me, (but^k) I do not stray (from^k) thy precepts.

(111)Thy testimonies are my heritage for ever; they^l are the joy of my heart.

(112)I incline my heart to perform thy statutes for ever, to the end.

(113)I hate double-minded men; I^m love thy law.

10   (114)Thou art my hiding-place and my shield; I hope in thy word*s*.

(115)Depart from me, you evildoers, that I may keep the commandmentⁿ of my God.

(116)Uphold me according to thy promise, that I may live,^o and let me not be put to shame *because of*^p my hope!

(117)Hold me up, that I may be safe, and *I will lift up*^q thy statutes continually!

(118)Thou dost spurn all who go astray from thy statutes; yea, their cunning is in vain.

15   (119)All the wicked of the earth *I discount*^r as dross; *wherefore*^s I love *all*^t thy testimonies.

(120)My flesh trembles for fear [of thee], and I am afraid of thy judgments.

---

^a RSV(MT) *word is*
^b RSV(MT) *and a*
^c RSV(MT) *to observe*
^d RSV(MT) *ordinances*
^e RSV(MT) *afflicted*
^f RSV(MT) *give me life*
^g RSV(MT) *word*
^h RSV = Q. MT *Accept now*
ⁱ RSV(MT) lack *from*. Q = Syr
^j RSV(MT) *but I*
^k Lacking in Q
^l RSV(MT) *yea, they*
^m RSV(MT) *but I*
ⁿ RSV(MT) *commandments*
^o RSV = Q. MT *and let me live*
^p RSV(MT) *in*
^q RSV(MT) *have regard for*
^r RSV *thou dost count*. MT *thou dost reject*
^s RSV(MT) *therefore*
^t Only in Q

Column XII

Ps. 119:128–142

Line

(128)על כן פקודי כול ישרתי כול אורח שקר שנאתי
(129)פלגי נפת עדוותיכה על כן נצרתם נפשי
(130)פתח דבריכה והאר מבין פותאים
(131)פי פערתי ואשאפה למצוותיכה תאבתי
(132)פנה אלי וחונני כמשפט לאוהבי שמכה
(133)פעמי הכן לאמרתכה ואל תשלט בי כול און
(134)פדני מעשק אדם ואשמורה פקודיכה
(135)פניכה האר בעבדכה ולמדני את חוקיכה
(136)פלגי מים ירדו עיני על כי לוא שמרו תורתכה
(137)צדיק אתה 𐤉𐤄𐤅𐤄 וישרים משפטיכה
(138)צויתה צדק עדוותיכה ואמונה מואדה
(139)צמתתני קנאתי כי שכחו דבריכה צרי
(140)צרופה אמרתכה מואדה עבדכה אהבה
(141)צעיר אנוכי ונבזה פקודיכה לוא שכחתי
(142)[ ]ות[ ]דקות עולם ותורתך אמת

Column XII

Ps. 119:128–142

Line

(128)Therefore I direct my steps *by complete precepts;*[a] I hate every false way.   Ps. 119

(129)Thy testimonies are *streams of honey:*[b] therefore my soul keeps them.

(130)*Unfold thy words, and enlighten him who*[c] imparts understanding to the simple.

(131)With open mouth I pant, I long[d] for thy commandments.

5   (132)Turn to me and be gracious to me, as is thy wont toward those who love thy name.

(133)Keep steady my steps *unto*[e] thy promise, and let no iniquity get dominion over me.

(134)Redeem me from man's oppression, that I may keep thy precepts.

(135)Make thy face shine upon thy servant, and teach me thy statutes.

(136)My eyes shed streams of tears, because men do not keep thy law.

10   (137)Righteous art thou, O LORD, and right are thy judgments.

(138)Thou hast appointed thy testimonies in righteousness and in all faithfulness.

(139)My zeal consumes me, because my foes forget thy words.

(140)Thy promise is well tried; thy[f] servant loves it.

(141)I am small and despised, yet I do not forget thy precepts.

15   (142)[   ] *righteous deeds*[g] for ever, and thy law is true.

---

[a] RSV(LXX, Lat) *by all thy precepts.* Q and MT uncertain
[b] Only in Q. RSV(MT) *wonderful*
[c] RSV(MT) *The unfolding of thy words gives light; it*
[d] RSV(MT) *because I long*
[e] RSV(LXX, Lat) *according to.* MT *in*
[f] RSV(MT) *and thy*
[g] RSV(MT) *Thy righteousness is righteous.* Q uncertain

Column xiii

Ps. 119:150–164

Line

(150) קרבו רודפי זמה מתורתכה רחקו
(151) קרוב אתה 𐤉𐤄𐤅𐤄 וכול מצוותיכה אמת
(152) קדם ידעתי מדעתכה כי לעולם יסדתני
(153) ראה עוניי וחלצני תורתכה לוא שכחתי
(154) ריבׄ (ה) ריבי וגאלני לאמרתכה חיני
(155) רחוק מרשעים (ישועה) כי חוקיכה לוא דרשו
(156) רחמיכה רבים 𐤉𐤄𐤅𐤄 כמשפטיכה חונני
(157) רבים רודפי וצרי מעדוותיכה לוא נטיתי
(158) ראיתי בוגדים ואתקוטטה אשר אמרתכה לוא שמרו
(159) ראה כי פקודיכה אהבתי 𐤉𐤄𐤅𐤄 כאמרתכה חונני
(160) רוֹ[ ] דבריכה אמת ולעולם כול משפט צדק
(161) שרים רדפוני חנום ומדבריכה פחד לבי
(162) שש אׄנוכי על אמרתכה ממוצא שלל רב
(163) שקׄ[ ]תי ואׄתׄעׄבה ותורתכה אהבתי
(164) [ ]ל [ ]שׄפׄטׄיׄ

Column XIII

Ps. 119:150–164

Line

(150)They draw near who persecute me with evil purpose; they are far from thy law.   Ps. 119

(151)But thou art near, O LORD, and all thy commandments are true.

(152)Long have I known from *knowledge of thee*^{a} that thou hast founded *me*^{b} for ever.

(153)Look on my affliction and deliver me; I^c do not forget thy law.

5   (154)Plead my cause and redeem me; give me life according to thy promise!

(155)Salvation is far from the wicked, for they do not seek thy statutes.

(156)Great is thy mercy, O LORD; *be gracious to me*^{d} according to thy justice.

(157)Many are my persecutors and my adversaries, but I do not swerve from thy testimonies.

(158)I look at the faithless with disgust, because they do not

10   keep thy *word.*^{e}

(159)Consider how I love thy precepts, *O LORD*^{ee}! *Be gracious to me*^{f} according to thy *promise.*^{g}

(160)The s[um] of thy word*s*^{h} is truth; and *every righteous ordinance*^{i} endures for ever.

(161)Princes persecute me without cause, but my heart stands in awe of thy words.

(162)I rejoice at thy word *more than*^{j} one who finds great spoil.

15   (163)I [hate] and abhor false[hood], but I love thy law.

(164)[Seven times a day I praise thee fo]r [thy righteous or]dinances.

---

^{a} RSV(MT) *thy testimonies*
^{b} RSV(MT) *them*
^{c} RSV(MT) *for I*
^{d} RSV(MT) *give me life*
^{e} RSV *commands.* Q = MT
^{ee} Lacking in RSV. Q = MT
^{f} RSV(MT) *Preserve my life*
^{g} RSV(MT) *steadfast love*
^{h} Or, *commandments.* RSV(MT) *word.* Q = LXX, Lat
^{i} RSV(MT) *every one of thy righteous ordinances*
^{j} RSV(MT) *like*

Column XIV

Pss. 119:171–176; 135:1–9

Line

(171)תבענה שפתי תהלה לכה כי תלמדני חוקיכה
(172)תענה לשוני אמרתכה כי כול מצוותיכה צדק
(173)תהי ידכה לעוזרני כי פקודיכה בחרתי
(174)תאבתי לישועתכה 𐤉𐤄𐤅𐤄 תורתכה שעשועי
(175)תחי נפשי ותהללכה ומ֯֯שפטיכה יעוזרני
(176)תעיתי כשה אובד בקש עבדכה כי עדוותיכה לוא שכחתי
135(1) הללו עבדי 𐤉𐤄𐤅𐤄 הללו את שם 𐤉𐤄𐤅𐤄 הללו יה
(2)ורוממו יה שעומדים בבית
𐤉𐤄𐤅𐤄 בחצרות בית אלוהינו ובתוכך ירושלים
(3)הללו את 𐤉𐤄𐤅𐤄 כי טוב זמרו שמו כי נעים (4)כי יעקוב
בחר לו וישראל לסגולה לו (5)אני ידעתי כי גדול 𐤉𐤄𐤅𐤄
ואלוהינו מכול אלוהים (6)אשר חפץ 𐤉𐤄𐤅𐤄 עשה
בשמים ובארץ לעשות יעשה אין כיה אין כ 𐤉𐤄𐤅𐤄
ואין שיעשה כמלך אלוהים בימים ובכול ת֯הומות (7)מעלה
נשיא֯[ ]ק֯צ֯ה הארץ ברקים למטר עשה מוציא רוח

] (8) [∘∘∘∘] (9)]ל[]

Column XIV

Pss. 119:171–176; 135:1–9

Line

(171)My lips will pour forth praise *to thee*[a] that thou dost teach me thy statutes.   Ps. 119

(172)My tongue will sing of thy word, for all thy commandments are right.

(173)Let thy hand be ready to help me, for I have chosen thy precepts.

(174)I long for thy salvation, O Lord, thy[b] law is my delight.

5   (175)Let me live, that I may praise thee, and let thy ordinances help me.

(176)I have gone astray like a lost sheep; seek thy servant, for I do not forget thy *testimonies.*[c]

(1)[d]*Give praise, O servants of the* Lord, *praise the name of the Lord, praise the* Lord.[d]   Ps. 135

(2)*And exalt the* Lord,[a] you that stand in the house

of the Lord, in the courts of the house of our God, *and in your midst, O Jerusalem!*[a]

10   (3)Praise the Lord, for *he*[e] is good; sing his[f] name, for he is gracious.[g] (4)*For Jacob*

he has chosen[h] *for himself, and*[i] Israel as *a possession for himself.*[j] (5)I[k] know that the Lord is great,

and that our *God*[l] is above all gods. (6)*What*[m] the Lord pleases he does,

in heaven and on earth, [n]*to do he does; there is none like the* Lord, *there is none like the* Lord,

and there is none who does as the King of gods,[n] in the seas and *in*[o] all deeps. (7)He it is who makes

15   the cloud[s] rise [at the] end of the earth, who makes lightnings for the rain and brings forth the

wind

[from his storehouses. (8)He it was who smote the first-born of Egypt, both of man and of beast;

⁹who] se[nt][p]

---

[a] Only in Q
[b] RSV(MT) *and thy*
[c] RSV(MT) *commandments*
[d–d] RSV(MT) *Praise the* Lord. *Praise the name of the* Lord, *give praise, O servants of the* Lord
[e] RSV(MT) *the* Lord
[f] RSV(MT) *to his*
[g] Or, *for it is pleasant so to do*
[h] RSV(MT) *For the* Lord *has chosen Jacob*
[i] Lacking in RSV(MT)
[j] RSV(MT) *his own possession*
[k] RSV(MT) *For I*
[l] RSV(MT) Lord
[m] RSV(MT) *Whatever*
[n–n] Only in Q
[o] Lacking in RSV(MT). Q = LXX, Lat
[p] Q = MT(RSV)

62 *The Dead Sea Psalms Scroll*

Column xv

Pss. 135:17–21; 136:1–16

Line

להם ולוא יאזינו ואין יש רוח בפיהם (18)כמוהם יהיו עושיהם וכול

אשר בטח בהם (19)בית ישראל ברכו את יהוה בית אהרון

ברכו את יהוה (20)בית הלוי ברכו את יהוה יראי

יהוה ברכו את יהוה (21)יברככה יהוה מציון שוכן

ירושלים הללו יה   5

136(1)הודו ל יהוה כי טוב כי לעולם חסדו (2)הודו לאלוהי האלוהים

כי לעולם חסדו (3)הודו לאדון האדונים כי לעולם חסדו

(4)לעושה נפלאות לבדו כי לעולם חסדו (5)לעושה השמים

בתבונה   כי לעולם חסדו (6)לרוקע הארץ על המים כי

לעולם חסדו (7)לעושה מאורות גדולים כי לעולם חסדו את   10

השמש   וירח כי לעולם חסדו (8)את השמש לממשלות יום

כי לעולם חסדו (9)ירח וכוכבים לממשלות בלילה כי לעולם חסדו

(10)למכה מצרים בבכוריהם כי לעולם חסדו (11)ויוציא ישראל

מתוכם כי לעולם חסדו (12)ביד חזקה ובאזרוע נטויה כי

לעולם חסדו (13)לגוזר ים סוף לגזרים כֹי לעולם חסדו (14)והעבר   15

ישׁראל בתוכו כי לעולם חסדו (15)נער פרעוה וחילו בים

[לֹ]ל[ ]בר כֹי ל[ ]ב[   ]לֹ[   ]   (16)למוליך עמו ב[   ]

Column xv

Pss. 135:17–21; 136:1–16

Line

they have (ears), but they hear not, nor is there any breath in their mouths. ⁽¹⁸⁾Like them   Ps. 135
be those who make them!—*and*^a every one

who trusts in them! ⁽¹⁹⁾O house of Israel, bless the Lord! O house of Aaron,

bless the Lord! ⁽²⁰⁾O house of Levi, bless the Lord! You that fear

the Lord, bless the Lord! ⁽²¹⁾*May the Lord bless you*^b from Zion, he who dwells

5 in Jerusalem! Praise the Lord!

⁽¹⁾O give thanks to the Lord, for he is good, for his steadfast love endures for ever. ⁽²⁾O   Ps. 136
give thanks to the God of gods,

for his steadfast love endures for ever. ⁽³⁾O give thanks to the Lord of lords, for his steadfast love
endures for ever;

⁽⁴⁾to him who alone does wonders,^c for his steadfast love endures for ever; ⁽⁵⁾to him who made the
heavens

by understanding, for his steadfast love endures for ever; ⁽⁶⁾to him who spread out the earth upon
the waters, for

10 his steadfast love endures for ever; ⁽⁷⁾to him who made the great *luminaries,*^d for his steadfast love
endures for ever;

^e*the sun and moon, for his steadfast love endures for ever;*^e ⁽⁸⁾the sun to rule^f the day,

for his steadfast love endures for ever; ⁽⁹⁾moon^g and stars to rule over the night, for his steadfast
love endures for ever;

⁽¹⁰⁾to him who smote the first-born of Egypt, for his steadfast love endures for ever; ⁽¹¹⁾and brought
Israel out

from among them, for his steadfast love endures for ever; ⁽¹²⁾with a strong hand and an outstretched
arm, for

15 his steadfast love endures for ever; ⁽¹³⁾to him who divided the Red Sea in sunder, for his steadfast
love endures for ever; ⁽¹⁴⁾and made Israel

pass through the midst of it, for his steadfast love endures for ever; ⁽¹⁵⁾overthrew^h Pharaoh and his
host in the Red

[Sea, for his steadfast love endures] for [ever;] ⁽¹⁶⁾to him who led his people through the [wilder]ness,
for [his steadfast love endures] for ev[er.]

---

^a RSV *yea*
^b RSV(MT) *Blessed be the Lord*
^c RSV(MT) *great wonders*
^d RSV(MT) *lights*
^{e–e} Only in Q
^f RSV(MT) *rule over*
^g RSV(MT) *the moon*
^h RSV(MT) *but overthrew*

Column XVI

Pss. 136:26; 118:1, 15, 16, 8, 9, 29; 145:1–7

Line

כי לעולם חסדו 118 1(?) הודו ל𐤉𐤄𐤅𐤄 כי טוב כי לעולם חסדו (15)קול
רנה וישועה באהלי צדיקים ימין 𐤉𐤄𐤅𐤄 עשה חיל (16)ימין
𐤉𐤄𐤅𐤄 רוממה ימין 𐤉𐤄𐤅𐤄 עשתה גבורה (8)טוב לבטוח
ב 𐤉𐤄𐤅𐤄 מבטוח באדם (9)טוב לחסות ב 𐤉𐤄𐤅𐤄 מבטוב
בנדיבים (?)טוב לבטוב ב 𐤉𐤄𐤅𐤄 מבטוח באלף עם (29)הודו
ל𐤉𐤄𐤅𐤄 כי טוב כי לעולם חסדו הללו יה
145 (1)תפלה לדויד ארוממכה 𐤉𐤄𐤅𐤄 אלוהי המלך
ואברכה שמכה לעולם ועד ברוך 𐤉𐤄𐤅𐤄 וברוך שמו
לעולם ועד (2)ברוך יום אברככה ואהללה שמכה לעולם ועד
ברוך 𐤉𐤄𐤅𐤄 ⸢וברוך⸣ שמו לעולם ועד (3)גדול 𐤉𐤄𐤅𐤄 ו⸢מ⸣הולל מואדה
לגדולתו אין חקר ברוך 𐤉𐤄𐤅𐤄 וברוך שמו לעולם ועד
(4)דור לדור ישבחו מעשיכה וגבורתיכה יגידו ברוך 𐤉𐤄𐤅𐤄
וברוך שמו לעולם ועד (5)הדר כבוד הודכה ידברו ונפלאותיכה
אשיח ברוך 𐤉𐤄𐤅𐤄 וברוך שמו לעולם ועד (6)ועזוז
נוראותיכה יואמרו וגדול⸢ו⸣תיכה אספר ברוך 𐤉𐤄𐤅𐤄
[ ]מו לעולם ועד (7)זכר רב טובכה [ ]

Column XVI

Pss. 136:26; 118:1, 15, 16, 8, 9, 29; 145:1–7

Line

for his steadfast love endures for ever. [1]O give thanks to the LORD, for he is good;   Ps. 136, Ps. 118
his steadfast love endures for ever! [15]Hark,

glad songs of victory in the tents of the righteous: "The right hand of the LORD does valiantly,
[16]the right hand

of the LORD is exalted, the right hand of the LORD *has wrought strength!*"[a] [8]It is better *to trust*[b]

in the LORD than to put confidence in man. [9]It is better to take refuge in the LORD than to put
confidence[c]

5   in princes. [d]*It is better to trust*[c] *in the LORD than to put confidence in a thousand people.*[d] [29]O
give thanks

to the LORD, for he is good; for his steadfast love endures for ever! *Praise the LORD!*[e]

[1]*A Prayer.*[f] Of David. I will extol thee,[g] my God and king,   Ps. 145

and bless thy name for ever and ever. *Blessed be the LORD and blessed be his name*

for ever and ever.[h] [2]*Blessed*[i] day I will bless thee, and praise thy name for ever and ever.

10   *Blessed be the LORD and blessed be his name for ever and ever.*[h] [3]Great is the LORD and greatly to,
be praised

his[j] greatness is unsearchable. *Blessed be the LORD and blessed be his name for ever and ever.*[h]

[4]One generation shall laud thy works to another, and shall declare thy mighty acts. *Blessed be the*
LORD

and blessed be his name for ever and ever.[h] [5]Of the glorious splendor of thy majesty *they will speak,*[k]
and of thy wondrous works,

I will meditate. *Blessed be the LORD and blessed be his name for ever and ever.*[h] [6]Men

15   shall proclaim the might of thy terrible acts, and I will *recount thy mighty acts.*[l] *Blessed be the LORD*

[*and blessed be*] *his* na[*me*] *for ever and ever.*[h] [7]They shall [pour forth] the fame of thy abundant
goodness

---

[a] RSV(MT) *does valiantly*
[b] RSV(MT) *to take refuge*
[c] Probable reading
[d–d] Only in Q
[e] Only in Q
[f] RSV(MT) *A Song of Praise*
[g] Q adds *O LORD*, but noted as a scribal error
[h] Only in Q: a constant refrain to each verse
[i] RSV(MT) *Every*
[j] RSV(MT) *and his*
[k] So Q, LXX and Lat. Lacking in RSV(MT)
[l] RSV *declare thy greatness*

Column XVII

Ps. 145:13–21+

Line

וברוך שמו לעולם ועד (13)מלכותכה מלכות כול עולמים וממשלתכה

בכול דור ודור ברוך 𐤉𐤄𐤅𐤄 וברוך שמו לעולם ועד נאמן

אלוהים בדבריו וחסיד בכול מעשיו ברוך 𐤉𐤄𐤅𐤄 וברוך
שמו לעולם ועד (14)סומך 𐤉𐤄𐤅𐤄 לכול הנופלים וזוקף לכול
הכפופים ברוך 𐤉𐤄𐤅𐤄 וברוך שמו לעולם ועד (15)עיני
כול אליכה ישברו ואתה נׄתן להמה א(את)וכלמה בעתו
ברוך 𐤉𐤄𐤅𐤄 וברוך שמו לעולם ועד (16)פותח אתה את
ידכה ומשביע לכול חי רצון ברוך 𐤉𐤄𐤅𐤄 וברוך שמו
לעולם ועד (17)צדיק 𐤉𐤄𐤅𐤄 בכול דרכיו וחסיד בכול
מעשיו ברוך 𐤉𐤄𐤅𐤄 וברוך שמו לעולם ועד (18)קרוב 𐤉𐤄𐤅𐤄
וברוך שמו לעולם ועד יקראוהו באמונה ברוך 𐤉𐤄𐤅𐤄
וברוך שמו לעולם ועד (19)רצון יראיו יעשה ואת שועתמה

ישמע ויושיעם ברוך 𐤉𐤄𐤅𐤄 וברוך שמו לעולם ועד
(20)שומר 𐤉𐤄𐤅𐤄 את כול יראיו ואת כול הרשעים ישמיד
ברוך 𐤉𐤄𐤅𐤄 וברוך שמו לעולם ועד
(21)תהלת 𐤉𐤄𐤅𐤄 ידבר פי ויברך כול בשׄר את שם קודשו
ברוך 𐤉𐤄𐤅𐤄 וברוך שמו לעולם ו[ ] זואת לזכרון
]]לׄ[ ]לׄ[ ]לׄ[ ]לׄ[[

Column XVII

Ps. 145:13–21+

Ps. 145

and blessed be his name for ever and ever.[a] (13)Thy kingdom is an everlasting kingdom, and thy dominion endures throughout all generations. *Blessed be the* LORD *and blessed be his name for ever and ever.*[a] [b]*God*[c] is faithful in his[d] words, and gracious in all his deeds.[b] *Blessed be the* LORD *and blessed be his name for ever and ever.*[a] (14)The LORD upholds all who are falling, and raises up all who are bowed down. *Blessed be the* LORD *and blessed be his name for ever and ever.*[a] (15)The eyes of all look to thee, and thou givest them their food in due season. *Blessed be the* LORD *and blessed be his name for ever and ever.*[a] (16) Thou openest thy hand, *and*[e] satisfiest the desire of every living thing. *Blessed be the* LORD *and blessed be his name for ever and ever.*[a] (17)The LORD is just in all his ways, and kind in all his doings. *Blessed be the* LORD *and blessed be his name for ever and ever.*[a] (18)The LORD is near[f] *and blessed be his name for ever and ever*; *they*[g] call upon him in *faithfulness.*[h] *Blessed be the* LORD *and blessed be his name for ever and ever.*[a] (19)He fulfills the desire of all who fear him, he also hears their cry, and saves them. *Blessed be the* LORD *and blessed be his name for ever and ever.*[a] (20)The LORD preserves all who *fear*[i] him; but all the wicked he will destroy. *Blessed be the* LORD *and blessed be his name for ever and ever.*[a] (21)My mouth will speak the praise of the LORD, and let all flesh bless his holy name.[j] *Blessed be the* LORD *and blessed be his name for ever and* [*ever.*[a]] [k]*This is for a memorial* . . .[k]

---

[a] Only in Q: a constant refrain to each verse
[b–b] Lacking in MT
[c] RSV *The* LORD
[d] RSV *all his*
[e] RSV *thou*
[f] RSV(MT) continues *to all who call upon him*
[g] RSV(MT) *to all who*
[h] RSV(MT) *truth*
[i] RSV(MT) *love*
[j] RSV(MT) continues *for ever and ever*
[k–k] Only in Q. A subscription?

Column XVIII

Ps. 154:3–19

Line

לטובים נפשתכמה ולתמימים לפאר עליון (4)החבירו יחד

להודיע ישעו ואל תתעצלו להודיע עוזו ותפארתו
לכול פותאים (5)כי להודיע כבוד 𐤉𐤄𐤅𐤄 נתנה חוכמה (6)ולספר
רוב מעשיו נודעה לאדם (7)להודיע לפותאים עוזו
להשכיל לחסרי לבב גדולתו (8)הרחוקים מפתחיה
הנדחים ממבואיה (9)כי עליון הואה אדון
יעקוב ותפארתו על כול מעשיו (10)ואדם מפאר עליון
ירצה כמגיש מנחה (11)כמקריב עתודים ובני בקר
כמדשן מזבח ברוב עולות כקטורת ניחוח מיד
צדיקים (12)מפתחי צדיקים נשמע קולה ומקהל חסידים

זמרתה (13)על אוכלמה בשבע נאמרה ועל שתותמה בחבר
יחדיו (14)שיחתם בתורת עליון אמריהמה להודיע עוזו
(15)כמה רחקה מרשעים אמרה מכול זדים לדעתה (16)הנה
עיני 𐤉𐤄𐤅𐤄 על טובים תחמל (17)ועל מפאריו יגדל חסדו

מעת רעה יציל נפש[(18)]𐤉𐤄𐤅𐤄 גואל עני מיד

זׄרׄ[ ]ל[(19)]קׄוׄבׄ ושופט

Column XVIII

Ps. 154:3–19

Line

^ayour souls with the good ones and with the pure ones to   Apocryphon: Ps. 154 or (Syriac) Ps. II^a
glorify the Most High. ⁽⁴⁾Form an assembly

to proclaim his salvation, and be not lax in making known his might and his majesty

to all simple folk. ⁽⁵⁾For to make known the glory of the LORD is Wisdom given, ⁽⁶⁾and for recounting

his many deeds she is revealed to man: ⁽⁷⁾to make known to simple folk his might,

5   to explain to senseless folk his greatness, ⁽⁸⁾those far from her gates,

those who stray from her portals. ⁽⁹⁾For the Most High is the LORD

of Jacob, and his majesty is over all his works. ⁽¹⁰⁾And a man who glorifies the Most High

he accepts as one who brings a meal offering, ⁽¹¹⁾as one who offers he-goats and bullocks,

as one who fattens the altar with many burnt offerings, as a sweet-smelling fragrance from the hand

10   of the righteous. ⁽¹²⁾From the gates of the righteous is heard her voice, and from the assembly of the
pious

her song. ⁽¹³⁾When they eat with satiety she is cited,^b and when they drink in community together,

⁽¹⁴⁾their meditation is on the law of the Most High, their words on making known his might.

⁽¹⁵⁾How far from the wicked is her word, from all haughty men to know here. ⁽¹⁶⁾Behold

the eyes of the LORD upon the good ones are^c compassionate, ⁽¹⁷⁾and upon those who glorify him
he increases his mercy;

15   from an evil time will he deliver [their] soul. ⁽¹⁸⁾[Bless] the LORD who redeems the humble from the
hand

of stranger[s and deliv]ers the pure from the hand of the wicked, ⁽¹⁹⁾[who establishes a horn out of
Ja]cob and a judge

---

^a Not in the Bible. See below, Part III, pp. 103–109
^b Heb. Syr *a true satiety*
^c Cn: Heb *is*

Column XIX

Plea for Deliverance

Line

כי לוא רמה תודה לכה ולוא תספר חסדכה תולעה

חי חי   יודה לכה יודו לכה כול מוטטי רגל בהודיעכה
חסדכה להמה וצדקתכה תשכילם כי בידכה נפש כול

חי נשמת כול   בשר אתה נתתה עשה עמנו 𐤉𐤄𐤅𐤄
כטובכה כרוב רחמיכה וכרוב צדקותיכה שמע

𐤉𐤄𐤅𐤄 בקול אוהבי שמו ולוא עזב חסדו מהמה
ברוך 𐤉𐤄𐤅𐤄 עושה צדקות מעטר חסידיו
חסד ורחמים שאגה נפשי להלל ש(את)מכה להודות ברנה
חסדיכה להגיד אמונתכה לתהלתכה אין חקר למות
הייתי בחטאי ועוונותי לשאול מכרוני ותצילני
𐤉𐤄𐤅𐤄 כרוב רחמיכה וכרוב צדקותיכה גם אני את
שמכה אהבתי ובצלכה חסיתי בזוכרי עוזכה יתקף
לבי ועל חסדיכה אני נסמכתי סלחה 𐤉𐤄𐤅𐤄 לחטאתי
וטהרנו מעווני רוח אמונה ודעת חונני אל אתקלה

בעווה אל תשלט בי שטן ורוח טמאה מכאוב ויצר
רע אל ירשו בעצמי כי אתה 𐤉𐤄𐤅𐤄 שבחי ולכה קויתי
כול היום ישמ̊חו אחי עמי ובית אבי השוממים בחונכה

◦ ◦ ◦]   ]◦לם אשמחה בכה

Column XIX

Plea for Deliverance

Line

a"Surely a maggot cannot praise thee nor a grave-worm   Apocryphon: Plea for Deliverance*a*
recount thy lovingkindness.

But the living can praise thee, all those who stumble can laud thee. In revealing

thy kindness to them and by thy righteousness thou dost enlighten them. For in thy hand is the
soul of every

living thing; the breath of all flesh hast thou given. Deal with us, O LORD,

5 according to thy goodness, according to thy great mercy, and according to thy many righteous
deeds. The LORD

has heeded the voice of those who love his name and has not deprived them of his lovingkindness.

Blessed be the LORD, who executes righteous deeds, crowning his saints

with lovingkindness and mercy. My soul cries out to praise thy name, to sing high praises

for thy loving deeds, to proclaim thy faithfulness—of praise of thee there is no end.*b* Near death

10 was I for my sins, and my iniquities had sold me to the grave; but thou didst save me,

O LORD, according to thy great mercy, and according to thy many righteous deeds. Indeed have I

loved thy name, and in thy protection have I found refuge. When I remember thy might my heart

is brave, and upon thy mercies do I lean. Forgive my sin, O LORD,

and purify me from my iniquity. Vouchsafe me a spirit of faith and knowledge, and let me not be
dishonored

15 in ruin. Let not Satan rule over me, nor an unclean spirit; neither let pain nor the evil

inclination take possession of my bones. For thou, O LORD, art my praise, and in thee do I hope

all the day. Let my brothers rejoice with me and the house of my father, who are astonished by
thy graciousness . . .

[   ] For e[ver] I will rejoice in thee.

---

a Not in the Bible. See below, Part III, pp. 119–121
b Or, *of thy praise* (or *praiseworthy act*) *there is no searching out*

Column xx

Pss. 139:8–24; 137:1

Line

שאול הנכה (9)אשאה כנפי שחר אשכונה באחרית ים (10)שם
ידכה תנחני ותאחזני ימינכה (11)ואומרה אך חושך ישופני
ולילה אזר בעדי (12)גם חושך   לוא יחשך ממכה ולילה
כיום יאיר כחושך כאור (13)כי אתה קניתה כליותי תסוכני בבטן
אמי (14)אודכה על כי נורא אתה נפלאו̊ת נפלאים מעשיכה
ונפשי ידעת מואדה (15)לוא נכחד עצבי ממכה אשר עשית̊י
בסתר רוקמתי בתחתיות ארץ (16)גלמי ראו עיניכה ועל
ספריכה כולם   יכתבו ימים יצרו ולו באח
מהמה (17)ולי מה יקרו רעיך אל על מה עצמו ראשיהם
(18)אספרם מחול ירבון הקיצותי ועוד עמכה (19)אם
תקטול אלה רשע אנשי דמים סור מני (20)אשר
יאמרוך למזמה נשאו לשוא עריך (21)הלוא משנאיכה
𐤉𐤄𐤅𐤄 אשנא וממתקוממיכה   אתקוטט
(22)תכלית שנאה שנאתים לאויבים היו לי (23)חקרני
אל ודע לבי בחנני ודע סרעפי (24)וראה אם דרך
עצב בי ונחני בדרך עולם
137(1) על נהרות בבבל שם ישב ו̊ג̊[ ] כ̇ב̇[   ] את ציון

Column xx

Pss. 139:8–24; 137:1

Line

in Sheol, thou art there! ⁽⁹⁾If I take the wings of the morning and dwell in the uttermost   Ps. 139
parts of the sea,

⁽¹⁰⁾there*ᵃ* thy hand shall lead me, and thy right hand shall hold me. ⁽¹¹⁾*And I said, " Surely darkness*
covers me,

and night has girded me about."ᵇ ⁽¹²⁾Even the darkness is not dark to thee, the night
is bright as the day; for darkness is as light with thee. ⁽¹³⁾For thou didst form my inward parts, thou
didst knit me together in my mother's

5   womb. ⁽¹⁴⁾I praise thee, *for thou art fearful. Wondrous,ᶜ* wonderful are thy works,
as my soul fully well knows.ᵈ ⁽¹⁵⁾*My pain isᵉ* not hidden from thee *by whom I wasᶠ* made
in secret, intricately wrought in the depths of the earth. ⁽¹⁶⁾Thy eyes beheld my unformed substance; in
thy book*s* were written, every one of them the days that were formed . . .

. . . *ᵍ* ⁽¹⁷⁾How precious to me are thy thoughts,*ʰ* O God! How vast is the sum of them!

10   ⁽¹⁸⁾If I would count them they are more than the sand. When I awake, I am still with thee.*ⁱ* ⁽¹⁹⁾O that
thou wouldst slay the wicked, O God, that*ʲ* men of blood would depart*ᵏ* from me, ⁽²⁰⁾men who
maliciously defy thee, who lift themselves up against thee for evil!*ˡ* ⁽²¹⁾Do I not hate them
that hate thee, O Lord? And do I not loathe them that rise up against thee?

⁽²²⁾I hate them with perfect hatred; I count them my enemies. ⁽²³⁾Search me,

15   O God, and know my heart! Try me and know my thoughts! ⁽²⁴⁾And see if there be any wicked
way*ᵐ* in me, and lead me in the way everlasting!

¹By the *rivers inⁿ* Babylon, there we sat down a[nd we]pt, [when we remembered] Zion.   Ps. 137

ᵃ RSV(MT) *even there*
ᵇ RSV *If I say, "Let only darkness cover me, and the light about me be night,"*
ᶜ RSV *for thou art fearful and wonderful.* MT and Q uncertain
ᵈ RSV (Grk, Lat) *Thou knowest me right well;* Q = MT
ᵉ RSV(MT) *my frame was*
ᶠ Or, *who (made) it.* RSV *when I was being*
ᵍ Q uncertain. RSV *for me, when as yet there was none of them.* MT uncertain
ʰ Or, (Grk, Lat) *friends.* Heb ambiguous
ⁱ Or, *Were I to come to the end I would still be with thee*
ʲ RSV(MT) *and that*
ᵏ Q uncertain
ˡ Heb uncertain
ᵐ Or, *idolatry*
ⁿ RSV(MT) *waters of*

Column XXI

Pss. 137:9; 138:1–8; Sirach 51:13ff. (1–11)

Line

ונפץ את עולליך אל הסלע 138(1) לדויד אודכה

𐤉𐤄𐤅𐤄 בכול לבי נגד 𐤉𐤄𐤅𐤄 אלוהים אזמרכה (2)אשתחוה
אל היכל קודשכה ואודה את שמכה על חסדכה ועל אמתכה
כי הגדלתה על כול שמכה אמרתכה (3)ביום קראתי ותענני

תרהיבני בנפשי עז (4)יודוך 𐤉𐤄𐤅𐤄 כול מלכי ארץ כי שמעו

אמרי פיכ (5)וישירו בדרכי 𐤉𐤄𐤅𐤄 כי גדול כבוד 𐤉𐤄𐤅𐤄

(6)כי רם 𐤉𐤄𐤅𐤄 ושפל יראה וגבה ממרחק ייֹדע (7)אם אלך

בתוך צרה תחיני על אף אויבי תשלח ידכה ותושיעני

ימינכה (8) 𐤉𐤄𐤅𐤄 יגמור בעדי 𐤉𐤄𐤅𐤄 חסדכה לעולם
מעשי ידיכה אל תרף
(1)אני נער בטרם תעיתי ובקשתיה (2)באה לי בתרה ועד

סופה אדורשנה (3)גם גרע נץ בבשול ענבים ישמחו לב
(4)דרכה רגלי במישור כי מנעורי ידעתיה (5)הטיתי כמעט

אוזני והרבה מצאתי לקח (6)ועלה היתה לי למלמדי אתן
הודי (7)זמותי ואשחקה קנאתי בטוב ולוא אשוב (8)חריתי
נפשי בה ופני לוא השׄיׄבותי (9)טרתי נפשי בה וברומיה לוא
אשלה (10)ידי פתׄחׄ[ ]מערמיה אתבונן (11)כפי הברותי אל?
לׄ

Column XXI

Pss. 137:9; 138:1–8; Sirach 51:13ff. (1–11)

Line

and dashes your little ones*ᵃ* against the rock! *⁽¹⁾*(A Psalm) of David. I give thee   Ps. 137, Ps. 138
thanks,

O LORD,*ᵇ* with my whole heart; before the gods*ᶜ* I sing thy praise; *⁽²⁾*I bow down

toward thy holy temple and give thanks to thy name for thy steadfast love and thy faithfulness;

for thou hast exalted above everything thy name and thy word.*ᵈ* *⁽³⁾*On the day I called, thou didst
answer me,

5   my strength of soul thou didst increase.*ᵉ* *⁽⁴⁾*All the kings of the earth shall praise thee, O LORD, for
they have heard

the words of thy mouth. *⁽⁵⁾*And they shall sing of the ways of the LORD, for great is the glory of the
LORD.

*⁽⁶⁾*For though the LORD is high, he regards the lowly; but the haughty he knows from afar. *⁽⁷⁾*Though
I walk

in the *middleᶠ* of trouble, thou dost preserve my life; thou dost stretch out thy hand against the
wrath of my enemies, and thy right hand

delivers me. *⁽⁸⁾*The LORD will fulfill his purpose for me; thy steadfast love, O LORD, endures for ever.

10   Do not forsake the work of thy hands.

*⁽¹⁾ᵍ*I was a young man before I had erred when I looked for her.   Apocryphon: Sirach 51: 13ff.*ᵍ*
*⁽²⁾*She came to me in her beauty when

finally I sought her out. *⁽³⁾*Even (as) a blossom drops in the ripening of grapes, making glad the heart,

⁽⁴⁾(So) my foot trod in uprightness; for from my young manhood have I known her. *⁽⁵⁾*I inclined
my ear

a little and great was the persuasion I found. *⁽⁶⁾*And she became for me a nurse; to my teacher I give

15   my ardor. *⁽⁷⁾*I purposed to make sport: I was zealous for pleasure, without pause. *⁽⁸⁾*I kindled

my desire for her without distraction. *⁽⁹⁾*I bestirred my desire for her, and on her heights I do not

waver. *⁽¹⁰⁾*I opened my hand(s)[. . .] and perceive her unseen parts. *⁽¹¹⁾*I cleansed my hands [. . .

ᵃ RSV *your little ones and dashes them.* Q = MT
ᵇ Q and other ancient witnesses: lacking in MT. RSV = Q
ᶜ Q *the* LORD *God,* but noted as a scribal error
ᵈ Or, *thou hast exalted thy word above every name of thine*
ᵉ Or, *thou didst embolden me in my soul with strength*
ᶠ RSV(MT) *midst*
ᵍ See below, Part III, pp. 112–117

Column XXII

Sirach 51:30; Apostrophe to Zion 1–18; Ps. 93:1–3

Line

שכרכם בעתו (1)אזכורך לברכה ציון בכול מודי

אני אהבתיך ברוך לעולמים זכרך (2)גדולה תקותך ציון ושלום
ותוחלת ישועתך לבוא (3)דור ודור ידורו בך ודורות חסידים

תפארתך (4)המתאוים ליום ישעך וישישו ברוב כבודך (5)זיז

כבודך יינקו וברחובות תפארתך יעכסו (6)חסדי נביאיך

תזכורי ובמעשי חסידיך תתפארי (7)טהר חמס מגוך שקר

ועול נכרתו ממך (8)יגילו בניך בקרבך וידידיך אליך נלוו

(9)כמה קוו לישועתך ויתאבלו עליך תמיך (10)לוא תובד תקותך

ציון ולוא תשכח תוחלתך (11)מי זה אבד צדק או מי זה מלט

בעולו (12)נבחן אדם כדרכו א יש כמעשיו ישתלם (13)סביב נכרתו

צריך ציון ויתפזרו כול משנאיך (14)ערבה באף תשבחתך ציון
מעלה לכול תבל (15)פעמים רבות אזכורך לברכה בכול לבבי אברכך

(16)צדק עולמים תשיגי וברכות נכבדים תקבלי (17)קחי חזון

דובר עליך וחלמות נביאים תתבעך (18)רומי ורחבי ציון
שבחי עליון פודך תשמח נפשי בכבודך
93 (1) הללויה 𐤉𐤄𐤅𐤄 מלך גאות לבש לבש 𐤉𐤄𐤅𐤄 [ ]ויתאזר אף

[ ]כ֯ן תבל בל טמוט (2)נכון כסאכה מ֯אז מ֯[ ]ל֯ם [ ](3)נש֯א֯ו נהרות

Column XXII

Sirach 51:30; Apostrophe to Zion 1–18; Ps. 93:1–3

Line

your reward in due season.   [(1)a]I remember   Apocrypha: Sirach 51:30; Apostrophe to Zion[a]

thee for blessing, O Zion; with all my might

have I loved thee. May thy memory be blessed forever! [(2)]Great is thy hope, O Zion; that peace

and thy longed-for salvation will come. [(3)]Generation after generation will dwell in thee and

generations of saints will be

thy splendor: [(4)]Those who yearn for the day of thy salvation that they may rejoice in the greatness

of thy glory. [(5)]On (the) abundance of

5   thy glory they are nourished and in thy splendid squares will they toddle. [(6)]The merits of thy

prophets

wilt thou remember, and in the deeds of thy pious ones wilt thou glory. [(7)]Purge violence from thy

midst: falsehood

and iniquity will be cut off from thee. [(8)]Thy sons will rejoice in thy midst and thy precious ones will

be united with thee.

[(9)]How they have hoped for thy salvation, thy pure ones have mourned for thee. [(10)]Hope for thee

does not perish,

O Zion, nor is hope in thee forgotten. [(11)]Who has ever perished (in) righteousness, or who has ever

survived

10   in his iniquity? [(12)]Man is tested according to his way; every man is requited according to his deeds;

[(13)]all about are thine enemies

cut off, O Zion, and all thy foes have been scattered. [(14)]Praise of thee is pleasing, O Zion,

cherished through all the world. [(15)]Many times do I remember thee for blessing; with all my heart I

bless thee.

[(16)]Mayst thou attain unto everlasting righteousness, and blessings of the honorable mayst thou

receive. [(17)]Accept a vision

bespoken of thee, and dreams of prophets sought for thee. [(18)]Be exalted, and spread wide, O Zion;

15   praise the Most High, thy saviour: let my soul be glad in thy glory.

[(1)]*Praise the LORD.*[b] The Lord reigns; he is robed in majesty; the LORD is robed, *and*[c] he is   Ps. 93

girded with strength. Yea

thou dost establish the world;[d] it shall never be moved; [(2)]thy throne is established from of old; [thou

art] from [ever]lasting. [(3)]The floods have lifted up

---

[a] Not in the Bible. See below, Part III, pp. 114–117 and 123–127

[b] Only in Q

[c] Lacking in RSV(MT). Q = LXX

[d] RSV(MT) *the world is established.* Q = LXX

Column XXIII

Pss. 141:5–10; 133:1–3; 144:1–7

Line

ויוכיחני שמן רואש אל יני רואשי כי עוד ותלפתי

ברעותיהמה (6)נשמטו בידי סלע שופטיהם ושמעו

אמרי כי נע מו (7)כמו פלח ובקע בארץ נפזרו עצמי לפי

אשאול (8)כי אליכה 𐤉𐤄𐤅𐤄 אדוני עיני בכה חסיתי אל
תער נפשי (9)שמורני מיד פח יקושו לי ומוקשות פועלי און

(10)יפולו במכמריו רשעים יחד אנוכי עד אעבוד
133(1) שיר ה מעלות לדויד הנה מה טוב ומה
נעים שבת אחים גם יחד (2)כשמן הטוב על הרואש
יורד על הזקן זקן אהרון שירד על פי מדיו (3)כטל חרמון

שיורד על הר ציון כי שמה צוה 𐤉𐤄𐤅𐤄 את הברכה עד
עולם שלום על ישראל
144(1) ברוך 𐤉𐤄𐤅𐤄 צורי המלמד ידי לקרב ואצבעותי למלחמה
(2)חסדי ומצודתי משגבי ומפלט לי מגני ובו חסיתי הרודד

עמים תחתי (3)אלוהים מה אדם ותדעהו בן אנוש
ותחושבהו (4)אדם להבל דמה וימיו כצל עובר (5)אלוהים הט

שמיכה ורד גע בה[ ]ויעשנו (6)ברק ברק ותפיצם שלח חצ°°°

?] (7)]כה ממרום פצני והציל[ ]

Column XXIII

Pss. 141:5–10; 133:1–3; 144:1–7

Line

or rebuke me (in kindness), but let the oil of the wicked never anoint my head;[a] for my prayer is continually[b] Ps. 141

against their wicked deeds. (6)When they are given over to those who shall condemn them, then they shall *hear*

my words how pleasant they are.[c] (7)As a rock which one cleaves and shatters on the land, so shall *my*[d] bones be strewn at the mouth

of Sheol. (8)But my eyes are toward thee, O LORD God;[e] in thee I see refuge; leave me

not defenseless! (9)Keep me from the trap which they have laid for me, and from the snares of evildoers!

(10)Let the wicked together fall into their own nets, while I escape.

(1)A Song of Ascents. Of David. Behold, how good and Ps. 133

pleasant it is when brothers dwell in unity! (2)It is like the precious oil upon the head,

running down upon the beard, upon the beard of Aaron, running down on the collar of his robes! (3)It is like the dew of Hermon,

which falls on the mountain[f] of Zion! For *thither*[g] the LORD has commanded the blessing, life for

evermore. *Peace be upon Israel.*[h]

(1)Blessed[i] be the LORD, my rock, who trains my hands for war, and my fingers for battle; Ps. 144

(2)*my steadfast love*[j] and my fortress, my stronghold and *deliverer for me,*[k] my shield and he in whom I take refuge, who subdues

peoples under *me.*[l] (3)O *God,*[m] what is man that thou dost regard him, or the son of man

that thou dost think of him? (4)Man is like a breath, *and*[n] his days are like a passing shadow. (5)Bow thy heavens, O *God,*[m]

and come down! Touch the moun[tains] that they smoke! (6)Flash forth the lightning and scatter them, send out

[thy arrows and rout them! (7)Stretch forth] thy [hand] from on high, rescue me and deliver [me from the many waters]

---

[a] Grk: Heb uncertain
[b] Or, *for still and my prayer is.* Q uncertain
[c] RSV *learn that the word of the LORD is true.* Q = MT
[d] RSV *their.* MT *our*
[e] Or, *O Yahweh, my Lord*
[f] RSV(MT) *mountains*
[g] RSV(MT) *there*
[h] Only in Q
[i] RSV(MT) *A Psalm of David. Blessed*
[j] RSV *my rock.* Q = MT
[k] RSV *my deliverer.* MT *my deliverer for me*
[l] RSV *him.* Q = MT
[m] RSV(MT) *LORD*
[n] Not in RSV(MT)

Column XXIV

Pss. 144:15; 155:1–19

Line

(15)אשרי העם שככה לו אשרי העם אשר 𐤉𐤄𐤅𐤄 אלוהיו
155(1) 𐤉𐤄𐤅𐤄 קראתי אליכה הקשיבה אלי (2)פרשתי כפי
למעון קודשכה (3)הט אוזנכה ותן לי את שאלתי (4)ובקשתי
אל תמנע ממני (5)בנה נפשי ואל תמגרה (6)ואל תפרע לפני
רשעים (7)גמולי הרע ישיב ממני דין האמת (8) 𐤉𐤄𐤅𐤄
אל תשפטני כחטאתי כי לוא יצדק לפניכה כול חי
(9)הבינני 𐤉𐤄𐤅𐤄 בתורתכה ואת משפטיכה למדני
(10)וישמעו רבים מעשיכה ועמים יהדרו את כבודכה
(11)זכורני ואל תשכחני ואל תביאני בקשות ממני
(12)חטאת נעורי הרחק ממני ופשעי אל יזכרו לי
(13)טהרני 𐤉𐤄𐤅𐤄 מנגע רע ואל יוסף לשוב אל (14)יבש
שרשיו ממני ואל ינצו ע[ ]יו בי (15)כבוד אתה 𐤉𐤄𐤅𐤄
על כן שאלתי מלפניכה שלמה (16)למי אזעקה ויתן לי
ובני אדם מה יוסיף אומ[ ] (17)מלפ[ ]יכה 𐤉𐤄𐤅𐤄 מבטחי
קראתי 𐤉𐤄𐤅𐤄 ויענני [ ] שבר לבי (18)נמתי
[ ]שנה חלמתי גם [ ]𐤉

Column XXIV

Pss. 144:15; 155:1–19

Line

Ps. 144

(15)Happy the people *for whom it is so*![a] Happy the people whose God is the LORD!

Apocryphon: Ps. 155 or (Syriac) Ps. III[b]

(1)[b]O LORD, I called unto thee, give heed to me. (2)I spread forth my palms toward thy holy dwelling. (3)Incline thine ear and grant me my plea, (4)And my request withhold not from me. (5)Edify my soul and do not cast it down, (6)And abandon (it) not in the presence of the wicked. (7)May the Judge of Truth remove from me the rewards of evil. (8)O LORD, judge me not according to my sins; for no man living is righteous before thee. (9)Grant me understanding, O LORD, in thy law and teach me thine ordinances, (10)That many may hear of thy deeds and peoples may honor thy glory. (11)Remember me and forget me not, and lead me into not situations too hard for me. (12)The sins of my youth cast far from me, and may my transgressions not be remembered against me. (13)Purify me, O LORD, from (the) evil scourge, and let it not turn again upon me. (14)Dry up its roots from me, and let its leaves not flourish within me. (15)Thou art (my) glory,[c] O LORD. Therefore is my request fulfilled before thee. (16)To whom may I cry and he would grant (it) me? And the sons of man—what more can [their] pow[er] do?— (17)My trust, O LORD, is befo[r]e thee. I cried "O LORD," and he answered me, [and he healed] my broken heart. (18)I slumbered [and sl]ept, I dreamt; indeed [I awoke. (19)Thou didst support me, O Lord, and I invoked the LOR]D . . .

---

[a] RSV *to whom such blessings fall*! Q = MT

[b] Not in the Bible. See below, Part III, pp. 109–112

[c] Heb. Syr *Great art thou*

Column xxv

Pss. 142:4–8; 143:1–8

Line

לי (5)אביטה ימין ואראה ואין לי מכיר אבד מנוס ממני אין

דורש לנפשי (6)זעקתי אליכה 𐤉𐤄𐤅𐤄 אמרתי אתה מחסי
חלקי בארץ החיים (7)הקשיבה אל רנתי כי דלותי מואדה
הצילני מרודפי כי אמצו ממני (8)הוצא ממסגר נפשי להודות

את שמכה בי יכת רו צדיקים כי תגמול עלי
(1)143 מזמור לדויד 𐤉𐤄𐤅𐤄 שמעה תפלתי
האזינה אל תחנוני באמונתכה ענני בצדקתכה (2)ואל
תבוא במשפט את עבדכה כי לוא יצדק לפניכה כול חי (3)כי
ירדוף אויב נפשי דכא לארץ חיתי הושיבני במחשכים
כמיתי עולם (4)ותתעטף עלי רוחי בתוכי וישתומם לבבי
(5)זכרתי ימים מקדם הגיתי בכול פועלכה במעשי ידיכה
אשיחה (6)פרשתי ידי א[ ]ה נפשי בארץ עיפה לכה סלה

(7)מהר ענני 𐤉𐤄𐤅𐤄 כ[ ]רוחי אל תסתר פניכה ממני
ונמשלתי עם יור[(8)]ש[ ]י בבוקר חסדכה
[ ]??? אליכה נשא[ ]

Column xxv

Pss. 142:4–8; 143:1–8

Line

for me. (4)I look to the right and watch,ᵃ but there is none who takes notice of me;   Ps. 142
                           no refuge remains to me, no man

cares for me. (5)I cry to thee, O LORD; I say, Thou art my refuge,

my portion in the land of the living. (6)Give heed to my cry; for I am brought very low!

Deliver me from my persecutors; for they are too strong for me! (7)Bring me out of prison, that I
                           may give thanks

5   to thy name! The righteous will surround me; for thou wilt deal bountifully with me.

                  (1)A Psalm of David. Hear my prayer, O LORD;   Ps. 143

give ear to my supplications! In thy faithfulness answer me, in thy righteousness! (2)Enter

not into judgment with thy servant; for no man living is righteous before thee. (3)For

the enemy *persecutes*ᵇ me; he has crushed my life to the ground; he has made me sit in darkness

10   like those long dead. (4)Therefore my spirit faints within me; *and*ᶜ my heart within me is appalled.

(5)I remember the days of old, I meditate on all that thou hast done; *on the works of thy hands*

*I contemplate.*ᵈ (6)I stretch out my hands t[o thee]; my soul thirsts for thee like a parched land.

                           Selah

(7)Make haste to answer me, O LORD! My spirit [fails]! Hide not thy face from me,

lest I be like those who go [down to the Pit. (8)Let me hear] in the morning of thy steadfast love,

15   [   ] to thee I lift up

ᵃ MT *Look to the right and watch.* Q = RSV
ᵇ RSV(MT) *has pursued*
ᶜ Only in Q
ᵈ RSV(MT) *I muse on what thy hands have wrought*

Column XXVI

Pss. 149:7–9; 150:1–6; Hymn to the Creator 1–9

Line

(7)לעשות נקמה בגויים תוכחות בלאומים (8)לאסור מלכיהם

בזקים ונכבדיהמה בכבלי ברזל (9)לעשות בהם משפט כתוב
הדר הוא לכול חסידיו לבני ישראל עם קודשו הללו יה
150(1) הללו אל בקודשו הללוהו ברקיע עוזו (2)הללוהו
בגבורותיו הללוהו כרוב גודלו (3)הללוהו בתקוע שופר הללוהו   5

בנבל וכנור (4)הללוהו בתוף ומחול הללוהו במנים ועוגב
(5)הללוהו בצלצלי שמע הללוהו בצלצלי תרועה (6)כול הנשמות

תהלליה הללויה
(1)גדול וקדוש 𐤉𐤄𐤅𐤄 קדוש קדושים לדור ודור (2)לפניו הדר

ילך ואחריו המון מים רבים (3)חסד ואמת סביב פניו אמת   10
ומשפט וצדק מכון כסאו (4)מבדיל אור מאפלה שחר הכין בדעת

לבו (5)אזראו כול מלאכיו וירננו כי   הראם את אשר לוא ידעו

(6)מעטר הרים תנובות   אוכל טוב לכול חי (7)ברוך עושה
ארץ בכוחו מכין תבל בחוכמתו (8)בתבונתו נטה שמים ויוצא

[   ] מאו[   ]ר עשה ויעל נשיא[   ]קצה[15

Column XXVI

Pss. 149:7–9; 150:1–6; Hymn to the Creator 1–9

Line

(7)to wreak vengeance on the nations and chastisement*s* on the peoples, (8)to bind their   Ps. 149
kings

with chains and their nobles with fetters of iron, (9)to execute on them the judgment written!

This is glory for all his faithful ones, *for the sons of Israel, his holy people.*^a Praise the Lord!

(1)Praise God^b in his sanctuary; praise him in his mighty firmament! (2)Praise him   Ps. 150

5   for his mighty deeds; praise him according to his exceeding greatness! (3)Praise him with trumpet
sounding; praise him

with lute and harp! (4)Praise him with timbrel and dance; praise him with strings and pipe!

(5)Praise him with sounding cymbals; praise him with loud clashing cymbals! (6)Let *all breathing*
things^c

praise the Lord! Praise the LORD!

(1)^dGreat and holy is the LORD, the holiest of holy ones for   Apocryphon: Hymn to the Creator^d
every generation. (2)Majesty precedes him

10   and following him is the rush of many waters. (3)Grace and truth surround his presence; truth

and justice and righteousness are the foundation of his throne. (4)Separating light from deep
darkness, he established the dawn by the knowledge

of his mind. (5)When all his angels had witnessed it they sang aloud; for he showed them what they
had not known:

(6)Crowning the hills with fruit, good food for every living being. (7)Blessed be he who makes

the earth by his power, establishing the world in his wisdom. (8)In his understanding he stretched out
the heavens, and brought forth

15   [wind] from his st[orehouses]. (9)He made [lightening for the rai]n, and caused mist[s] to rise [from]
the end [of the earth].

---

^a Only in Q
^b RSV(MT) *Praise the Lord! Praise God*
^c RSV(MT) *everything that breathes*
^d Not in the Bible. See below, Part III, pp. 129–131

Column XXVII

II Sam. 23:7; David's Compositions; Ps. 140:1–5

Line

ועץ ח֯יצנ֯ית ובאש שרף ישרפו בשבת
ויהי דויד בן ישי חכם ואור כאור השמש וסופר

ונבון ותמים בכול דרכיו לפני אל ואנשים ויתן
לו 𐤉𐤄𐤅𐤄 רוח נבונה ואורה ויכתוב תהלים
שלושת אלפים ושש מאות ושיר לשורר לפני המזבח על עולת
התמיד לכול יום ויום לכול ימי השנה ארבעה וששים ושלוש
מאות ולקורבן השבתות שנים וחמשים שיר ולקורבן ראשי
החודשים ולכול ימי המועדות ולי ם הכפורים שלושים שיר
ויהי כול השיר אשר דבר ששה ואבעים וארבע מאות ושיר
לנגן על הפגו֯עים ארבעה ויהי הכול ארבעת אלפים וחמשים
כול אלה דבר בנבואה אשר נתן לו מלפני העליון
140 (1) למנצח מזמור לדויד (2) חלצני 𐤉𐤄𐤅𐤄
מאדם רע מ[ ]יש חמסים תצרני (3) אשר חשבו רעות בלב כול
היום יגרו֯ [ ]ל[ ]מות (4) שננו לשונם כמו נחש חמת עכביש תחת

] [(5) שו֯מרני 𐤉𐤄𐤅𐤄 מידי ר֯שע֯ מאיש] [

Column XXVII

II Sam. 23:7; David's Compositions; Ps. 140:1–5

Line

and the wood of an outside room,[a] and they are utterly consumed with fire *in the sitting.*[b]   II Sam. 23

[c]And David, the son of Jesse, was wise, and a light   Apocryphon: David's Compositions[c]
like the light of the sun, and literate,

and discerning and perfect in all his ways before God and men. And the LORD gave

him a discerning and enlightened spirit. And he wrote

5   3,600 psalms; and songs to sing before the altar over the whole-burnt

perpetual offering every day, for all the days of the year, 364;

and for the offering of the Sabbaths, 52 songs; and for the offering of the New

Moons and for all the Solemn Assemblies and for the Day of Atonement, 30 songs.

And all the songs that he spoke were 446, and songs

10   for making music over the stricken, 4. And the total was 4,050

All these he composed through prophecy which was given him from before the Most High.

[1]To the choirmaster. A Psalm of David. Deliver me, O LORD,   Ps. 140

from evil men; preserve me from violent men, [2]who plan evil things in their heart,

and stir up wars continually. [3]They make their tongue sharp as a serpent's, and under their lips is
the poison of *a spider.*[d]

15   [4]Guard me, O LORD, from the hands of the wicked; [preserve me] from [violent] men . . .

---

[a] RSV *and the shaft of a spear*. Heb uncertain
[b] Lacking in RSV. Q = MT. Heb uncertain
[c] Not in the Bible. See below, Part III, pp. 133–137
[d] RSV(MT) *vipers. Selah*

Column XXVIII

Pss. 134:1–3; 151A, B

Line

𐤉𐤄𐤅𐤄 העומדים בבית 𐤉𐤄𐤅𐤄 בלילות (2)שאו ידיכם קודש וברכו

את שם 𐤉𐤄𐤅𐤄 (3)יברככה 𐤉𐤄𐤅𐤄 מציו[ ] עושה שמים וארץ

151 A הללויה לדויד בן ישי (1)קטן הייתי מאחי וצעיר מבני אבי וישימני

רועה לצונו ומושל בגדיותיו (2)ידי עשו עוגב ואצבעותי כנור

ואשימה ל𐤉𐤄𐤅𐤄 כבוד אמרתי אני בנפשי (3)ההרים לוא יעידו

לו והגבעות לוא יגידו עלו העצים את דברי והצואן את מעשי

(4)כי מי יגיד ומי ידבר ומי יספר את מעשי אדון הכול ראה אלוה

הכול הוא שמע והוא האזין (5)שלח נביאו למושחני את שמואל

לגדלני יצאו אחי לקראתו יפי התור ויפי המראה (6)הגבהים בקומתם

היפים בשערם לוא בחר 𐤉𐤄𐤅𐤄 אלוהים בם (7)וישלח ויקחני

מאחר הצואן וימשחני בשמן הקודש וישימני נגיד לעמו ומושל בבני

בריתו

151 B תחלת גב[ ]רה ל[ ]יד משמשחו נביא אלוהים (1)אזי רא[ ]תי פלשתי

מחרף ממ[ ]אנוכי [ ] את [ ] [

Column XXVIII

Pss. 134:1–3; 151A, B

Line

of the Lᴏʀᴅ, who stand by night in the house of the Lᴏʀᴅ! ⁽²⁾Lift up your hands to the holy   Ps. 134
place, and bless

*the name of*ᵃ the Lᴏʀᴅ. ⁽³⁾May the Lᴏʀᴅ bless you from Zion, he who made heaven and earth!

ᵇA Hallelujah of David the Son of Jesse. ⁽¹⁾Smaller was I than my   Apocryphon: Ps. 151Aᵇ
brothers and the youngest of the sons of my father, so he made me

shepherd of his flock and ruler over his kids. ⁽²⁾My hands have made an instrument and my fingers
a lyre;

₅   And (so) have I rendered glory to the Lᴏʀᴅ, thought I, within my soul. ⁽³⁾The mountains do not
witness

to him, nor do the hills proclaim; The trees have cherished my words and the flock my works.

⁽⁴⁾For who can proclaim and who can bespeak and who can recount the deeds of the Lord? Everything has God seen,

everything has he heard and he has heeded. ⁽⁵⁾He sent his prophet to anoint me, Samuel

to make me great; My brothers went out to meet him, handsome of figure and appearance. ⁽⁶⁾Though
they were tall of stature

₁₀   and handsome by their hair, The Lᴏʀᴅ God chose them not.⁽⁷⁾ But he sent and took me

from behind the flock and anointed me with holy oil, And he made me leader of his people and
ruler over the sons

of his covenant.

⁽¹⁾ᵇAt the beginning of David's power after the prophet of God had   Apocryphon: Ps. 151Bᵇ
anointed him. Then I [saw] a Philistine

uttering defiances from the r[anks of the enemy.]   I . . . the . . .

ᵃ Only in Q
ᵇ Not in the Bible. See below, Part III, pp. 94–103

PART III

The Apocryphal Compositions

PSALMS KNOWN
IN ANCIENT TRANSLATIONS

AMONG the eight compositions contained in the Psalms Scroll which are not in the modern Bibles (see the discussion on the contents of the scroll in Part I, above) are four poems that had been known, prior to the recovery of the scroll, in ancient translations. The scroll now gives us the Hebrew text on which those translations were based. All four poems (one, Psalm 151, is in two sections) were originally composed in Hebrew, and we have every right to hope that in the scroll we have texts very close to what the author-poets actually created.

Why do we say "very close"? Why not say "the original poems"? In academic parlance the original composition is called the autograph. For writings that derive from antiquity autographs of materials copied and preserved through the centuries are very difficult to come by. Autographs are sometimes discovered in stone or clay-tablet inscriptions, but those are materials which had usually been unknown before their discovery in modern times. The word autograph is reserved for the material as it was under the hand, or at the dictation, of its author.

While we do not have the actual autographs, therefore, of the four poems in question, we may well have texts that reflect the autographs quite accurately. None of the four poems was written in the first century A.D., the date of the scroll itself; in fact, the very youngest of the four may have been composed two or more centuries before the scroll was written! The scroll contains but copies of copies of the conjectured autographs of the poems. Even so, considerable confidence can be placed in our first-century copies if the reader will read them with tolerance for scribal errors. Scribal errors are sometimes intentional and sometimes unintentional. Only a comparison with the auto-graphs would indicate exactly where errors have been made and which type they are, and since we do not have the autographs scholars will allow themselves considerable debate as to how close to the original our copies come. But for the present we ought to assume a stance of confidence in the texts we now have.

Comparison of our texts of the four poems with their conjectured autographs is not the only comparison that can be made. They must be compared with their ancient translations, and this comparison, while less interesting perhaps, can be done with considerably more confidence. It must be borne in mind that we no more have the autographs of the ancient translations than of the original poems; in the case of the translations we must be content with copies of copies of the work of the actual translator. And the first question a scholar has when he finds an original-language text of an ancient translation is whether he has found the *Vorlage* of the translation, or at least something very close to it, that is, if he has now the original-language text which the translator used in making his autograph-translation.

Of our four poems two seem to be in the class of *Vorlagen*: Psalms 154 and 155 are almost verbatim parallels to the Syriac translations of them which had been known before the scroll was discovered and unrolled. That is, we now have in the scroll the texts of Psalms 154 and 155 almost precisely as they lay before the eyes of the Syriac translator. These two psalms, known heretofore only as Syriac Apocryphal Psalms Nos. II and III, existed only in Syriac and (now) their original-language Hebrew. The other two poems (Psalm 151 and the Sirach piece) existed in Greek, Syriac, and Latin translations, and in both cases the Syriac and Latin translations were almost certainly made from the Greek translation, the oldest in each case. There is even a medieval Hebrew translation of the canticle in Sirach 51, made for the most part from the Syriac, which had itself been translated most probably from the Greek. All this is to say that these four poems, including Psalm 151, ceased to be copied sometime after the first century A.D. in their original Hebrew form and subsisted for a while only in Greek, from which the Latin and Syriac forms then were derived.

The three heretofore unknown psalms, as well as the prose insert in column XXVII, also ceased to be copied sometime after the first century A.D., and we must suppose were simply never rendered into any other language until the English translations which appear on these pages.

Psalm 151

Psalm 151 was known, before the recovery of this scroll, in Greek, Latin, and Syriac translations, the latter two based on the first, or Greek. But Psalm 151 in the scroll is radically different from the old translations and considerably more fascinating. To begin with, it is actually two poems, and that is the reason that we must subdivide 151 into 151A and 151B. The old translations are all preserved as units without a suspicion of being divided into two poems originally, which is to say that the earliest, or Greek, translation represents a dramatic transformation of the text of Psalm 151A, B into a shorter and amalgamated Psalm 151 as it has been known in the old Greek Bibles.

The layman can imagine what excitement such a discovery as this causes among scholars—the recovery of the original language of a known psalm but in a far fuller text! What are the "new" elements? Why were they omitted from the Greek? Why were the two poems amalgamated and epitomized into shorter form? These are questions which will be debated by interested experts for some time to come: we can only hint at answers now.

All the poetry in the scroll is copied out as though it were prose: only Psalm 119 is in metric arrangement, but that is due not to any effort on the part of the ancient scribe to make poetry but to show clearly the alphabetic arrangement of the first letters of each bicolon. The poetry of Psalm 151A is not at all difficult to scan, however: it is made up of seven pairs, or couplets, of bicolons preceded by a short title. Hebrew poetry can be measured in sense-accented feet, or stresses; the bicolons in our psalm generally have the 3/2 meter save for verses 4 and 7, which have bicolons in 3/3. The 3/2 meter is particularly dramatic in verse 6b, where the negative assertion is made that God did not choose David's brothers even though they were handsome in every way. God instead chose the humble good-shepherd musician, little David, playing on his harp. Psalm 151A has two strophes clearly indicated by the slightly longer verses 4 and 7, each of which closes a strophe. All this will be indicated in the metered arrangements of the text and the translation below. Since much of our understanding of the psalm depends on a comparison with the old Greek translation, line-by-line parallels are here offered both for the Hebrew and Greek texts and for their corresponding English translations. Clearly distinctive elements in each are underlined in order to indicate, even at a glance, two important observations: the scroll's Hebrew text is considerably fuller than the Greek version of it; and it contains every thought and phrase present in the Greek. (Only two or three totally insignificant Greek words stand alone and they can be accounted for in terms of translation techniques.) There is no underlining in either Psalm 151B or the Greek Psalm 151:6–7, where only the word "Philistine" appears in both texts.

(For other possible translations see below, the "Variant Translations of Psalm 151A," pp. 100–103.)

It is clear from the parallels that the Hebrew psalm is complete in itself. One might ordinarily expect that the longer-known Greek translation would inform our understanding of the newly recovered original. On the contrary, beside the Hebrew psalm the Greek version appears so desiccated as to be very nearly meaningless in its first five verses. Verse 3 in the Greek is a good case of how truncated the Greek text is; its parallel in Hebrew verse 4 is a beautifully complete Hebrew couplet of bicolons. The Hebrew asks, in essence, who could possibly recount the totality of God's mighty acts: he is omniscient. The Greek parallel is comparatively ridiculous: it changes the idea of man's inability to proclaim all of God's deeds to the very rigid idea that man cannot proclaim anything *to* God because God himself can hear! Beside the Hebrew the Greek is now seen as patently absurd in verse 3. Verses 4 and 5 in the Greek come off a bit better but against the Hebrew it is now clear that they are so jumbled that Greek verse 5 has lost its thrust.

The poem is a poetic midrash on I Sam. 16:1–13, the attractively simple account of how the shepherd David, Jesse's eighth and youngest son, was made ruler of Israel. Just as in I Kings 3:5–15 Solomon protested his youth, so David here begins by noting his. But the point of David's election in the Bible is the crux of the poetic midrash: "The Lord looks upon the heart" (I Sam. 16:7). However, the biblical passage fails to state what God saw in David's heart, and it is just that which the poetic midrash supplies. Even though David is insignificant in external appearance, he, in his soul or heart or to himself, has said the significant thing: he would give glory to the Lord (verse 2); and the Lord who can see into the heart has seen and heard everything David has done and said (verse 4). Therefore, God heeded David's piety of soul by sending the prophet Samuel to take him from behind the flock to make him a great ruler.

The first strophe (verses 1–4) deals with David and what he thought and did to praise God and how God, who sees into the heart, heeded David's soul prayer. What David thought and did, his "words" and "works" (verse 3b), are represented by the scroll itself and the 4,050 psalms and songs of column xxvii, lines 2–11. The second strophe (verses 5–7) deals with God's response, through Samuel, to David's desire, by making David great where he had been insignificant (verses 1 and 5), and by anointing him ruler of his people, where he had been only a ruler of flocks (verses 1b and 7b).

The beauty and integrity of the Hebrew psalm may be seen, for example, in the parallelism of thought between Hebrew verses 1 and 7. Whereas Jesse, David's father, had made the lad shepherd and ruler over his flocks, God made him leader and ruler over his people. This parallel structure is truncated in the Greek to the bland statement in Greek verse 1, "I tended my father's flock." Notice that the superscription, or title, in Hebrew says nothing about the fight with Goliath; the Hebrew

psalm (151A) has nothing to do with Philistines. Psalm 151A follows the story of David as it is in I Samuel 16; Psalm 151B takes its material from I Samuel 17, where the Goliath episode is recorded. The Greek combines the two into one psalm.

It is obvious by now that we are here dealing with a case where, as noted above, we do not actually have the precise Hebrew *Vorlage* from which the Greek translation was made. The Greek translation was made from a truncated amalgamation of the two Hebrew psalms. In reducing the two psalms in size down to about the length of the first, both psalms were abused. We have no way of knowing how long Psalm 151B originally was; the bottom third of each column in the scroll is lacking. Only the word Philistine appears in both the Hebrew and the Greek. Greek verses 6 and 7 probably represent a considerable compression of Psalm 151B into the two verses, which would correspond only to some four Hebrew colons, if the compressing and amalgamation took place in a Hebrew edition or recension before translation into Greek —a very likely hypothesis. On the other hand, the original Psalm 151B, as we now know, had a rather full superscription, and starts out, not as Greek verse 6 with the actual altercation between the lad and the giant (I Sam. 17:40–49) but with the point where David first entered the Israelite camp and saw the Philistine challenging the ranks of Israel (I Sam. 17:23). Indeed, one should rather expect a poem based on the exciting events of I Samuel 17 to include a bit of its main point: that rare combination in David of both humility and bravado, born of his experiences as a lonely shepherd caring and fighting for his sheep— experiences, according to the biblical story, which formed his apprenticeship for becoming king. The superscription prepares the reader of Psalm 151B for what took place, recounted in I Samuel 17, after the spirit of God left Saul and went mightily upon David, as noted in the last dozen or so verses of I Samuel 16: one expects to hear something of the wonderful consternation registered in the Israelite camp of a mere shepherd-musician (Psalm 151A = I Samuel 16) wanting to fight the giant. The point of the second psalm undoubtedly had to do with the wonderful force of "manhood" and gallantry which had come to David upon being anointed by Samuel and upon receiving the spirit (force, strength) of God, a

Psalm 151A

LXX

Q

Οὗτος ὁ ψαλμὸς ἰδιόγραφος εἰς Δαυεὶδ
καὶ ἔξωθεν τοῦ ἀριθμοῦ, ὅτε ἐμονο-
μάχησεν τῷ Γολιάδ.

הללויה לדויד בן ישי

151⁽¹⁾ Μικρὸς ἤμην ἐν τοῖς ἀδελφοῖς μου,

καὶ νεώτερος ἐν τῷ οἴκῳ τοῦ πατρός μου·
ἐποίμαινον τὰ πρόβατα τοῦ πατρός μου.

⁽²⁾ αἱ χεῖρές μου ἐποίησαν ὄργανον,

οἱ δάκτυλοί μου ἥρμοσαν ψαλτήριον.

[Lacking]

⁽³⁾ καὶ τίς ἀναγγελεῖ

τῷ κυρίῳ μου

αὐτὸς κύριος, αὐτὸς πάντων εἰσακούει.

⁽⁴ᵃ⁾ αὐτὸς ἐξαπέστειλεν τὸν ἄγγελον αὐτοῦ

⁽⁵ᵃ⁾ οἱ ἀδελφοί μου

καλοὶ καὶ

μεγάλοι

⁽⁵ᵇ⁾ καὶ οὐκ εὐδόκησεν

κύριος

ἐν αὐτοῖς

⁽⁴ᵇ⁾ καὶ ἦρέν με ἐκ τῶν προβάτων τοῦ πατρός μου,

⁽⁴ᶜ⁾ καὶ ἔχρισέν με ἐν τῷ ἐλαίῳ τῆς χρίσεως αὐτοῦ.

*Verse
no.*

⁽¹⁾ 3–4

קטן הייתי מן אחי
וצעיר מבני אבי
וישימני רועה לצונו
ומושל בגדיותיו

⁽²⁾ 4–5

ידי עשו עוגב
ואצבעותי כנור

⁽³⁾ 5–6

ואשימה ליהוה כבוד
אמרתי אני בנפשי
ההרים לוא יעידו לו
והגבעות לוא יגידו
עלו העצים את דברי
והצואן את מעשי

⁽⁴⁾ 7–8

כי מי יגיד ומי ידבר
ומי יספר את מעשי אדון
הכול ראה אלוה
הכול הוא שמע והוא האזין

⁽⁵⁾ 8–9

שלח נביאו למושחני
את שמואל לגדלני
יצאו אחי לקראתו
יפי התור ויפי המראה

⁽⁶⁾ 9–10

הגבהים בקומתם
היפים בשערם
לוא בחר יהוה
אלוהים בם

⁽⁷⁾ 10–12

וישלח ויקחני מאחר הצואן
וימשחני בשמן הקודש
וישימני נגיד לעמו
ומושל בבני בריתו

---

¹ I Sam. 16: 11; 17: 14.
² Judg. 6: 15; Ps. 119: 141. The opening phrases of
Psalm 151A recur verbatim in Pseudo-Philo's *Liber
Antiquitatum Biblicarum*, edited by Guido Kisch (1949),
paragraph lxii, line 5: "Minimus inter fratres meos, et
pascens oves patris fui."
³ I Sam. 16: 11.
⁴ Isa. 42: 12.
⁵ Eccles. 2: 1, 15; 3: 17, 18. Hebrew idiom meaning "to
myself," using the figure of soul or heart. With the word
"heart" it normally precedes the thought expressed,
meaning "I had (wrongly) thought"; see the variant

translations of Skehan and Rabinowitz, below. Here,
however, because of the context and general meaning of
the poem, it is read with the preceding lines to express the
thought in David's heart or soul, which God saw there
when he directed Samuel to choose David as king (I Sam.
16: 7). See the frequent and facile interchange of the
words "heart" and "soul" in column IV of the Thanksgiving Hymns.
⁶ Contrast Mic. 6: 1–2, Isa. 44: 23 and 55: 12, etc.
⁷ A little-used word in Neo-Hebrew meaning "lift up"
or "hold high" or "appreciate." See the Damascus
Document v 5 (7: 7), "They esteemed the deeds of David."

Psalm 151A

Greek	11QPs[a] column XXVIII, lines 3–12 *Hebrew*
This psalm, though supernumerary, is truly written by David when he single-handedly fought Goliath.	A Hallelujah of David the Son of Jesse.
(1) I was small among my brothers and the youngest *in* my father's *house*. I tended my father's flock.	(1) Smaller was I than my brothers[1] and the youngest *of the sons* of my father,[2] So he made me shepherd of his flock[3] *and ruler over his kids.*
(2) My hands made a musical instrument and my fingers *fashioned* a lyre.	(2) My hands have made an instrument and my fingers a lyre; And (so) have I rendered glory to the Lord,[4] thought I, within my soul.[5]
	(3) The mountains do not witness to him, nor do the hills proclaim;[6] The trees have cherished[7] my words and the flock my works.
(3) And who shall proclaim *to (for) my* Lord? *the Lord himself*, he hears everything.[10]	(4) For who can proclaim *and who can bespeak* *and who can recount the deeds of the* Lord?[8] *Everything has God seen*,[9] everything has he heard[10] *and* he *has heeded.*
(4a) He sent his *messenger*	(5) He sent his *prophet to anoint me*, *Samuel to make me great*;
(5a) My brothers were handsome and tall	My brothers *went out to meet him*, handsome *of figure and appearance*. (6) Though they were tall *of stature* *and handsome by their hair*,
(5b) But the Lord did not take pleasure in them.	The Lord *God* chose them not.[11]
(4b) And he took me from *my father's* sheep (4c) and anointed me with the oil *of his anointing*.	(7) *But he sent* and took me from behind the flock[12] and anointed me with *holy* oil,[13] *And he made me leader to his people* *and ruler over the sons of his covenant.*[14]

---

[8] In the spirit of Isa. 40:12–13 and Sirach 16:26 (not of Ps. 118:17).

[9] Note in the photograph of column XXVIII at line 7 that the conjunction "and," with a scribal correction dot over it, has been erased just before the word "God."

[10] Most ancient versions read simply, "he hears," while others (LXX$^{\aleph}$ OL$^{Y\ Gall}$) read, "he hears everything," a very good translation of the Hebrew as here presented. Prof. Isaac Rabinowitz and others, however, prefer to read the Hebrew quite independently by introducing "the God of the Universe" in translating the Hebrew, which is, of course, possible on the face of it (but see P. W. Skehan in the *Catholic Biblical Quarterly*, XXV (1963), pp. 407–408, for decisive arguments against it). The point of I Sam. 16:7, however, is undoubtedly the climax of the first strophe of Psalm 151—God sees everything, even what is on the heart, or in the soul of man; and he has heeded David's humble desire and efforts to praise him, as expressed in verse 2 above.

[11] Verses 5 and 6 reflect I Sam. 16:4–10, using the very Hebrew words found there.

[12] Ps. 78:70–71; II Sam. 7:8 (Amos 7:15).

[13] Ps. 89:21.

[14] Parallel to verse 1 above.

Psalm 151B

LXX	Q	*Col.* XXVIII *lines*
	תחלת גב[ו]רה ל[דו]יד משמשחו נביא אלוהים	13
151(6) ἐξῆλθον εἰς συνάντησιν τῷ ἀλλοφύλῳ καὶ ἐπικατηράσατό με ἐν τοῖς εἰδώλοις αὐτοῦ	(1) אזי רא֯[י]תי פלשתי מחרף ממ[ערכות האיוב]	13–14
(7) ἐγὼ δὲ σπασάμενος τὴν παρ' αὐτοῦ μάχαιραν ἀπεκεφάλισα αὐτόν, καὶ ἦρα ὄνειδος ἐξ υἱῶν 'Ισραήλ	(2) ...אנוכי.....את....	14

transformation which no man could see but which is the very theological essence of I Samuel 17. (The reader can by this point share the frustrated sense of loss one feels when he finds only a few words of an ancient composition.)

The loss of most of Psalm 151B cannot detract, however, from the full recovery of Psalm 151A. The poetry of it indicates that not a word is missing: we can have every confidence that the scribe has transmitted the whole to the leather of our scroll; we can also be grateful that neither worm nor rodent has consumed a jot or a tittle of his work.

The most interesting omission in the Greek is the rather long section appearing in the Hebrew in verses 2b and 3. Not a word of this survives in the Greek version. The lines seem innocent enough at first blush: David says to himself, within his soul, that he would with his homemade lyre make such music as to render glory to God; and while nature cannot praise God or witness to him, David's flock and the plants among which it grazes greatly appreciate the shepherd's music. In other words, David is fully capable of praising God and, although nature about him cannot do so, nature's response heightens the musical praise which David renders to God. One cannot escape a picture of a shepherd out in the field surrounded by his flock in a pastoral setting: the flock and plants attend to the music as David plays to the glory of God. It is the well-known theme of the good shepherd so often portrayed in early Jewish and Christian art in which David or the Davidic Christ has replaced Orpheus, the original shepherd musician of Greek mythology.

(It should be stressed that the suggestion that Psalm 151 exhibits meager overtones of Orphic vocabulary depends entirely on how one understands verses 2b to 4, especially verse 3, which are subject to three quite different translations. For the reader's convenience in his own searches on the matter, several of the available possibilities are noted below under "Variant Translations of Psalm 151 A." In any event, please note that no suggestion has been made from any quarter that Orphic thinking in any way affected the essential theology of the Essenes at Qumran.)

One understands his religion and his faith by hearing it expressed in familiar and known images: this is the good kind of syncretism involved in apologetics. In folk-imagery, God is sung of in modern times as the pilot of one's soul, one who safely guides the ship of soul to its port, sea-air-spiritual. We know from literary records that Moses was praised by second-century B.C. Jewish apologists of Alexandria in Orphic terms, specifically as being Musaeus, the tutor of Orpheus. And we know from archaeology of a number of nonliterary references to David, in mosaics and paintings, using Orphic images. All this was really quite normal and of widespread usage in hellenistic times. Well-meaning Jews would say to understanding Greeks and Romans, "You see, David is our Orpheus—a shepherd, a musician, and one who praised God in every virtue of soul." They used current vocabulary to speak of their great king of antiquity. Paul and other early Christians delighted in explaining Christ in the language of the first-century Mediterranean world. But referring to the unknown in terms of the known or the

David-Christ, the Good Shepherd depicted as Orpheus. This Jerusalem mosaic of the second century A.D. was found by M.-J. Lagrange in 1901. (From the frontispiece of M.-J. Lagrange, *L'Orphisme* [1937].)

Psalm 151B

Greek	11QPs[a] column XXVIII, lines 13–14 *Hebrew*
	At the beginning of David's power after the prophet of God had anointed him.[15]
(6) I went out to meet the Philistine and he cursed me by his idols.	(1) Then I (saw)[16] a Philistine uttering defiances from the r[anks of the enemy].[17]
(7) But drawing his sword from him I beheaded him and removed shame from the sons of Israel.	(2) . . . I . . . . . the . . . .

strange in terms of the familiar was perhaps nowhere better illustrated than at Lystra in Lycaonia, where according to Acts 14:12, "Barnabas they called Zeus, and Paul, because he was the chief speaker, they called Hermes." At Lystra, Paul had told a crippled man to walk, and the man did, according to the text. For Jews under Greek influence to speak of David in terms of Orpheus would be quite understandable. In fact, the amazing observation, perhaps, is that until the recovery of our Psalm 151A there had been no literary evidence of an Orphic David: one would certainly expect it, since the parallels between David and Orpheus need not be strained for comparison. And yet, the allusion in our psalm is so timid as to be disappointing. Scientifically speaking, we must admit that the evidence of an Orphic allusion in verses 2b and 3 is at best tenuous.

The first thing about verses 2b and 3 which strikes the student of the Bible is that they are quite nonbiblical in tone. The Bible delights in insisting that nature, mountains, hills, trees, and the sea do, poetically speaking, praise God and witness to him (see, e.g., Isaiah 40 and 55). This observation was the first I had made when Father J.-P. Audet of the French School of Bible and Archaeology in Jerusalem, upon seeing the text, not only agreed with the observation but made the intriguing suggestion that on the basis of his years of study of the good-shepherd theme in early Christianity he would advise me to investigate the possibility of Orphic imagery lying back of the six colons of poetry which failed to survive into the Greek version. Discovering numerous mosaics and paintings from Jewish antiquity depicting David in Orphic poses but absolutely no literary reference to David in Orphic vocabulary, I have ventured to suggest that the missing literary link has been tenuously supplied.[18] David's expression, in the psalms, "Let me render glory to the Lord, said I, within my soul," demands to be compared to the expression Josephus puts into the mouth of God when God is speaking to Samuel on his choice of a successor to Saul—the very subject matter of Psalm 151A: "I make not the kingdom a prize for comeliness of body, but for virtue of soul, and I seek one who in full measure is distinguished by this, one adorned with piety, justice, fortitude and obedience, qualities whereof beauty of soul consists" (*Antiquities* VI, 160). Psalm 151A makes a great point of insisting that David, unlike his brothers, is small, unattractive, and humble (verses 5 and 6), but in his soul wants only to glorify God with his homemade lyre. The climax of Psalm 151A is in the staccato affirmation that God chose not the brothers: rather he chose the little shepherd behind Jesse's flock and exalted him as leader of the covenant people.

---

15 Drawn from I Sam. 16:13 and 18.

16 Drawn from I Sam. 17:23–25.

17 Drawn from I Sam. 17:8, 10, 45; cf. 17:26, 36, and the Qumran War Scroll column III, line 7 and *passim*.

18 "Ps 151 in 11Q Pss" in *Zeitschrift für die alttestamentliche Wissenschaft*, LXXV (1963), pp. 73–85; see now *Discoveries in the Judaean Desert of Jordan*, Vol. IV (1965), pp. 54–64. On the influence of hellenism on ancient Jewish orthodoxy see the critical article by Elias Bickerman, "Symbolism in the Dura Synagogue," *Harvard Theological Review*, LVIII (1965), pp. 127–151; and on Orphic influence, see especially pp. 136–141.

When David had been anointed by Samuel and had received the spirit of God upon him he became thereby infused with something like supernatural strength even though he was still but a lad (I Sam. 16:13ff.). He was thus prepared to meet the giant Goliath on the field of battle, for now, according to Psalm 151B, he had *geburah* (a substantive related to *gibbor*, mighty warrior), used of David in I Sam. 16:18 just after the events noted in Psalm 151A. It was because of his anointment by Samuel that David received his immense fortitude, which enabled him to meet and defeat the Philistine. Unfortunately we are at the bottom of the column at this point in Psalm 151B without much hope ever of recovering the remainder of the psalm. We know, of course, what happened when the shepherd David met the giant according to the account in I Samuel 17, but we shall probably never know how our poet went on to express it in his language and thought forms. The Greek in verses 1 to 5 is already so disappointingly different from the Hebrew of Psalm 151A that the Greek of verses 6 and 7 inspires no confidence whatever as a basis for conjecturing what the remainder of Psalm 151B would have been.

We should, nonetheless, be grateful for what has been recovered of these exciting poems. They open doors to new avenues of investigation in a number of directions of interest to technicians, scholars, and experts in the field of intertestamental Jewish literature, especially Greek translations of Jewish works. And for the layman they provide a gem of poetry quite worthy of being called Psalm 151.

Variant Translations of Psalm 151A

Psalm 151 was the first of all the psalms in the scroll to be published. Because of its irresistible fascination I wrote a translation and commentary

for it and sent them off to a European biblical journal while I was in Jerusalem still working on very basic aspects of the study of the scroll as a whole. The article appeared in February 1963,[19] and immediately the psalm commanded the attention it deserves. Several scholars responded with translations of their own, and it soon became apparent that lines 5 to 7 of column XXVIII, our verses 2b to 4, were amenable to more than one understanding. This is due in part to the fact that the ancient scribe who copied the scroll did not always clearly distinguish two of the smallest letters in the Hebrew alphabet, the *waw* and the *yod*; it is due also to the fact that since such ancient Hebrew scrolls have no punctuation provided, some words may be read with one phrase to render one sense or with another to yield quite a different meaning. Finally, the sense one attributes to a text of poetry may depend to some limited extent on how one scans the poetry itself; there are different schools of thought on the question. All three of these observations are operative in the various translations, and understandings, of Psalm 151 so far offered.

Raphael Weiss, of Hebrew University in Israel, agrees with the translation above in all respects except for verse 4, which he prefers to read:

> But who can proclaim and who can tell,
>   and who can recount the works of the Lord of
>   the Universe?
> The God of the Universe has seen—
>   He has heard and he has heeded.[20]

Professor Patrick W. Skehan, of the Catholic University of America, who is working on all the Psalter material from Cave 4, agrees with our understanding of verse 4 but disagrees on two matters relating to verses 2 and 3, and on where the second strophe begins.

---

[19] See note 18, above.

[20] See Weiss' article (in Hebrew) in *Massa* for May 15, 1964, and an interesting sequel in *Massa* for January 29, 1965. Reading the word "all" in lines 7 and 8 as a genitive, following the words there for deity, cannot be supported in the ancient versions which, where they are clear, read "all" (*hakkōl*) as accusative.

Quite pertinent to this point is an Arabic "anti-psalm," called to my attention by Prof. John Strugnell; see O. C. Krarup, *Auswahl pseudo-Davidischer Psalmen arabisch und deutsch herausgegeben* (Kopenhagen, 1909), pp. 25ff.:

"O David, if the mountains did not glorify me
  then would I surely pluck them out.
And if the trees did not glorify me
  then would I surely reduce their fruit.

But there is nothing which does not render me glory....
Act so then, ye people, for I see everything...."
Such a psalm presents God as saying, in direct response to ideas such as are expressed in Psalm 151A, that mountains and all nature had jolly well better witness to and glorify God. Prof. Strugnell has remarked, "Our Arab had access to Psalm 151A and corrected 'David's' unorthodox thoughts." In agreement with Psalm 151A, however, our Arab also notes that God sees everything.

Quite beside the point perhaps, but nonetheless interesting in this regard, are the opening lines of Tablet I of the Gilgamesh Epic:

"All things he saw, even to the ends of the earth....
He peered through all secrets....
What was hidden he saw...."

SKEHAN Psalm 151A

A Hallelujah of David the son of Jesse

(1) I was the least of my brothers
and the youngest of my father's sons;
And he made me shepherd of his flock,
and ruler of his little goats.
(2) My hands fashioned a reed pipe
and my fingers a lyre,
and I gave to the Lord glory.
(3) I had said to myself,
the mountains cannot witness to Him,
nor the hills relate;
Neither the boughs of trees, my words,
nor the flock, my compositions:
Who indeed can relate, and who can tell,
and who can recount the works of the Lord?
Everything, God saw;
everything He heard—and He gave heed.
(4) He sent His prophet to anoint me,
Samuel to exalt me.
(5) My brothers went out to meet him,
handsome of presence, handsome to see—
Though they were tall of stature,
with handsome heads of hair,
not them did the Lord God choose;
((4))But He sent and took me from after the flock
and anointed me with the holy oil,
And He made me leader of His people,
and ruler of the sons of His covenant.[21]

Professor William H. Brownlee, of the Claremont Graduate School in California, agrees with our translation of the psalm but has provided a much fuller and more literary English rendering of it.[22]

Professor Isaac Rabinowitz, of Cornell University, disagrees considerably with our understanding of the psalm and has, through quite different punctuation, different readings of *waw*s and *yod*s, and quite a different scansion of the poetry, been able to render a sense remarkably at variance with those noted above.

RABINOWITZ Psalm 151A

A Hallelujah of David the son of Jesse

(1) I was less important than my brothers,
being younger than my father's sons,
so he made me shepherd of his flock
and ruler over his kids.

(2) My hands made a flute,
and my fingers a lyre,
and I gave the Lord glory.
(3) I said in my soul:
"The mountains will not bear witness for me,
nor the hills;
the trees will not report my words on my
behalf,
nor the flock my deeds;
but O that someone would report,
O that someone would speak about,
and O that someone would recount my
deeds!"
(4) The Master of the universe saw;
the God of the universe—
He Himself heard,
and He Himself gave ear.
(5) He sent His prophet to anoint me,
Samuel to magnify me;
and my brothers went forth to meet him.
(6) The handsome in form
and handsome in appearance,
who were tall in their height
and who were comely because of their hair—
not them did the Lord God choose,
but He sent and took me from following the
flock;
and having anointed me with the holy oil,
He made me prince for His people
and ruler over the sons of His covenant.[23]

Abbé Jean Carmignac, editor in Paris of the international journal, *Revue de Qumrân*, who at first supported our translation (but not our scansion), is now in essential agreement with Rabinowitz, and his translation differs only in certain questions of poetic scansion. (The following is translated from French.)

CARMIGNAC Psalm 151A

First Strophe

1 I was smaller than my brothers
2 and younger than the sons of my father.

3 He made me sphepherd of his flock
4 and ruler over his kids.

5 My hands have fashioned a flute,
6 my fingers a lyre
7 and I have rendered glory to the Lord.

8 I said to myself:
9 "The mountains will not witness for me

[21] "The Apocryphal Psalm 151," *Catholic Biblical Quarterly*, XXV (1963), pp. 407–409.
[22] "The 11Q Counterpart to Psalm 151, 1–5," *Revue de Qumrân*, No. 15 (1963), pp. 379–387.
[23] "The Alleged Orphism of 11QPss Col. 28, 3–12," *Zeitschrift für die alttestamentliche Wissenschaft*, LXXVI (1964), pp. 193–200.

10 and the hills will not proclaim on my behalf,
11 the trees (will not proclaim) my words
12 nor the flock my works.

13 Who indeed will proclaim,
14 who will express,
15 who will recount my works?"

Second Strophe

16 The Lord of the universe has seen,
17 the God of the universe, he has heard
18 and he has heeded.

19 He sent his prophet to consecrate me,
20 Samuel to make me great.

21 My brothers went out to meet him,
22 of handsome appeal
23 and of handsome figure,
24 with their fine height
25 with their comely hair.

26 The Lord God did not choose them,
27 but he sent to take me from behind the flock
28 and he consecrated me with holy oil.

29 He made me leader to his people
30 and ruler over the sons of his covenant.[24]

Professor John Strugnell, who has done the most detailed and completely thorough textual critique to date of Psalm 151A,[25] agrees closely with Skehan's translation, and so to that extent with my own, but renders the crucial verses 3 and 4 thus:

> The mountains cannot witness to Him,
>   nor the hills proclaim about Him;
> Nor the trees (proclaim) His words,
>   nor the flocks His deeds.
> For who can relate, who can tell
>   and who can recount the works of the Lord?
> But God saw all, all He heard,
>   and He gave ear.

It should be stressed again, finally, that the suggestion of the slight reflection of Orphic thinking in the poem depends entirely on how one understands lines 5 to 7 of column XXVIII, that is, our verses 2b to 4, but especially verse 3. Professor Rabinowitz is particularly concerned that it be shown that there is no basis for the Orphic sugges-

tion whatever, and his translation is partly designed to rule it out. Abbé Carmignac's translation follows Rabinowitz' very closely, and although he has not addressed himself to the question of Orphic influence he has eliminated the necessity of doing so in his translation. Monsignor Skehan's translation, which is very close to ours except in two particulars, and Professor Strugnell's, which is similar, nonetheless proved no real basis for a discussion of Orphism. Those of Professors Weiss and Brownlee retain our essential understanding of the psalm even though they have not pronounced themselves on the question of the possible meager Orphic overtones.

Professor Avi Hurvitz has given support to Rabinowitz' and Weiss's reading of line 7, our verse 4, in an article arguing that one should read "Lord of the Universe" and "God of the Universe" (rather than "Everything has God seen") because such a reading can be established in the hellenistic period.[26] All such arguments, however, ignore those ancient Greek and Latin versions of Psalm 151 which clearly understood the words to mean "Everything has God seen" (i.e., everything in David's heart or soul—adhering, as one must, to the subject matter of the poem).

Professor A. Dupont-Sommer, of the University of Paris, is convinced that Psalm 151A exhibits Orphic influence and is of Essene origin, as well. His translation is perhaps the closest to my own of those here noted, but there is still a notable difference in lines 5 and 6 (the lines are numbered below).[27]

DUPONT-SOMMER Psalm 151A

3Alleluia! Of David, son of Jesse.
I was the least of my brothers
  and the youngest of the sons of my father.
And (the latter) made of me 4the shepherd of his flock
  and the leader of his goats.
My hands fashioned an instrument of music
  and my fingers, a lyre;
5and I rendered glory to Yahweh,
  having said to myself:

[24] "La forme poétique du Psaume 151 de la grotte 11," *Revue de Qumrân*, No. 15 (1963), pp. 371–378, and "Précisions sur la forme poétique du Psaume 151," *Revue de Qumrân*, No. 18 (1965), pp. 249–252.
[25] "Notes on the Texts and Transmission of the Apocryphal Psalms 151, 154 and 155," forthcoming in the *Harvard Theological Review*.
[26] See Hurwitz' article (in Hebrew) in *Tarbitz* for 1965, pp. 224–227.
[27] "Le Psaume cli dans 11QPs^a et le problème de son origine essénienne," *Semitica*, XIV (1964), pp. 25–62.

" Do the mountains not witness 6to Him?
  And do not the hills proclaim (Him)? "
The trees esteemed my words
  and the flock, my poems.
7For who will proclaim and who will celebrate
  and who will recount the works of the Lord?
The universe, Eloah sees it;
  8the universe, He hears it, and He heeds.
He sent His prophet to annoint me,
  Samuel 9to make me great.

My brothers went out to meet him,
  they who were of handsome form and handsome
                                              mien,
who were tall of stature,
  10who had handsome hair:
    Yahweh chose them not.
But He sent to take me 11from behind the flock,
  and He anointed me with holy oil,
and He made of me the prince of His people
  and the leader of the sons 12of His covenant.

Psalms 154 and 155

Psalms 154 and 155 have been known heretofore only by those scholars interested in Syriac studies, and they referred to the two psalms as Nos. II and III of the Five Syriac Apocryphal Psalms. Only very recently have we known to label them Psalms 154 and 155: for thus are they numbered in the oldest extant Syriac manuscript of the Psalter which has only in the past few years come to light and which is as yet unpublished. Psalms 152 and 153 in the medieval manuscript were known by scholars as Nos. IV and V of the Syriac apocryphal psalms, but Psalms 152 and 153 do not appear in our scroll, and we have no Hebrew text for them.

Thus we skip over Psalms 152 and 153 (Syriac psalms dealing with David's prowess as a shepherd, guarding his flock and fighting preying beasts—see Appendix I) and take up Psalms 154 and 155. These psalms have nothing to do with David whatever, despite the fact that they are preserved in Syriac in conjunction with three psalms about David as a shepherd. The order in which they are found in the medieval Syriac manuscript from which we get their numbers (151–155) is more logical than the order in which they are preserved in the later Syriac manuscripts (as Nos. I–V, with our two psalms of this section coming second and third). The medieval Syriac manuscript is the oldest Syriac manuscript having these apocryphal psalms, and is the only Syriac manuscript of the biblical Psalter which contains the five apocryphal psalms, and is the only Syriac manuscript which gives them all the numbers 151–155. But even if the order is both logical (the three psalms about David and then the two not about him) and the most ancient preserved of the Syriac group, we still cannot state unequivocally that the order was

the original one in which they were first found when first grouped together: we cannot really be sure that they are by the same author—indeed, they probably were not composed by the same poet.

But despite the uncertainty of our answers to such questions of order, date and authorship, one thing is clear: our newly found Hebrew texts of Psalms 154 and 155 are the *Vorlagen* of the Syriac texts of them; that is, Psalms 154 and 155 in the scroll are the Hebrew psalms from which the Syriac translations were made. This does not mean that the Syriac translator of them had our very scroll in his hands when he translated these psalms into Syriac—whenever it was—but it does mean that he had copies very much like ours when he did so. Here is one of those rare cases in scholarship, then, where we now know, without further ado, what lay back of a translated text. The Syriac translation corresponds to the Hebrew original at about 95 per cent, or better, correspondence.

The Syriac translation of Psalm 154 indicates that the psalm is only slightly longer than what we actually have in the scroll. The Hebrew text of Psalm 154 in the scroll takes up all of column XVIII, but it must be remembered that only about two-thirds of the column survived the decomposition which over the centuries ravaged one end of the rolled-up scroll in the cave. There are about four verses of the psalm lacking, two which would have been at the bottom of column XVII, and two in the last third of column XVIII: hence, the great bulk of the psalm has been preserved, and the four verses that are lacking are rather easily reconstructed on the basis of the Syriac translation and the extant Hebrew text.

Psalm 154

(Verses 1–3*a* and 17*b*–20 reconstructed from the Syriac)

Meter			Verse no.	Syr lines	Col. XVIII lines
3/3	בקהל רבים השמיעו תפארתו	[בקול גדול פארו אלוהים	(1)	1–2	
3/3	ועם אמונים ספרו גדולתו]	ברוב ישרים פארו שמו	(2)	3–4	

(11QPsᵃ column XVIII)

Meter			Verse no.	Syr lines	Col. XVIII lines
3/3	ולתמימים לפאר עליון	[חברו] לטובים נפשתכמה	(3)	5–6	1
3/3/3	ואל תתעצלו להודיע עוזו	החבירו יחד להודיע ישעו ותפארתו לכול פותאים	(4)	7–8	1–2
3/2	נתנה חוכמה	כי להודיע כבוד יהוה	(5)	9	3
3/2	נודעה לאדם	ולספר רוב מעשיו	(6)	10	3–4
3/3	להשכיל לחסרי לבב גדולתו	להודיע לפותאים עוזו	(7)	11–12	4–5
2/2	הנדחים ממבואיה	הרחוקים מפתחיה	(8)	13–14	5–6
3/3	ותפארתו על כול מעשיו	כי עליון הואה אדון יעקוב	(9)	15–16	6–7
3/3	ירצה כמגיש מנחה	ואדם מפאר עליון	(10)	17–18	7–8
	כמקריב עתודים ובני בקר		(11)	19	8
	כמדשן מזבח ברוב עולות				9
3/3/3	כקטורת ניחוח מיד צדיקים				9–10

Psalm 154

(1) [With a loud voice glorify God;
    in the congregation of the many proclaim his majesty.
(2) In the multitude of the upright glorify his name
    and with the faithful recount his greatness.]

(11QPs^a column XVIII)

(3) [Bind][28] your souls with the good ones
    and with the pure ones to glorify the Most High.
(4) Form an assembly to proclaim his salvation
    and be not lax in making known his might
    and his majesty to all simple folk.

(5) For to make known the glory of the Lord
    is Wisdom[29] given,
(6) and for recounting his many deeds
    she is revealed to man:
(7) to make known to simple folk his might
    and to explain to senseless folk his greatness,
(8) those far from her gates,
    those remote from her portals.

(9) For the Most High is the Lord of Jacob
    and his majesty is over all his works.
(10) And a man who glorifies the Most High,
    he accepts as one who brings a meal offering
(11)   as one who offers he-goats and bullocks,
    as one who fattens the altar with many burnt offerings,
    as a sweet-smelling fragrance from the hand of the righteous.[30]

---

[28] Verses 1 and 2, the first word of verse 3, some of verses 18–19, and all of 20 are reconstructed from the Syriac on the basis of the style of the Hebrew scroll text.

[29] The Psalms Scroll offers the first clear evidence of the personification of Wisdom, as a woman, in the nonbiblical literature at Qumran. In the Bible see, e.g., Prov. 8:34; also Sirach 1:15.

[30] Essentially the biblical idea of God's looking favorably upon the righteous who cannot or do not offer many sacrifices, reflected at Qumran in 1QS ("Manual of Discipline") ix 4–5.

Psalm 154—*continued*

Col. XVIII *lines*	*Syr lines*	*Verse no.*			
10–11	22–23	(12)	מפתחי צדיקים נשמע קולה	ומקהל חסידים זמרתה	3/3
11–12	24–25	(13)	על אוכלמה בשבע נאמרה	ועל שתותמה בחבר יחדיו	3/3
12	26–27	(14)	שיחתם בתורת עליון	אמריהמה להודיע עוזו	3/3
13	28–29	(15)	כמה רחקה מרשעים אמרה	מכול זדים לדעתה	3/3
13–14	30	(16)	הנה עיני יהוה	על טובים תחמל	3/3
14–15	31–32	(17)	ועל מפאריו יגדל חסדו	מעת רעה יציל נפש[ם]	3/3
15	33–35	(18)	[ברכו את] יהוה		
15–16			גואל עני מיד ז֯ר֯[ים	ומצי]ל [תמימים מיד רשעים]	3/3/3
16	36–37	(19)	[מקים קרן מיע]ק֯ו֯ב֯	ושופט [עמים מישראל]	3/3
	38–39	(20)	[נוטה אהלו בציון	ויועד לנצח בירושלים]	[3/3]

Psalm 154—*continued*

(12) From the gates of the righteous is heard her voice
    and from the assembly of the pious her song.[31]
(13) When they eat with satiety she is cited,[32]
    also when they drink in community together,
(14) Their meditation is on the Law of the Most High
    their words on making known his might.[33]
(15) How far from the wicked is her word
    from all haughty men to know her.[34]

(16) Behold the eyes of the Lord
    upon the good ones are compassionate,
(17) and upon those who glorify him he increases his mercy;
    from an evil time will he deliver [their] soul.
(18) [Bless] the Lord
    who redeems the humble from the hand [of strangers]
    [and deliv]ers the pure from the hand of the wicked,
(19) [Who establishes a horn out of Ja]cob
    and a judge [of peoples out of Israel;]
(20) [He will spread his tent in Zion
    and abide forever in Jerusalem.][35]

---

[31] Wisdom's voice, song, and word. The Syriac misinterprets these verses to refer to God himself directly.

[32] The Syriac says "true" or "faithful."

[33] This is the point, verses 13–14, at which the psalm seems most sectarian: see 1QS vi 4–7 and 1QSa ii 11–22.

[34] Wisdom's voice, song, and word, as in verse 12, above.

[35] Some of verses 18–19 and all of 20 are reconstructed from the Syriac in the style of the Hebrew scroll text.

Psalm 154 has five strophes of excellent biblical-style Hebrew poetry. There are twenty verses, including those reconstructed from the Syriac, most of which are bicolons. The psalm seems to be of the type used in worship, which might be called a "Call to Worship." The first strophe has seven verbs, all in the imperative mode, which call the faithful to glorify God by assembling to proclaim God's greatness and to instruct the uninitiated. The second strophe affirms that the task of the assemblage is the God-given and Wisdom-endowed duty of informing senseless and simple folk, that is, those who are far from Wisdom, of God's mighty acts. In the third strophe those who thus glorify God are compared to those who offer many sacrifices, and even to sweet-smelling incense offered by the truly righteous. The fourth strophe notes that Wisdom's voice may be heard in the assembly of the righteous and pious, who meditate on Torah, and in the mission of proclaiming God's might, even while they eat and drink together. The fifth strophe contains the assurance that God's special protection is over the good, the pure, the glorifiers, and the poor, who though presently experiencing an evil time will surely know God's compassion, loving faithfulness, and deliverance from the hands of strangers and wicked men. Verse 18 reverts to the call-to-worship theme of the first strophe, a directive to bless the Lord who is redeemer, deliverer, and sustainer.

The psalm is highly sapiential, that is, it belongs to a corpus of Jewish writings called Wisdom literature. Wisdom is here personified as a woman who sings (verse 12). She has gates of her own, but her voice may be heard in the gateways of the righteous (verses 8 and 12). Wicked and insolent men do not know her (verse 15), although she is intimately known by the righteous ones, who are supposedly called into assembly by this psalm. Wisdom's principal function here is to aid man in proclaiming the glory of God (verse 5).

There are three groups mentioned in the psalm: the righteous, the wicked, and the senseless, these last being neither among the initiated or their enemies. Only the first group, the glorifiers, have Wisdom, but Wisdom is theirs for the purpose of the teaching of God's mighty acts to the uninitiated—the simple folk. Of the wicked and insolent we hear very little: they lack Wisdom (verse 15), and they seem to be responsible for the evil

times that apparently have befallen the good group—according to the last strophe.

If the Syriac of verses 19 and 20 can be trusted to reflect the intent of the psalm, then the goal of the whole piece seems to be in the hope there expressed, namely that God will spread his tent on Zion and abide continually in Jerusalem. Zion and Jerusalem are synonymous, as well as the ideas of spreading the tent and abiding: the two colons of verse 20 are in synonymous parallelism. The tent would in all likelihood be a poetic allusion to the temple or, perhaps, a truly pure temple. Verse 20 does not necessarily indicate that the temple in Jerusalem does not exist. If it did imply the nonexistence of the temple, then certain possibilities for dating the composition of the psalm would thereby be suggested. Sane caution is in order in dealing with a verse of Hebrew reconstructed from Syriac: it is quite out of order to jump to brilliant conclusions on such a basis.

Certain scholars will surely insist that Psalm 154 is Essenian because of certain words and ideas contained in it, and those words and ideas cannot be overlooked as possible indices of the epithets and practices of the Qumran sect called Essenes. Such expressions as the "good ones" and the "pure ones" are attested elsewhere in Qumran literature as names used at Qumran of the sect. The fourth strophe will appeal to some students of Qumran literature as reflective of the pious practices of the Qumran sect during meal times—while eating and drinking to meditate on the Law and to speak of the task of proclaiming God's might (verses 13–14). Other scholars will go on to suggest that the wicked men here mentioned were the Hasmonaean priests in Jerusalem, because of whom the Sons of Zadok of Qumran exiled themselves to the Dead Sea shore wastes. They may further say that the third strophe contains compensative and consoling assurances for exiled priests who do not have access to the holy altar in Jerusalem. We know, by the way, that some scholars will say these things because at least two very respectable scholars had already said them on the basis of the Syriac text before the scroll was unrolled.

It cannot be denied that the psalm lends itself to thoughts about the Qumran sect. In fact, anyone who in studying the psalm did not think of the other Qumran literature and passages in it about the practices of the sect probably is not very familiar with it. Soon after I had unrolled the scroll and began to study it I grew very excited about this psalm and wrote a paper on it arguing all of the inferences cited above. I read the paper before a very august gathering of scholars in the library of the American School of Oriental Research in Jerusalem, Jordan, and in the discussion that followed was confronted with the sobriety and maturity of second thoughts on the matter. In the months that followed, as I reworked the paper for publication in a European journal, I came to realize that although Psalm 154 may have been proto-Essenian and may have originated in early circles which later became part of the Qumran group, the psalm itself lacks any characteristic that should be called exclusively Essenian. It is biblical in vocabulary and tone, not Essenian or Qumranian. It cannot have been written by the Qumranian Teacher of Righteousness, as some might suggest, and also be included in a scroll of psalms attributed to the ancient King David.

It is in fact very difficult to date a psalm such as Psalm 154. The scroll contains compositions, such as Psalm 151, which would not have contributed anything to the theology of the Qumran sect. The presence of Psalm 154 in the scroll says nothing about its provenance or origins; and still, its affinities to known ideas and practices of the Qumran Essenes suggest that it may have originated in Hasidic or proto-Essenian circles, perhaps in the second quarter of the second century B.C.

Whether or not Psalm 154 originated in proto-Essenian circles, its position in the scroll, with respect to what precedes and what follows, is very interesting in terms of its probable use in worship at Qumran. Psalm 145 in columns XVI and XVII, Psalm 154 in column XVIII, and the "Plea for Deliverance" in column XIX all in one way or another deal with the theme of praising God for his mighty and victorious acts of deliverance and redemption.

As suggested above in the Introduction, one of the most unusual and fascinating facets of the scroll is the prose notation following Psalm 145. Although it is undoubtedly a subscription to Psalm 145, it should be noted that if it was a rather lengthy prose statement, such as the one in column XXVII, it would also have preceded Psalm 154; that is, it alone would have come between the two

psalms. A short psalm might have intervened, but it would be shear conjecture to determine which (Psalm 117? Psalm 120?), since we have no way of knowing how long the prose notation actually was. Be that as it may, the few words preserved of it fit very well into the theme of the psalms present in columns XVI to XIX, praise of God's mighty acts in Israel's history.

Psalm 155 is about as biblical as a psalm can be: its poetry is like that of the biblical psalms; its vocabulary is biblical; and its content is like that of biblical psalms of thanksgiving in which the psalmist includes his prayer for deliverance which has now been granted. The great resolution is recorded in verse 17: "I cried 'O Lord' and he answered me, and he healed my broken heart."

Psalm 155 is a Psalm of Thanksgiving with a Plea for Deliverance imbedded in it. One cannot but think of psalms such as 22 and 51 when reading this beautiful poem. The first strophe is metered in staccato cries directed at God in desperation and despair. In dire straits a man pleads in clipped and pitiful tones not to be left in the hands of wicked men. He spreads his hands in prayer to the temple ("thy holy dwelling" of verse 2) and begs that his life be renewed and not cast down (verse 5).

The poet readily admits of the justice of God's ways and his own desert of punishment for the sins of his youth (verse 12). Perhaps quoting Ps. 143:2, he says "no man living is righteous" before God. His plea is based on the argument that God would do better to edify his soul, renew his life (verse 5), by teaching him of the ordinances of the Law in this experience (verse 9), than by abandoning him to wicked men and the fate to which they would subject him (verse 6); for thus he in turn would teach the congregation of God's glory (verse 10), as a result of divine deliverance. Psalm 22 (verses 23ff.) concludes with the same argument. Other biblical psalms follow the same pattern.

The psalm includes a number of memorable phrases not the least of which is in verses 13 and 14: "Purify me, O Lord, from the evil scourge and let it not turn again upon me. Dry up its roots from me and let its leaves not flourish within me." The phrase in verse 11, "Lead me not into situations too hard for me" reminds one of the similar phrase in the Lord's Prayer, "Lead me not into

Psalm 155

Meter			Verse no.	Syr lines	Col. XXIV lines
2/2	הקשיבה אלי	יהוה קראתי אליכה	(1)	1	3
2/2	למעון קודשכה	פרשתי כפי	(2)	2	3–4
2/2	ותן לי את שאלתי	הט אוזנכה	(3)	3–4	4
2/2	אל תמנע ממני	ובקשתי	(4)	5	4–5
2/2	ואל תמגרה	בנה נפשי	(5)	6	5
2/2	לפני רשעים	ואל תפרע	(6)	7	5–6
2/2/2	דין האמת	גמולי הרע ישיב ממני	(7)	8	6
3/3	כי לוא יצדק לפניכה כול חי	יהוה אל תשפטני כחטאתי	(8)	9–10	6–7
3/3	ואת משפטיכה למדני	הבינני יהוה בתורתכה	(9)	11–12	8
3/3	ועמים יהדרו את כבודכה	וישמעו רבים מעשיכה	(10)	13–14	9
3/3	ואל תביאני בקשות ממני	זכורני ואל תשכחני	(11)	15–16	10
3/3	ופשעי אל יזכרו לי	חטאת נעורי הרחק ממני	(12)	17–18	11
3/3	ואל יוסף לשוב אלי	טהרני יהוה מנגע רע	(13)	19–20	12
3/3	ואל ינצו ע[ל]יו בי	יבש שורשיו ממני	(14)	21–22	12–13
3/3	על כן שאלתי מלפניכה שלמה	כבוד אתה יהוה	(15)	23–24	13–14
3/3	ובני אדם מה יוסיף אומ[צם]	למי אזעקה ויתן לי	(16)	25–26	14–15
	קראתי יהוה ויענני	מ̊לפ̊[נ]יכה יהוה מבטחי	(17)	27–28	15–16
3/3/3		[וירפא את] שבר לבי		29	16
	חלמתי גם [הקיצותי]	נמתי [ואי]שנה	(18)	30	16–17
	ואקרא יהו[ה] [מפלטי]	[סמכתני יהוה	(19)	31–33	17
	חסיתי בכה ולוא אבוש]	[עתה אראה בושתם	(20)	34–35	
	ובית יעקוב בחיריכה]	[פדה את ישראל חסידיכה יהוה	(21)	37–38	

---

[36] The first strophe, verses 1–7, is a staccato plea to God: "O Lord," here, serves the whole strophe and falls outside the meter—anacrusis. See verse 17, "I cried 'O Lord' and he answered me," which is a reference to the "O Lord" here.

[37] See Ps.143:2.

[38] The Hebrew text introduces an alphabetic acrostic arrangement at this point commencing with the fifth letter of the Hebrew alphabet.

[39] See Matt. 6:13 and J. Carmignac's article in *Revue biblique*, LXXII (1965), pp. 218–226.

Psalm 155

11QPs[a] column XXIV, lines 3–17

(1) O Lord,[36] I called unto thee,   give heed to me.

(2) I spread forth my palms   toward thy holy dwelling.

(3) Incline thine ear   and grant me my plea,

(4) And my request   withhold not from me.

(5) Edify my soul   and do not cast it down

(6) And abandon (it) not   in the presence of the wicked.

(7) May the Judge of Truth   remove from me   the rewards of evil.

(8) O Lord, judge me not according to my sins;
    for no man living is righteous before thee.[37]

(9) Grant me understanding,[38] O Lord, in thy law,
    and teach me thine ordinances,

(10) that many may hear of thy deeds
    and peoples may honor thy glory.

(11) Remember me and forget me not
    and lead me not into situations too hard for me.[39]

(12) The sins of my youth cast far from me
    and may my transgressions not be remembered against me.

(13) Purify me, O Lord, from the evil scourge
    and let it not turn again upon me.

(14) Dry up its roots from me
    and let its leaves not flourish within me.[40]

(15) Thou art glory,[41] O Lord.
    Therefore is my request fulfilled before thee.

(16) To whom may I cry and he would grant (it) me?
    And the sons of man—what more can [their] pow[er] do?—

(17) My trust, O Lord, is befo[r]e thee.
    I cried "O Lord" and he answered me,
    [and he healed] my broken heart.

(18) I slumbered [and sl]ept,
    I dreamt; indeed [I awoke.][42]

(19) [Thou didst support me, O Lord,
    and I invoked] the Lord, [my deliverer.][43]

(From the Syriac)   *Syr lines*

(20) Now shall I behold their shame;   34
    I have trusted in thee and shall not be abashed.   35

(Render glory for ever and ever.)   36

(21) Deliver Israel, O Lord, thy faithful ones,   37
    and the house of Jacob, thy chosen ones.   38

---

[40] A figure, borrowed perhaps from Ezek. 17:7–9, referring to what sin can do inside a man. Cf. Ps. 32:5, and lines 15 and 16 of "Plea for Deliverance" in column XIX.

[41] See Ps. 3:4. The Syriac reads "Great art thou" (cf. Job 36:5). See also 1QH ("Thangksgiving Hymns") iv 40, "For thou art truth . . . ."

[42] A shout or cry of defiance of enemies—see Pss. 3:2 and 118:6.

[43] Verses 17 to 19 are readily reconstructed on the basis of the Hebrew and Syriac (especially Mosul 1113) texts. The remainder of the Hebrew psalm is lacking because of the condition of the scroll.

temptation." But certainly the most moving lines come at the beginning of the psalmist's testimony that God had delivered him (verse 17): "I cried 'O Lord' and he answered me, and he healed my broken heart."

Verses 9 through 16 present an alphabetic acrostic arrangement which probably continued through to the end of the psalm. Professor Patrick W. Skehan, of the Catholic University of America in Washington, agrees that the lost lines at the bottom of column XXIV contained the last three verses, 19 to 21 (*samekh*, '*ayin*, *pe*), as reconstructed above: indeed much of the reconstruction I owe to him. But Monsignor Skehan also thinks that our verses 1 to 8 are only four verses and that the whole poem is an alphabetic acrostic beginning not with the Hebrew letter *he*, as I perceive it, but with the first letter '*alef*.[44]

Whereas Psalm 154 has a number of affinities with the sect at Qumran of antiquity, Psalm 155 has none whatever. Psalm 154 can be thought of as proto-Essenian but certainly not Psalm 155. The psalm is so "biblical" (or archaized) in tone, content, and spirit that one must assume it simply was not very widely known in general Jewish worship in the first century, that it was excluded from the Psalter, as it manifestly was, in the rabbinical decisions at Jamnia, around A.D. 90-100. One almost wishes he could reverse the decision of the council and add these psalms to our present Psalter. At any rate, Psalm 155 is about as biblical as a nonbiblical psalm can get, and there is no certainty as to the date of its composition.[45]

Sirach 51:13ff.

The fourth of the previously known poems in the scroll is identifiable as the second canticle after the epilogue of Ecclesiasticus, or the Wisdom of Ben Sira, or Sirach. Sirach is found in the Old Testament of Catholic Bibles and among the Apocrypha of Protestant Bibles; it enjoys neither canonical nor deutero-canonical status in Jewish Bibles, but among Jews and Christians it has been an oft-read and favored book through the centuries. Recent English editions of Sirach are those available in the *Confraternity of Christian Doctrine Bible* of 1955 and in the Revised Standard Version *Apocrypha* of 1957, and in them beginning at chapter 51, verse 13, are studious translations of our canticle, based on the then available Greek, Latin, Syriac, and medieval Hebrew texts. Now, if one compares the canticle as located there with the canticle as it appears in our scroll, he will discover rather radical differences. The differences are so great, in fact, that in my early preliminary report on the unrolling of the Psalms Scroll I did not mention the presence in it of the canticle.

It was not until Monsignor Patrick W. Skehan saw the text of the poem in the scroll that it was definitely identified: Professor Skehan, with Father Louis Hartman, had translated Sirach for the *Confraternity Bible*. But even he was quite amazed over the differences the new text offers.

The first observation one makes about the canticle in the scroll is the rather obvious one of its presence there. The Psalms Scroll is clearly Davidic in the sense that the scribe who penned it in the first century A.D. believed that all the poetic compositions in it were authored by the ancient King David: columns XXVII and XXVIII fall short only of making an outright statement to that effect. And yet the canticle heretofore was known only in conjunction with the much later Jerusalem sage, Jesus the Son of Sira, of the second century B.C. It occurs in his work, which we call Sirach, after the epilogue, and some scholars have voiced suspicions as to its authorship, but the same scholars sometimes interpreted certain words or ideas in it according to our knowledge of Sirach.[46] This is

---

[44] See Skehan, "A Broken Acrostic and Psalm 9" in the *Catholic Biblical Quarterly*, XXVII (1965), pp. 1–5.

[45] Avi Hurvitz and others have attempted, by linguistic analysis, to date Psalm 155 no earlier than the Persian period (Hurvitz, "Observations on the Language of the Third Apocryphal Psalm from Qumran," *Revue de Qumrân*, No. 18 (1965), pp. 225–232). His work appeared too late to receive consideration here.

[46] Copies in Hebrew of Sirach, or Ecclesiasticus, have been found in Cave 4 at Qumran and in one of the chambers of the fortress wall at Masada. The Qumran fragment contains only eleven or so verses of Sirach chapter 6, and not much is yet known about it, but Professor Yigael Yadin, who in 1963 conducted the excavations at Masada, has reported that the five chapters preserved of the Masada scroll of Sirach date to the first century B.C., i.e., only a

but to observe, I suppose, that those in antiquity who appended it to Sirach had fairly good reason to do so: the setting of the canticle fits very well that of a "sung" confession by a Wisdom teacher who exhorts his disciples "to go and do likewise." One's feeling might well be that if Ben Sira did not pen it as a closing lecture for a graduating class then at least he should have used it, or one like it. It fits Ben Sira's context better perhaps than David's; consorting with Wisdom and taking her as a mistress are themes of the later period. And yet the biblical witness gives us some useful clues on David's attested relation to Wisdom. The prose inset in column xxvii asserts that King David was wise, bright as sunlight, literate, and discerning (xxvii 2–3). These Davidic attributes derive from the Bible itself. The wise woman of Tekoa said that David had "wisdom like the wisdom of the angel of God to know all things that are on the earth" (II Sam. 14:20). One of Saul's young men testified that David was prudent or discerning of speech (I Sam. 16:18), and David himself is reported to have sung of how the spirit of God spoke through him (II Sam. 23:2). It is not at all gauche, therefore, to have David in mind while reading the psalm. Its presence in a Davidic psalter is as acceptable as its presence in Sirach, if one is willing to think of David in the manner of Wisdom thinkers.

The poem is an alphabetic acrostic (each verse begins with sequential letters of the Hebrew alphabet), and its stichotic arrangement is, therefore, easily established. It was known heretofore in ancient Greek, Latin, and Syriac as well as in a medieval Hebrew version. The medieval Hebrew text was perhaps a translation from the Syriac, just as the Latin was based on the Greek. Although none of the versions or recensions accurately reflects our scroll text of the canticle, the Greek is manifestly the oldest among them and the one which affords the most fruitful comparisons.

Just as we did the Greek and the Hebrew of Psalm 151, so we put the Greek and the Hebrew of Sirach 51:13ff., side by side, underlining the distinctive elements of each text, that is, the words or phrases that have no corresponding words or phrases in the parallel column. Whereas in the case of Psalm 151 we noted that the Hebrew contained every salient idea and most every word of the Greek text, here we must note that the two texts are quite different at some crucial points. The Greek, it may be quickly observed, has no line corresponding either to Hebrew verse 8b or verse 9b; and at that point it becomes quite difficult to match up the colons of the two texts: verse 10b of the Hebrew ambiguously relates to the sense of the Greek placed opposite it, while verses 9a and 10a are unmistakably parallel. The first really telling distinction of the sort occurs already in verses 1 and 2. Verse 13a of the Greek is an excellent translation of Hebrew verse 1a, but Greek verse 13b adds a note of piety totally lacking in Hebrew verse 1b. And then Greek verse 14a, it must be admitted, simply fails to translate Hebrew verse 2a; the Greek is highly pious while the Hebrew begins to border on the erotic. The other versions, it may be pointed out, follow the Greek lead in this regard, presenting essentially pious ideas in lieu of those phrases in the Hebrew which suggest erotic figures and nuances. Even the medieval Hebrew text reflects the difference noted between the Qumran text and the Greek, right up, that is, until what we may now call verse 13 (Hebrew letter *mem*) of the medieval Hebrew text, which is itself erotic enough: "My bowels are astir like a firepot for her, to gaze upon her, that I may own her, a pleasant possession." But that sentence is in the medieval text of the canticle aready known by scholars for sixty-five years. Here now are the Greek and Hebrew parallels followed by their respective translations.

---

matter of some decades after its supposed composition date, around 200 B.C. Yadin further reports that the Masada text is practically identical with the medieval copy of Sirach found in the old Karaite synagogue of Cairo in the late nineteenth century. This is far from the case with our Qumran text of the canticle in Sirach 51, which is remarkably different from the Cairo text. It should be observed, however, that the Cairo text and the ancient Greek text of the canticle are in very close agreement, though not

"practically identical," exhibiting the same compatibility in the canticle as in the rest of Sirach. Yadin is of the opinion that the Masada text shows that the medieval Cairo text represents the original, since his text and the medieval text are in such close agreement. Such a judgment is probably correct for chapters 1 to 50 of Sirach, but definitely not for our canticle. See Yadin's report in the *Illustrated London News* for October 31, 1964, pp. 696–697, and text in *The Ben Sira Scroll from Masada* (1965).

Sirach 51:13ff.

	LXX (*apud* Swete)	Q	*Verse no.*	*Col.* XXI *lines*
(13)	Ἔτι ὢν νεώτερος πρὶν ἢ πλανηθῆναί με	אני נער בטרם תעיתי	(1)	11
	ἐζήτησα σοφίαν προφανῶς ἐν προσευχῇ μου	ובקשתיה		
(14)	ἔναντι ναοῦ ἠξίουν περὶ αὐτῆς	באה לי בתרה	(2)	11–12
	καὶ ἕως ἐσχάτων ἐκζητήσω αὐτήν.	ועד סופה אדורשנה		
(15a)	ἐξ ἄνθους ὡς περκαζούσης σταφυλῆς	גם גרע נץ בבשול ענבים	(3)	12
	εὐφράνθη ἡ καρδία μου ἐν αὐτῇ	ישמחו לב		
(15b)	ἐπέβη ὁ πούς μου ἐν εὐθύτητι	דרכה רגלי במישור	(4)	13
	ἐκ νεότητός μου ἴχνευον αὐτήν.	כי מנעורי ידעתיה		
(16)	ἔκλινα ὀλίγον τὸ οὖς μου καὶ ἐδεξάμην	הטיתי כמעט אוזני	(5)	13–14
	καὶ πολλὴν εὗρον ἐμαυτῷ παιδείαν.	והרבה מצאתי לקח		
(17)	προκοπὴ ἐγένετό μοι ἐν αὐτῇ·	ועלה היתה לי	(6)	14–15
	τῷ διδόντι μοι σοφίαν δώσω δόξαν.	למלמדי אתן הודי		
(18)	διενοήθην γὰρ τοῦ ποιῆσαι αὐτὴν	זמותי ואשחקה	(7)	15
	καὶ ἐζήλωσα τὸ ἀγαθόν	קנאתי בטוב		
	οὐ μὴ αἰσχυνθῶ.	ולוא אשוב		
(19aα)	διαμεμάχισται ἡ ψυχή μου ἐν αὐτῇ	חריתי נפשי בה	(8)	15–16
(?)		ופני לוא השיבותי		
(20aα)	τὴν ψυχήν μου κατεύθυνα εἰς αὐτὴν	טרתי נפשי בה	(9)	16–17
		וברומיה לוא אשלה		
(19bα)	τὰς χεῖράς μου ἐξεπέτασα πρὸς ὕψος	ידי פ̊ת̊ח[תי . . .]	(10)	17
(19bβ(?))	καὶ τὰ ἀγνοήματα αὐτῆς ἐπενόησα	[ו]מערמיה אתבונן		
		כפי הברותי אל . . .	(11)	17

			Verse no.	*Col.* XXII *line*
(30b)	(καὶ δώσει) τὸν μισθὸν ὑμῶν ἐν καιρῷ αὐτοῦ.	. . . .] שכרכם בעתו	(23b)	1

---

[47] For a discussion of the textual problems see *Discoveries in the Judaean Desert of Jordan*, Vol. IV, pp. 81ff. Both the Greek and the Hebrew verbs can mean both "travel" and "err."

[48] A possible alternative translation is "in her searches."

[49] The Hebrew verb means also "to exegete," related to the word *midrash*, and something of that meaning undoubtedly is intended. "Finally" also means "her end."

[50] Similar to the figure in Gen. 40:10, here meaning the maturity of young manhood.

[51] See Ps. 104:15.

[52] "Foot" in Hebrew, on occasion, is used euphemistically to indicate the phallus. See, e.g., Judg. 3:24; II Kings 18:27; Isa. 7:20; Ezek. 16:25.

[53] Or, "in smoothness."

[54] The verb "to know" in Hebrew can imply sexual intercourse; here the erotic metaphor continues.

[55] The Hebrew word here can mean seductive speech as in Prov. 7:21 and 16:21.

[56] Literally "one who gives suck," supposedly a mother- or nurse-figure. Wisdom is called both mother and bride in Sirach 15:2, and either bride or mistress in Prov. 8:30, 9:1–6; Sirach 24:21; and Wisdom of Solomon 71:2 and 8:2. See also Prov. 5:18–19. Incidentally, Zion is viewed as

Sirach 51:13ff.

LXX

(13) When I was young before I had wandered
I sought Wisdom *openly in my prayer.*
(14) *I prayed for her before the temple*
and finally will I seek her out.
(15a) Even from the flower until the ripening of a grape
my heart has delighted *in her.*
(15b) My foot trod in uprightness;
from my youth *have I sought* after her.

(16) I inclined my ear but a little *and received* (her),
and great was the *learning* I found.
(17) There was *profit* for me *in her*;
to him who gives me Wisdom give I *glory.*
(18) I purposed *to act after her*:
and I was zealous for good,
and shall not *be ashamed.*
(19aα) My soul *has wrestled* with her

(20aα) I directed my soul toward her
(19aβ) *and in my deeds I was exact.*
(19bα) I stretched my hands *on high*
(19bβ) and perceived her *secrets.*

(30b) . . . your reward in his season.

11QPs^a column XXI, lines 11–17

Q

(1) I was a young man before I had erred[47]
when I looked for her.
(2) *She came to me in her beauty*[48]
when finally I sought her out.[49]
(3) Even (as) a blossom drops in the ripening of grapes,[50]
making glad the heart,[51]
(4) (So) my foot[52] trod in uprightness;[53]
for from my young manhood *have I known her.*[54]
(5) I inclined my ear but a little

and great was the *persuasion*[55] I found.
(6) And she became for me *a nurse*;[56]
to my teacher[57] I give my *ardor.*[58]
(7) I purposed *to make sport*:[59]
I was zealous for pleasure,[60]
without *pause.*[61]
(8) *I kindled* my desire[62] for her[63]
without distraction.
(9) I bestirred my desire[64] for her,[65]
and on her heights I do not waver.[66]
(10) I spread my hand(s)[67] . . .
and perceive her *unseen parts.*[68]
(11) *I cleansed my hand(s)*[69] . . .

11QPs^a column XXII, line 1

(23b) . . . your reward in his season.

---

a mother who gives suck in Isa. 66:1–11 and in the Apostrophe to Zion, column XXII.

57 Wisdom, just called nurse, is now called teacher.

58 The Hebrew word can mean "manhood" and "virility," or "glory" and "majesty." See Prov. 5:9.

59 Wisdom besported herself before God at creation: so Prov. 8:30.

60 A word which in Hebrew can also mean "good."

61 The last colons of verses 7, 8 and 9 serve to indicate the passion of concentration and dedication.

62 Literally "soul" or "self."

63 Possibly "in her" or, remotely, "with her."

64 "Soul" or "self," as in verse 8.

65 Possibly "in her" or "with her," as above.

66 The figure is borrowed from Prov. 9:3–14.

67 The word "hand," as well as the word "foot," can connote the phallus: see Isa. 57:8.

68 Or "her nakedness." The Greek translator would have understood "the unknown things about her." See Sirach 42:18 in Yadin, *The Ben Sira Scroll*, p. 27. (The Hebrew word for "perceive" can also mean "pierce".)

69 Again, the word "hand" can suggest the phallus, as above.

The poem in the scroll, in the right-hand column marked Q, has many ambiguities throughout. The double entendres suggest a deliberate literary quality intended by the poet. Manifestly the Greek recension understands only one sense throughout. Whether the Greek translator chose to ignore the underlying nuances or whether the Greek is based on an intermediate Hebrew which had somehow excised the erotic overtones is difficult to determine. It is the same question we faced when dealing with Psalm 151 and the great differences there between the Hebrew and the Greek. In both these cases one may say that the Greek recension is ostensibly more biblically orthodox or pious than the Hebrew, but that would be a rather superficial observation, for while there may be a rather weak image of Orpheus superimposed on the figure of David in Psalm 151A, the poem itself, as well as Psalm 151B which follows it, is based firmly on I Samuel 16 and 17 in the Old Testament: only the imagery can be said to bé in any sense nonbiblical. And our present canticle is as completely biblical, even in imagery, as any psalm in the scroll: every figure and image in it has a similar one in Genesis or Proverbs or the Song of Songs in the Old Testament, or Sirach itself, which is about as "orthodox" in theology and piety as any book in the Bible. Erotic figures and images are not really rare in the Bible, particularly in so-called biblical Wisdom literature; our canticle is a part of apocryphal Wisdom literature.

What needs to be pointed out here is a fact of Hebrew vocabulary of which the layman may be unaware: both the word "hand" and the word "foot" may in Hebrew suggest the phallus. The word basically meaning "hand" is translated "nakedness," with a footnote indicating the uncertainty of it, in the Revised Standard Version at Isa. 57:8. The word basically meaning "foot" is used euphemistically in Judg. 3:24, I Sam. 24:3, II Kings 18:27, Isa. 7:20, Isa. 36:12, and perhaps as well in Isa 6:2 and Ruth 3:14. The double meaning in verse 4 of the Hebrew canticle becomes rather prominent when it is also realized that the Hebrew word meaning "uprightness" can also mean "smoothness" and that the Hebrew word translated there as "have I known" can connote sexual intercourse. If the word "hand(s)" is euphemistic in verses 10 and 11, then the singular should be understood instead of the plural.

The word translated "persuasion" in verse 5 can mean "learning," as with the Greek opposite; it can also mean "doctrine" and can connote the idea of discipline. But in Wisdom literature it is found in erotic contexts meaning "persuasion" (Prov. 7:21, 16:21) or even "seductive speech." The word meaning "ardor" in verse 6 (Prov. 5:9) can mean also "manhood," "strength," or, with the Greek, "glory" or "majesty." The word translated "desire" in verses 8 and 9 basically means "self," and in the Bible is most often translated by "soul," which is the only one of the meanings surviving in the Greek. The word meaning "pleasure" in verse 7 most often in the Bible means simply "good," as the Greek has it. The words "spread" and "perceive" in verse 10 could possibly mean "distend" and "pierce." Another possible translation of "unseen parts" would be "unknown parts," which leads into the Greek meaning "ignorance of Wisdom."

The quality of literary ambiguity is present other than in words with possible sexual connotations. The first and most striking is that in the Hebrew word of verse 1 meaning "to err"; it can indeed mean "wander" or "travel," as the Greek has it: the Greek of verse 13a is an excellent translation of Hebrew verse 1a, for the Greek word itself shares some of the ambivalence of the Hebrew. Hebrew verse 2b and Greek verse 14b are also very close in meaning; only the tense of the Hebrew verb may be different. Seeking Wisdom out in the Hebrew carries with it the connotation of doing an exegesis of Wisdom, or of a midrash or homiletical exposition on Wisdom—as well as the idea of searching for her. The Greek idea of finding profit in Wisdom, of Greek verse 17, entails only a very slight misreading of the Hebrew, just as in the case of Greek verse 18c, which is only a minor misunderstanding of the Hebrew, based on a metathesis of consonants of the verb in Hebrew verse 7c. Hebrew verses 7c and 8b say the same thing; they speak of a young man's passionate attention to the object of his devotion, and the repetition of the idea renders literary quality.

Our poem is of a literary type well known in Jewish Wisdom literature, in which Wisdom is personified as a woman. In Wisdom of Solomon 8:2 we read:

> I loved her and sought her from my youth,
> and I desired to take her for my bride,
> and I became enamored of her beauty.

And in Sirach 15:2 we find the mother or nurse idea of verse 6 of our canticle:

She will come to meet him like a mother,
  and like the wife of his youth she will welcome him.

Our verse 6 says that Wisdom has been the young man's nurse and teacher, and she now becomes his mistress.

In the Bible, Proverbs chapter 9 provides the pattern for thinking of Wisdom as a mistress or a harlot whom man should take. She is contrasted in 9:1–6 with a human harlot whose water is stolen and whose bread must be eaten in secret (9:13–18). The word "heights" in our verse 9 is found also in Prov. 8:2 as well as Prov. 9:3: Wisdom and her maids appeal to passersby from the high places of the town just as do actual harlots (Prov. 9:14; cf. Sirach 24:19–22).

Our song tells of a young man, who before he had erred, had sought Wisdom, and who, while maturing from childhood into young manhood, as the blossom drops in the ripening of grapes, dedicated himself to Wisdom. She who in his minority had been his mother, or nurse, and teacher, in his majority becomes his mistress. As soon as passions develop, they are sublimated in the pursuit of Wisdom.

One can readily understand how the pious at Qumran would appreciate such a poem. By all indications celibacy was the usual practice there, and a poem such as this or the one in Proverbs 9 would have strong spiritual significance for them. Actually, if the versions are to be trusted for the second half of the psalm, from what would have been the fourteenth verse on to the end, the context is that of a Wisdom teacher setting his own experience of maturing youth as an example for his disciples to follow.

It is, of course, quite difficult to determine what the rest of the poem would have been in the missing lines of column XXI of the scroll. Verse 12 undoubtedly started with the word heart as the versions indicate and verse 13 almost certainly was very close to what we have in the Syriac and the medieval Hebrew at that point:

My bowels are astir like a firepot for her,
                              to gaze upon her,
  that I may own her, a pleasant possession.

Originally verses 14 through 23 were probably very much like Sirach 51:22–30, the first letters of each line continuing through the Hebrew alphabet and then a final and extra verse beyond the alphabetic acrostic reading (in the medieval Hebrew):

Do your work in righteousness
  and he will give you your reward in his season.

And that was the end of the original poem as well, for at the top of col. XXII the same final words appear: *your reward in his season.*

The strong indication, therefore, is that the last part of the song was an exhortation by the supposed Wisdom teacher to his students that they follow his example and in their puberty dedicate themselves also to the pursuit and acquisition of Wisdom, so that as they mature they, like their teacher, may direct their human passions toward righteousness. Professor Taylor in 1899 translated the medieval Hebrew of the last verses of the canticle thus:

Turn unto me, O foolish ones;
  and lodge in my house of learning.
How long shall ye lack these things,
  and your soul be very thirsty?
I opened my mouth and spake to her,
  Get ye wisdom in possession without money.
And bring your necks into her yoke;
  and let your soul take up her burden.
She is nigh to them that seek her;
  and he that giveth his soul findeth her.
See with your eyes that I was a little one;
  and I laboured in her and found her.
Hear, ye many, my teaching in my youth;
  and ye shall get silver and gold by me.
My soul shall rejoice in my age;
  and ye shall not be ashamed of my song.
Work your works in righteousness;
  and he shall give you *your reward in his season.*

The italicized words in the last line above appear in the Psalms Scroll at the top of column XXII, guaranteeing to us the presence in the scroll of the full canticle. Calculations easily indicate that the missing lines at the bottom of Column XXI would have contained the amount of Hebrew necessary to reach the end of the last line of the song. Therefore, while some twelve and a half verses of the poem are lacking in the scroll, reconstruction of the whole piece on the basis of what is there, plus what we have in the versions and in the medieval copy, is now virtually assured.

PSALMS HERETOFORE UNKNOWN

Plea for Deliverance

COLUMN XIX of the Psalms Scroll contains twenty or so verses of a prayer for deliverance from sin and Satan, with a praise of thanksgiving for past experiences of salvation embedded within the prayer. The original full psalm probably had some twenty-four or twenty-five verses, judging from the arrangement of the materials preceding and following it in columns XVIII and XX.

The psalm is quite biblical in vocabulary, style, form, and ideas. The oft-met biblical argument, that God spare a man his life because in death no man can praise him, is here poignantly stated, making use of phrases familiar from Isa. 38:18–19, Ps. 6:4–5, and so on. Some words and ideas known from earliest rabbinic, Tannaitic, literature find expression in lines 15 and following. Nonetheless, it would be extremely precarious to attempt to date the psalm on the basis of such words.

Another copy of this psalm has been located by Father J. van der Ploeg among the fragments of 11QPs[d] (see Appendix II, p. 145). It indicates that there was at least one line preceding our first line and perhaps a few words following what we have at the bottom of column XIX. A judicious guess might be that our line 18 is very close to the end of the psalm but that four or five verses at the beginning are lost to us from the bottom four or five lines of column XVIII.

Plea for Deliverance

Col. XIX *lines*

כי לוא רמה תודה לכה 1
ולוא תספר חסדכה תולעה
חי חי יודה לכה 2
יודו לכה כול מוטטי רגל
בהודיעכה חסדכה להמה 2–3
וצדקתכה תשכילם
כי בידכה נפש כול חי 3–4
נשמת כול בשר אתה נתתה
עשה עמנו יהוה כטובכה 4–5
כרוב רחמיכה
וכרוב צדקותיכה
שמע יהוה בקול אוהבי שמו 5–6
ולוא עזב חסדו מהמה
ברוך יהוה עושה צדקות 7–8
מעטר חסידיו חסד ורחמים
שאגה נפשי להלל את שמכה 8–9
להודות ברנה חסדיכה
להגיד אמונתכה 9
לתהלתכה אין חקר
למות הייתי בחטאי 9–10
ועוונותי לשאול מכרוני
ותצילני יהוה 10–11
כרוב רחמיכה
וכרוב צדקותיכה
גם אני את שמכה אהבתי 11–12
ובצלכה חסיתי
בזוכרי עוזכה יתקף לבי 12–13
ועל חסדיכה אני נסמכתי
סלחה יהוה לחטאתי 13–14
וטהרני מעווני
רוח אמונה ודעת חונני 14–15
אל אתקלה בעווה
אל תשלט בי שטן 15
ורוח טמאה
מכאוב ויצר רע 15–16
אל ירשו בעצמי
כי אתה יהוה שבחי 16–17
ולכה קויתי כול היום
ישמ̊חו אחי עמי 17
ובית אבי השוממים בחונכה
[ ]
[ ]לם אשמחה בכה 18

---

[1] The dead cannot praise God: so Isa. 38:18–19; Ps. 6:4–5, and often elsewhere in the Bible.
[2] Very close to the phrasing in Isa. 38:19.
[3] Very similar to Job 12:10.

Col. XIX lines	Plea for Deliverance 11QPs[a] column XIX
1	Surely a maggot cannot praise thee nor a grave-worm recount thy lovingkindness.[1]
2	But the living can praise thee[2] (even) those who stumble can laud thee.
2–3	In revealing thy kindness to them and by thy righteousness thou dost enlighten them.
3–4	For in thy hand is the soul of every living thing; the breath of all flesh hast thou given.[3]
4–5	Deal with us, O Lord, according to thy goodness, according to thy great mercy, and according to thy many righteous deeds.
5–6	The Lord has heeded the voice of those who love his name and has not deprived them of his lovingkindness.
7–8	Blessed be the Lord who executes righteous deeds, crowning his saints with lovingkindness and mercy.[4]
8–9	My soul cries out to praise thy name, to sing high praises for thy loving deeds,
9	To proclaim thy faithfulness— of praise of thee there is no end.
9–10	Near death was I for my sins, and my iniquities had sold me to the grave;
10–11	But thou didst save me, O Lord, according to thy great mercy, and according to thy many righteous deeds.
11–12	Indeed have I loved thy name and in thy protection have I found refuge.
12–13	When I remember thy might my heart is brave, and upon thy mercies do I lean.
13–14	Forgive my sin, O Lord, and purify me from my iniquity.[5]
14–15	Vouchsafe me a spirit of faith and knowledge and let me not be dishonored in ruin.
15	Let Satan not rule over me, nor an unclean spirit;
15–16	neither let pain nor the evil inclination take possession of my bones.
16–17	For thou, O Lord, art my praise, and in thee do I hope all the day.
17	Let my brothers rejoice with me and the house of my father, who are astonished by thy gracious[6]... [. . . . .]
18	[For e]ver I will rejoice in thee.

[4] Very similar to Ps. 103:4.
[5] See Ps. 51:4 and Jer. 33:8.
[6] Or, "appalled by thy grace"—a rare if not unique phrase unanticipated in the text.

Apostrophe to Zion

Zion is in the prayers of all who love her, and in those prayers God is put in remembrance of the promises spoken of prophets for her future. This apostrophe to Zion is not a prayer addressed to God; that is, it is not a Promethean prayer in itself, but it refers to such prayers in an attempt to console Jerusalem because of her enemies. "Accept a vision bespoken of thee, a dream of prophets sought for thee" (verse 17).

The poem is complete in column XXII; it is preceded and followed by known compositions. Furthermore, it is an alphabetic acrostic, like the preceding canticle from Sirach, and the acrostic is complete. Only the Apostrophe to Zion, Psalm 151A (column XXVIII) and the prose insert on David's compositions (column XXVII) are complete among the apocryphal compositions in the scroll, though Psalms 154 and 155 are certainly not far from whole.

Since the Psalms Scroll was first published, another copy of our "Apostrophe to Zion" has come to light in a Psalter manuscript from Cave 4 (4QPs^f).[7] The Cave 4 manuscript is quite fragmentary, however, so that not until the summer of 1965 was the discovery made that it contained other than biblical psalms. The first seven columns of 4QPs^f, which contain Psalms 22, 107, and 109, were assigned to Monsignor Patrick W. Skehan because of their biblical nature, while (what can now be called) columns VII to X were assigned to Abbé Jean Starcky because they contain non-biblical materials (three apocryphal psalms): such was the basis of division of labor, back in 1953–55, within the international team of scholars who are working on the tens of thousands of fragments from Cave 4. It was due to the keen perception of Professor John Strugnell that the Skehan and Starcky materials were identified as belonging to the same original manuscript: the

script and leather are identical. The Cave 4 manuscript dates from the middle of the first century B.C. and includes about half the text of the Apostrophe to Zion in columns VII and VIII of the extant fragments. It offers some twenty variants, none of which alters the sense of the poem but some of which bring improvements to the Hebrew text. The readings that are clearly superior are signaled in the notes below, to the text: a complete list of the variants may be found in Father Starcky's preliminary publication of the Cave 4 fragments.

There are three strophes in the poem. Verses 1 through 6 assure Zion, in the address to her, of her future, of the generations of children who will play in her parks and the faithful citizens in whom she will be proud. Verses 7 through 13 refer to Zion's sorrow and plight and the men of violence and iniquity whom God will in his sure justice banish from her midst. Verses 14 to the end pick up the opening theme of prayers for and praise of Zion. Zion will surely attain the blessings sought for her by her men of honor, her prophets:

Mayst thou attain unto everlasting righteousness,
    and blessings of the honorable mayst thou receive.
Accept a vision bespoken of thee,
    a dream of prophets sought for thee. [vv. 16–17]

The poem is beautifully "biblical." It is written in the style of apostrophes to Zion found in the Bible: Isa. 54:1–8; 60:1–22; and 62:1–8. But much of the vocabulary and the imagery of the poem is taken from Isa. 66:10–11:

> Rejoice with Jerusalem, and be glad for her,
>   all you who love her;
> rejoice for her in joy,
>   all you who mourn over her;
> that you may suck and be satisfied
>   with her consoling breasts;
> that you may drink deeply with delight
>   from the abundance of her glory.

---

[7] J. Starcky, "Psaumes apocryphes de la grotte 4 de Qumrân," *Revue biblique*, LXXIII (1966).

Apostrophe to Zion

Meter		*Verse no.*		*Col.* XXII *lines*
	אזכורך לברכה ציון	(1)	א	1–2
	בכול מודי אני אהבתיך		ב	
3/3/3	ברוך לעולמים זכרך			
	גדולה תקותך ציון	(2)	ג	2–3
3/4	ושלום ותוחלת ישועתך לבוא			
	דור ודור ידורו בך	(3)	ד	3–4
3/3	ודורות חסידים תפארתך			
	המתאוים ליום ישעך	(4)	ה	4
3/3	וישישו ברוב כבודך		ו	
	זיז כבודך יינקו	(5)	ז	4–5
3/3	וברחובות תפארתך יעכסו			
	חסדי נביאיך תזכורי	(6)	ח.	5–6
3/3	ובמעשי חסידיך תתפארי			
	טהר חמס מגוך	(7)	ט	6–7
3/4	שקר ועול נכרתו ממך			
	יגילו בניך בקרבך	(8)	י	7
3/3	וידידיך אליך נלוו			
	כמה קוו לישועתך	(9)	כ	8
3/3	ויתאבלו עליך תמיד			
	לוא תובד תקותך ציון	(10)	ל	8–9
3/3	ולוא תשכח תוחלתך			
	מי זה אבד צדק	(11)	מ	9–10
3/3	או מי זה מלט בעולו			

Apostrophe to Zion

11QPs^a column XXII, lines 1–10

(1)   I remember thee[8] for blessing, O Zion;

    with all my might have I loved thee.[9]

    May thy memory be blessed for ever!

(2)   Great is thy hope, O Zion;

    that peace and thy longed-for salvation will come.

(3)   Generation after generation will dwell in thee

    and generations of saints will be thy splendor:[10]

(4)   those who yearn[11] for the day of thy salvation

    that they may rejoice in the greatness of thy glory.[12]

(5)   On (the) abundance of thy glory they are nourished[13]

    and in thy splendid squares will they toddle.[14]

(6)   The merits of thy prophets wilt thou remember,

    and in the deeds of thy pious ones wilt thou glory.[15]

(7)   Purge[16] violence from thy midst;

    falsehood and evil will be cut off from thee.

(8)   Thy sons will rejoice in thy midst[17]

    and thy precious ones will be united with thee.

(9)   How they have hoped for thy salvation,

    thy pure ones have mourned for thee.[18]

(10)   Hope for thee does not perish, O Zion,

    nor is hope in thee forgotten.

(11)   Who has ever perished (in) righteousness,

    or who has ever survived[19] in his iniquity?

---

[8] The reading in 4QPs^f is *qal* not *hifil*; I had mistakenly read the *waw* in 11Q as a *yod* here and in verse 15.

[9] See Isa. 66:10 (also 65:18–19).

[10] See Isa. 60:19 and 62:3.

[11] See Ps. 132:13–14.

[12] Cf. Isa. 65:18–19; 66:10.

[13] Borrowed directly from Isa. 66:11. Literally "they suck".

[14] A rare word perhaps meaning "hopple" when in reference to a camel (so Arabic). Here the figure is that of an infant playing in a park.

[15] The allusion here could well be to the "sure promises" of God in covenant contexts: see the notes in *Discoveries in the Judaean Desert of Jordan*, Vol. IV, p. 88.

[16] The Hebrew is uncertain: the word here may be a *piel* infinitive with imperative force, a *pual* form, possibly a noun; or the text may be defective. It is unlikely that it is a *pual* perfect since the scribe is consistent in providing the *mater lectionis* necessary for that form.

[17] Cf. Isa. 65:18–19; 66:10.

[18] *Ibid.*

[19] The Hebrew verb is rare but clear in the context. The two colons of this verse begin, in 4QPs^f, with a very interesting Aramaic orthography: see Starcky's article referred to above.

Apostrophe to Zion—*continued*

Meter		*Verse no.*		*Col.* XXII *lines*
	נבחן אדם כדרכו	(12)	נ	10
3/3	איש כמעשיו ישתלם			
	סביב נכרתו צריך ציון	(13)	ס	10–11
3/3	ויתפזרו כול משנאיך			
	ערבה באף תשבחתך ציון	(14)	ע	11–12
3/3	מעלה לכול תבל			
	פעמים רבות אזכורך לברכה	(15)	פ	12
3/3	בכול לבבי אברכך			
	צדק עולמים תשיגי	(16)	צ	13
3/3	וברכות נכבדים תקבלי			
	קחי חזון דובר עליך	(17)	ק	13–14
3/3	וחלמת נביאים תתבעך			
	רומי ורחבי ציון	(18)	ר	14–15
	שבחי עליון פודך		ש	
3/3/3	תשמח נפשי בכבודך		ת	

Apostrophe to Zion—*continued*

11QPs^a column XXII, lines 10–15

(12) Man is tested according to his way;
every man is requited according to his deeds;
(13) all about are thine enemies cut off, O Zion,
and all thy foes have been scattered.

(14) Praise of thee is pleasing,[20] O Zion,
cherished through all the world.
(15) Many times do I remember thee for blessing;
with all my heart I bless thee.[21]
(16) Mayst thou attain unto everlasting righteousness,
and blessing of the honorable mayst thou receive.
(17) Accept a vision bespoken of thee,
a dream[22] of prophets sought for thee.[23]
(18) Be exalted, and spread wide, O Zion;[24]
praise the most high, thy saviour:
let my soul be glad in thy glory.

---

[20] Literally "pleasing to the nose," an expression used in the Bible to refer to sacrifices pleasing to God. Here the reference is to the love, esteem, and praise held by Jews throughout the world for Jerusalem: Zion is cherished through all the world as incense is pleasing to God. See "cherished" in Ps. 151:3 (xxviii 6). Cf. A. Dupont-Sommer, *Semitica*, XV (1965), pp. 74–77. For M'LH LKWL TBL 4QPs^f reads M'L KL TBL.

[21] Verse 15 in 4QPs^f reads: "Many times do I remember thee for blessing, *O Zion*; with all my *might have I loved* thee." The 4Q scribe's memory of verse 1 misguided him.

[22] 11QPs^a reads "and dreams," but 4QPs^f preserves the parallelism and the correct form, "a dream."

[23] The two verbs in this verse present difficulties; 4QPs^f has N'MR in place of DWBBR (?MDUBBR) but also has the strange TTB'K.

[24] See Isa. 51:17; 52:2; 54:2; 60:1; and Micah 4:13.

Hymn to the Creator

Column XXVI contains a Wisdom psalm of praise of God as Creator. There are barely nine verses or bicolons of it preserved.

Verses 7–9 are made up of phrases which are also found in Jer. 10:12–13 (51:15–16) and Ps. 135:7. These verses may have originally belonged to some very familiar liturgy of praise of the Creator, easily quotable and frequently used; for they are found equally well at home in Jeremiah, the Psalter, and this poem. Such "floating" bits of liturgical poetry may have been even more common than we had heretofore thought.

The poem is sapiential, belonging to Jewish Wisdom literature of the period between the testaments, in a category with Psalm 154 and Sirach 51:13ff. It does not represent the best poetry in the scroll.

Hymn to the Creator

	Verse no.	*Col.* XXVI *lines*
גדול וקדוש יהוה	(1)	9
קדוש קדושים לדור ודור		
לפניו הדר ילך	(2)	9–10
ואחריו המון מים רבים		
חסד ואמת סביב פניו	(3)	10–11
אמת ומשפט וצדק מכון כסאו		
מבדיל אור מאפלה	(4)	11–12
שחר הכין בדעת לבו		
אז ראו כול מלאכיו וירננו	(5)	12
כי הראם את אשר לוא ידעו		
מעטר הרים תנובות	(6)	13
אוכל טוב לכול חי		
ברוך עושה ארץ בכוחו	(7)	13–14
מכין תבל בחוכמתו		
בתבונתו נטה שמים	(8)	14–15
ויוצא [רוח] מאו[צרותיו]		
[ברקים למט]ר עשה	(9)	15
ויעל נ̇ש̇א̇[ים מ]ק̇צ̇ה [ארץ]		

Hymn to the Creator

11QPs^a column xxvi, lines 9–15

(1) Great and holy is the Lord,

the holiest of holy ones for every generation.[25]

(2) Majesty precedes him,

and following him is the rush of many waters.[26]

(3) Grace and truth surround his presence;

truth and justice and righteousness are the foundation of his throne.[27]

(4) Separating light from deep darkness,

by the knowledge of his mind[28] he established (the) dawn.

(5) When all his angels had witnessed (it) they sang aloud;

for he showed them what they had not known:

(6) Crowning (the) hills with fruit,

good food for every living being.

(7) Blessed be he who makes (the) earth by his power,

establishing (the) world in his wisdom.

(8) In his understanding he stretched out (the) heavens,

and brought forth [wind] from his st[orehouses].

(9) He made [lightning for the rai]n,

and caused mist[s] to rise [from] the end of [the earth].[29]

[25] The reference is to the "assembly of the holy ones" as in Ps. 89:5–7 (see Zech. 14:5). In Hos. 11:12 (Hebrew text 12:1) God is "the Holy One."

[26] Jer. 10:13 (51:13, 16).

[27] Ps. 97:2.

[28] Literally "heart." Rare and possibly unique in reference to God. But see column iv, especially, of the Thanksgiving Hymns from Qumran, where the thought, way, and purpose of the heart of God are frequently mentioned.

[29] See Jer. 10:12–13 (51:15–16) and Ps. 135:7 for the same poetic elements in different sequences.

A PROSE INSERT

David's Compositions

THE prose insert in column XXVII is interesting from three different points of view: the calendars of early Judaism, the liturgies of this period, and beliefs concerning David around the time of Christ.

According to the insert David wrote 3,600 psalms and 450 songs, making a total of 4,050 compositions credited to Israel's great king.

Psalms (line 5)		3,600
Songs for daily offerings (l.6)	364	
Songs for Sabbath offerings (l.7)	52	
Songs for festivals, holy days (l.8)	30	
"Songs for the stricken" (l.10)	4	
Total number of songs	450	450
Grand total		4,050

Of only passing interest to scholars is the challenge this figure seems to offer Solomon's record of I Kings 5:12. According to the Hebrew Bible, Solomon wrote 3,000 proverbs and 1,005 songs, for a total of 4,005. This would give David a surplus of 45. However, according to early Greek translations of the Bible, Solomon wrote 5,000 songs, for a total of 8,000. What perhaps is of some interest in these figures is the category of "song". According to these differing traditions both David and Solomon wrote songs, and it is the number of songs that varies in the traditions about Solomon. Furthermore, it is the song that is of real cultic interest in the scroll insert (cf. "song" in II Sam. 22 [Ps. 18]:1; Amos 6:5; I Chron. 6:16; 16:7–42; 25:7, II Chron. 7:6; 29:26–30).

Of immediate interest to students of early Jewish calenders will be the figures above relating to the number of songs David wrote and for what purpose: they indicate a 52-week, 364-day year. Lunar calendars are normally reckoned to have 354 days, such as the calendar, used in early rabbinical literature and surviving in modern Judaism, which must include intercalated months seven years out of nineteen in order to adjust the calendar to the movement of the earth in its solar orbit. A modified lunar calendar of 364 days is known from the sectarian, non-rabbinic books of Enoch and Jubilees, and several scholars have since 1953 been correct in claiming that the Qum-

ran sect used this calendar. Although the Psalms Scroll was not necessarily written or copied at Qumran but may possibly have been brought in by an initiant when he first entered the community there, the presence in the scroll of this prose insert with its cultic and calendaric references is nonetheless of considerable importance.

David is credited with both prophecy and Wisdom in composing his psalms and songs. Some of the attributes of David listed in lines 2–4 are found also noted of him in II Samuel 22 and 23. The psalm in II Samuel 23:1–7 was included in the Psalms Scroll in the (lost) last lines of column XXVI and the (extant) top line of column XXVII:

Now these are the last words of David:
The oracle of David, the son of Jesse,
  the oracle of the man who was raised on high,
the anointed of the God of Jacob,
  the sweet psalmist of Israel:
"The spirit of the Lord speaks by me,
  his word is upon my tongue.
The God of Israel has spoken,
  the Rock of Israel has said to me:
When one rules justly over men
  ruling in the fear of God,
he dawns on them like the morning light,
  like the sun shining forth upon a cloudless
                                        morning,
  like rain that makes grass to sprout from
                                        the earth.
Yea, does not my house stand so with God?
  For he has made with me an everlasting
                                        convenant,
  ordered in all things and secure.
For will he not cause to prosper
  all my help and my desire?
But godless men are all like thorns that are
                                        thrown away;
  for they cannot be taken with the hand;
but the man who touches them
  arms himself with iron and the shaft of a
                                        spear,
and they are utterly consumed with fire."

The psalm, found only in II Samuel 23 in the Bible, is here included among biblical and apocryphal psalms. And manifestly our prose insert draws on the psalm for some of its phrases in lines 2–4 about David's great wisdom and enlightenment.

Biblical allusions to David's wisdom are limited to the psalm above, the few expressions in I Sam. 16:12–23, and the speech of the wise woman of Tekoa in II Samuel 14, already noted above in reference to the canticle of Sirach 51:13ff. But the tradition of David's wisdom and his allegiance to Wisdom are very important in this scroll. Psalm 154, Sirach 51:13ff., and the Hymn to the Creator, all join the ranks now of Hebrew Wisdom literature, and in this scroll they also form a part of the "Davidic" literature as it was conceived in the first century A.D.

David's Compositions

ויהי דויד בן ישי חכם ואור כאור השמש וסופר

ונבון ותמים בכול דרכיו לפני אל ואנשים ויתן

לו י ה ו ה רוח נבונה ואורה ויכתוב תהלים

שלושת אלפים ושש מאות ושיר לשורר לפני המזבח על עולת

התמיד לכול יום ויום לכול ימי השנה ארבעה וששים ושלוש

מאות ולקורבן השבתות שנים וחמשים שיר ולקורבן ראשי

החודשים ולכול ימי המועדות ולים הכפורים שלושים שיר

ויהי כול השיר אשר דבר ששה ואבעים וארבע מאות ושיר

לנגן על הפגועים ארבעה ויהי הכול ארבעת אלפים וחמשים

כול אלה דבר בנבואה אשר נתן לו מלפני העליון

5

10

David's Compositions

11QPs^a column XXVII, lines 2–11

Line

And David, the son of Jesse, was wise, and a light like the light of the sun, and literate,

and discerning and perfect in all his ways before God and men.[1] And the Lord gave

him a discerning and enlightened spirit. And he wrote

5 3,600 psalms; and songs to sing before the altar over the whole-burnt

perpetual offering every day, for all the days of the year, 364;[2]

and for the offering of the Sabbaths, 52 songs;[3] and for the offering of the New

Moons and for all the Solemn Assemblies and for the Day of Atonement, 30 songs.

And all the songs that he composed were 446, and songs

10 for making music over the stricken, 4.[4] And the total was 4,050.

All these he composed through prophecy which was given him from before the Most High.

---

[1] The elements in the first two lines relate especially to II Samuel 14 and 23:1–7 (see column XXVII, line 1), as well as to I Sam. 16:12–23.

[2] See the literature quoted in *Discoveries in the Judaean Desert of Jordan*, Vol. IV, p. 91.

[3] Several documents from Caves 4 and 11, and now from Masada, relate to Sabbath liturgy poetry: 4QS1 37–39 and 4QBt have been published in *Vetus Testamentum*, Suppl. VII (1959), pp. 318–345, and in *Revue Biblique*, LXVII (1961), pp. 212, 233. See also Yigael Yadin's report on Masada in the *Illustrated London News* for October 31, 1964, pp. 696–697.

[4] Psalm 91 is noted in rabbinic literature as a psalm to be recited over those stricken by demons or evil spirits. A text of Psalm 91 in a recension from Qumran Cave 11 has been published by J. van der Ploeg in *Revue Biblique*, LXXII (1965), 210–217.

The scroll unrolled. The delicate task of unrolling was completed November 20, 1961. (Copyright by the Palestine Archaeological Museum, Jerusalem, Jordan; reproduced by permission.)

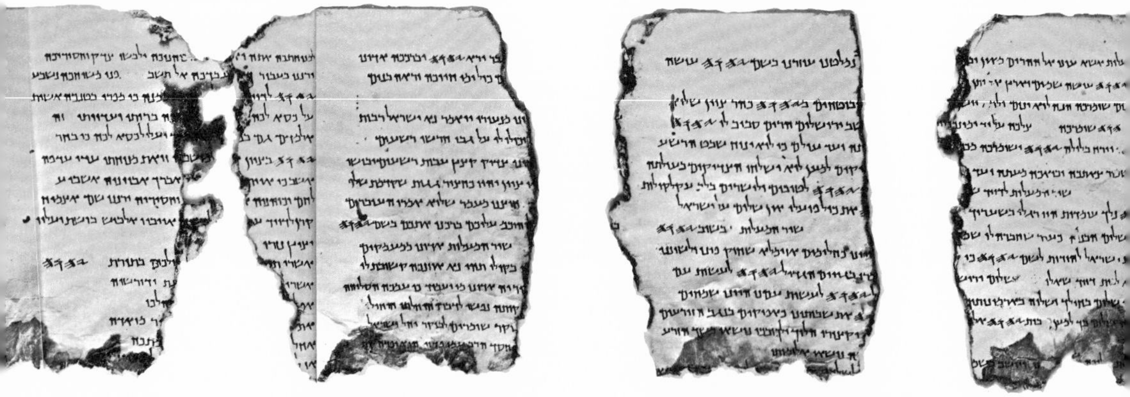

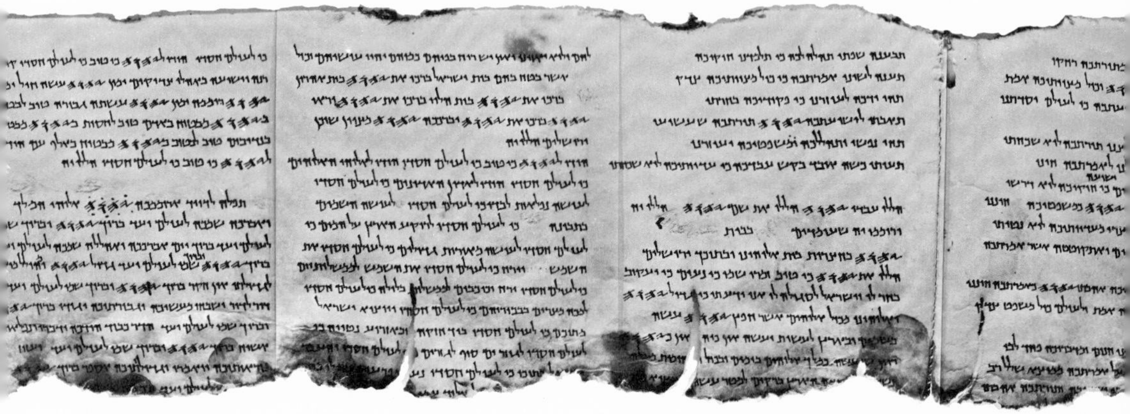

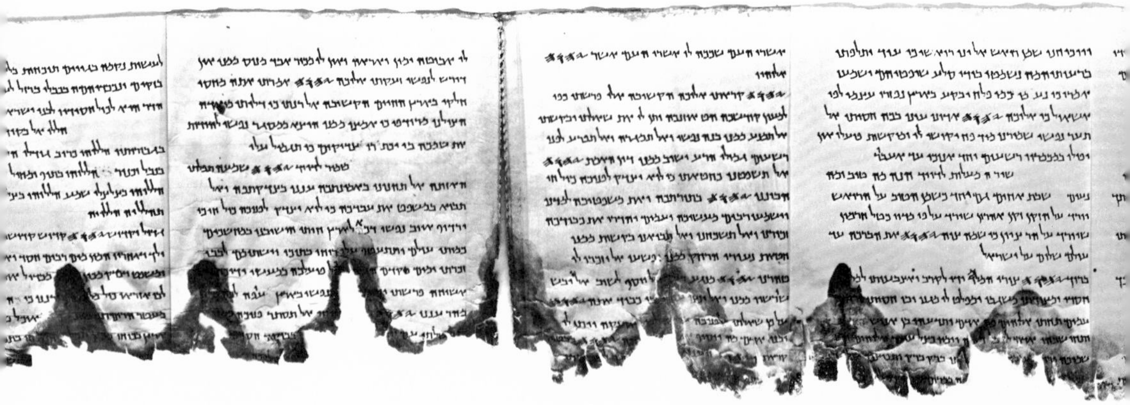

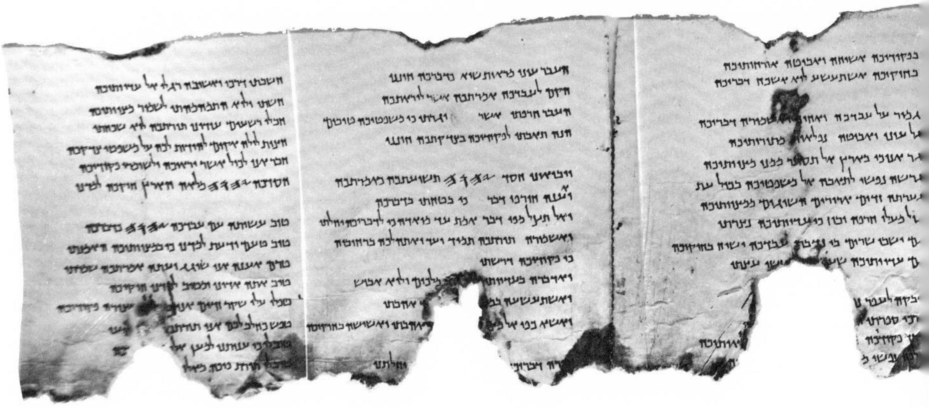

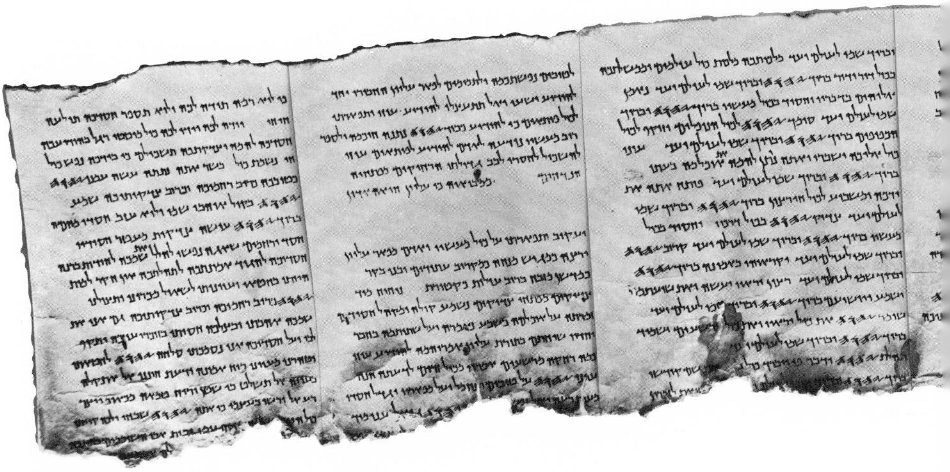

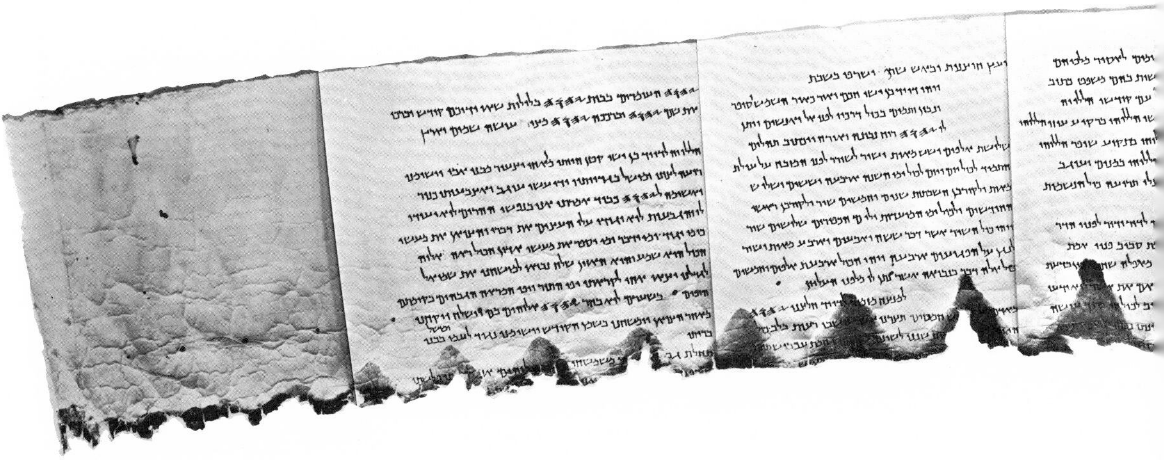

APPENDIXES

APPENDIX I

Psalms 152 and 153

(*Syriac Pss. IV and V*)

OF the five Syriac apocryphal psalms which are normally numbered by roman numerals I through V, the Psalms Scroll contains Nos. I, II, and III in their original-language Hebrew (columns XXVIII, XVIII, and XXIV). For clarity's sake we have in this volume numbered the five psalms according to the numbering in the oldest Syriac manuscript found of them to date (Mosul, Library of the Chaldaean Patriarchate, 1113). Mosul 1113, dating to the twelfth century A.D., is, in fact, not only the oldest manuscript containing the five Syriac psalms; it is also the only one in which the five psalms are contained in a biblical Psalter.[1] But because we now have in the Psalms Scroll the original Hebrew of three of the psalms, at least in a first-century A.D. recension, we know that Mosul 1113 offers the most faithful Syriac version of the five psalms as well as the oldest copy of that version. Providentially, one might say, Mosul 1113 also offers the most sensible and certainly the easiest system of numbering the five psalms, by appending them as supernumerary psalms at the end of the Psalter itself. The other, and younger, Syriac manuscripts which contained the five psalms were, for the most part, copies of a "Handbook of Discipline" as drawn up by a Syrian Christian, Bishop Elijah of al-Anbar, who lived in the tenth century A.D., the psalms being appended as filler material.

Prior to recovery of the Psalms Scroll, Psalms II–V were known only in Syriac. Psalm I, however, was known also in Greek and Latin, as Psalm 151. That is, in the Greek and Latin Psalter traditions, it was attached to the Psalter as supernumerary

and labeled as such. Only Mosul 1113 in the Syriac tradition numbers Psalm I as Psalm 151, but it is also the only Psalter manuscript anywhere in any language, aside from the Psalms Scroll itself, which has apocryphal psalms other than 151, and it is the only manuscript in existence which *numbers* psalms beyond 151. The following list gives the Mosul 1113 numbering as it corresponds to the more customary roman numbering:

Ps. 151 = Ps. I
Ps. 152 = Ps. IV
Ps. 153 = Ps. V
Ps. 154 = Ps. II
Ps. 155 = Ps. III

Psalms 152 and 153 do not appear in the extant Psalms Scroll: there is no ancient Hebrew text available for them. Whether they appeared in the Psalms Scroll in its original and complete state is a moot question. Those scholars who feel strongly that the Syrian Christians first got the five psalms from Karaite Jews, who reportedly found scrolls in a cave south of Jericho in the eighth century A.D., will tend to think that Psalms 152 and 153 were definitely included in the ancient library at Qumran.[2] Whether they were in the Qumran library is still, nonetheless, a moot question. Be that as it may, it seems appropriate to offer translations of Psalms 152 and 153 as an appendix to this edition of the Psalms Scroll, so that the reader who does not have access to texts of the five apocryphal psalms might be introduced to all of them under one cover. The translations here offered are based on the oldest and best available Syriac manuscripts, especially Mosul 1113.[3]

---

[1] See the *List of Old Testament Peshitta Manuscripts*, edited by the Peshitta Institute (Leiden, 1961), p. 113.

[2] See J. Strugnell, "Notes on the Text and Transmission of the Apocryphal Psalms 151, 154 and 155,"

forthcoming in the *Harvard Theological Review*.

[3] I am indebted to P. W. Skehan for his invaluable assistance in collating the Mosul manuscripts.

Psalm 152

Sung by David when he fought with the lion and the wolf which
ravished sheep from his flock.

(1) O God, O God, come to my aid; help me and save me;
    deliver my soul from the killers.
(2) Shall I descend to Sheol at the mouth of a lion
    or shall a wolf devour (me) so that I am no more?
(3) Was it not enough for them to ambush my father's flock
    and tear to pieces a sheep from his fold,
        that my own life they should also seek to destroy?

(4) Have mercy, O Lord, on thy chosen one,
    and save thy devoted one from destruction
(5) That he may faithfully and constantly praise thee
    and may glorify thy majestic name,
(6) When thou hast redeemed him from the hands of the destroyer death
    and hast delivered me from consignment to the mouths
        of the wild beasts.

(7) Quickly, O my Lord, send from thy presence a deliverer,
    and pull me from the yawning pit
    which would imprison me in its depths.

Psalm 153

Sung by David when he gave thanks to God that he had saved him
from the lion and the wolf both of which he had killed.

(1) Praise the Lord, all peoples:
    glorify him and bless his name.
(2) For he has saved the life of his elect one from the hands of death
    and delivered his devoted one from destruction,
(3) Saved me from the snares of Sheol
    and released my soul from the unfathomable abyss.

(4) Before my help had departed from his presence
    I was almost torn in two by two wild beasts.
(5) But he sent his angel and shut for my sake the gaping mouths
    and rescued my life from destruction.
(6) So shall my soul glorify and exalt him
    for all his acts of kindness he has done
        and still does for me.

APPENDIX II

Pre-Masoretic Psalter Texts

THERE are 30 Psalter texts from the eleven caves of Qumran, and three from ancient sites in Israel; in addition, there are four Bible-commentary (*pesher*) texts from Qumran containing Psalter textual readings. These account for all available Hebrew Psalter texts which are older than the Cairo Geniza (Firkowitch-Leningrad) materials.[1]

The following catalogue and index have been assembled from the published literature and, by correspondence, from the scholars whose assigned materials are as yet unpublished. For the latter information I am most grateful, for their generosity and thoughtfulness, to Monsignor Patrick W. Skehan (4QPs^{a-q}), Father J. van der Ploeg (11QPs^{b-d} and 11QPsAp^{a}), Professor Yigael Yadin (Masada and 11QPs^{a} Frag. E) and Abbé Jean Starcky (4QPs^{f} columns VII to X).

It should be carefully noted that in many of the manuscripts noted below there are only portions of the texts preserved: where only a word or even parts of letters are available, the citation is nonetheless given. To date, four Qumran Psalter manuscripts have been recovered containing both biblical and apocryphal psalms (4QPs^{f}, 11QPs^{a,d} and 11QPsAp^{a}). Full contents of the scroll are noted in the catalogue, but only the biblical psalms are noted in the index. A complete bibliography of all materials so far published appears in Appendix III, pp. 151–153.

Catalogue

Psalms Manuscripts from Qumran

(*the dash — means "continuous with the following"*)

1. 1QPs^{a} (1Q10)	Ps. 86:5–8
	92:12–14
	94:16
	95:11—
	96:1–2
	119:31–34, 43–48, 77–79
2. 1QPs^{b} (1Q11)	126:6
	127:1–5
	128:3
3. 1QPs^{c} (1Q12)	44:3–5, 7, 9, 23–24, 25
4. 2QPs (2Q14)	103:2–11
	104:6–11
5. 3QPs (3Q2)	2:6–7
6. 4QPs^{a}	5:9–13—
	6:1–4
4QPs^{a}	Ps. 25:15
	31:24(–25)—
	[Ps. 32 lacking]
	33:1–12
	35:2, 14–20, 26–28—
	36:1–9
	38:2–12, 16–23—
	71:1–14 [Note order]
	47:2
	53:4–7—
	54:1–6
	56:4
	62:?13—
	63:2–4
	66:16–20—

[1] The material in this appendix appeared earlier as an article in the *Catholic Biblical Quarterly*, XXVII (1965), pp. 114–123; 1QH means the Scroll of *Hodayot* or Hymns from Cave 1, 1QM the War Scroll from Cave 1, and 1QS the Manual of Discipline from Cave 1. See Paul Kahle, *The Cairo Geniza* (1959), pp. 5ff. and 131ff.

4QPs^{a}	Ps. 67:1–7
	69:1–19
7. 4QPs^{b}	91:5–8, 12–15
	92:4–8, 13–15
	93:5
	94:1–4, 8–14, 17–18, 21–22
	96:2
	98:4
	99:5–6
	100:1–2
	?102:5
	102:10–29—
	103:1–6, 9–14, 20–21
	[Pss. 104–111 lacking]
	112:4–5
	113:1
	115:2–3
	116:17–19
	118:1–3, 6–11, 18–20, 23–26, 29
8. 4QPs^{c}	16:7–9
	18:3–14, 16–18, 33–41
	27:12–14—
	28:1–2, 4
	35:27–28
	37:18–19
	45:8–11
	49:1–17
	50:14–23—
	51:1–5
	52:6–11—
	53:1
9. 4QPs^{d}	?146:10
	147:1–3, 13–17, 20—
	104:1–5, 8–11, 14–15, 22–25, 33–35 [Note order]
10. 4QPs^{e}	76:10–12
	77:1
	78:6–7, 31–33
	81:2–3
	86:10–11
	88:1–4
	89:44–46, 50–53
	(?34:2a)—
	104:1–3, 20, 21
	105:22–24, 36–45
	109:13
	115:15–18—
	116:1–3

4QPs^{e}	Ps. 120:6
	125:2–5—
	126:1–5
	129:8—
	130:1–3
11. 4QPs^{f}	22:14–17
	107:2–4, 8–11, 13–15, 18–19, 22–30, 35–42
	109:4–6, 25–28
Col. vii–viii	Apostrophe to Zion
ix	Eschatological Hymn
x	Apostrophe to Judah
12. 4QPs^{g}	Ps. 119:37–43, 44–46, 49–50, 73, 81–83, 90–92
13. 4QPs^{h}	119:10–21
14. 4QPs^{j}	48:1–7
	49:6, 9–12, ?15, ?17
15. 4QPs^{k}	26:7–12—
	27:1
	30:9–13
	135:7–16
16. 4QPs^{l}	104:3–5, 11–12
17. 4QPs^{m}	93:3–5
	95:3–6
	97:6–9
	98:4–8
18. 4QPs^{n}	135:6–8, 11–12
	136:23
19. 4QPs^{o}	114:7–8
	115:1–4
	116:5–10
20. 4QPs^{p}	143:6–8
21. 4QPs^{q}	31:25—
	[Ps. 32 lacking]
	33:1–18
	35:4–20
21a. 4QPs frag. 1	42:5
4QPs frag. 2	88:12
4QPs frag. 3	99:1
21b. 4QPs89	89:20–22, 26–28, 31
22. 5QPs (5Q5)	119:99–101, 104, 113–120, 138–142
23. pap6QPs (pap6Q5)	78:?36–37
24. 8QPs (8Q2)	17:5–9, 14
	18:6–9, 10–13
25. 11QPs^{a}	THE PSALMS SCROLL [note order]
Frags. A–E	Ps. 101:1–8
	102:1–2, 18–29—

Frags. A–E	Ps. 103:1
	109:21–31
	118:25–29—
	104:1–6, 21–35—
	147:1–2, 18–20—
	105:1–12
Col. i	Ps. 105:25–45
ii	146:9–10—
	148:1–12
iii	121:1–8—
	122:1–9—
	123:1–2
iv	124:7–8—
	125:1–5—
	126:1–6—
	127:1
v	128:4–6—
	129:1–8—
	130:1–8—
	131:1
vi	132:8–18—
vi–xiv	119:1–6, 15–25, 37–49, 59–73, 82–96, 105–120, 128–142, 150–164, 171–176—
xiv–xv	135:1–9, 17–21—
xv–xvi	136:1–16, 26—
	?118:1, 15, 16, 8, 9, 29—
xvi–xvii	145:1–7, 13–21
xviii	154:3–19
xix	Plea for Deliverance
xx	Ps. 139:8–24—
xx–xxi	137:1, 9—
	138:1–8
xxi–xxii	Sirach 51:13–30—
	Apostrophe to Zion—
	Ps. 93:1–3
xxiii	141:5–10—
	133:1–3—
xxiii–xxiv	144:1–7, 15—
	155:1–19
xxv	142:4–8—
	143:1–8
xxvi	149:7–9—
	150:1–6—
	Hymn to the Creator
xxvii	II Sam. 23:7—
	David's Compositions—
	Ps. 140:1–5
xxviii	134:1–3—

Col. xxviii	Ps. 151A, B
26. 11QPs^{b}	2:1–6
	9:3–7
	12:5–8—
	13:2–6—
	14:1–2, 3–6
	17:9–15—
	18:1–12
	43:1–3
	59:5–8
	7:18–21—
	78:1
27. 11QPs^{c}	35:15–28—
	36:1–13
	37:1–40—
	38:1–23—
	39:1–14—
	40:1
	68:3
	78:5–7, 8–11
	81:2–9
27a.11QPs^{d}	141:10—
	133:1–3
	Plea for Deliverance
27b.11QPsAp^{a}	Ps. 91:1–16

In addition to the above texts of psalms, as such, there are four manuscripts from Qumran which contain ancient commentaries, of sorts, to portions of Psalms 1, 2, 37, 45, 57, and 68, and hence afford some textual readings in those psalms. Three have been published and the fourth reported.

28. 1QpPs57 (1Q16)	Ps. 57:1
1QpPs68 (1Q16)	68:13, 26, 27, 30, 31
29. 4QFlorilegium	1:1
	2:1
30. 4QpPs37	37:8–17, 19–26, 32–36, 38
31. 4QpPs45(?)	45:1f.

Psalms Manuscripts in Israel

The Qumran materials listed above are all housed in the Palestine Archaeological Museum in Jerusalem, Jordan. Three manuscripts of psalms have been found in Israel since the discovery of the Qumran Scrolls.

On April 3, 1960, during the course of a systematic search of caves south of historic 'En Gedi, a group under the direction of Professor Yigael Yadin, of the Hebrew University, found a small fragment, a little over one and a half by two inches in size, containing portions of Psalms 15 and 16. It is later than most Qumran scrolls and should be dated late in the first century A.D. A short report and a plate are available in the *Israel Exploration Journal*, XI (1961), p. 40 and Plate 20.

32. No siglum (Nahal Hever) Ps. 15:1–5—
                              16:1

During the course of Professor Yadin's massive archaeological attack on, and siege of, in the winters of 1963–1965, the ancient Judaean natural fortress at Masada, which is located south of 'En Gedi and north of Sodom on the desert cliffs overlooking the Dead Sea, two psalms manuscripts were found.[2]

33. M1039–160 (Masada) Ps. 81:3–17—
                             82:1–8—
                             83:1–19—
                             84:1–13—
                             85:1–6

34. M1103–1742 (Masada)[3]   150:1–6

Index

---

[2] See, e.g., the *New York Times* for December 1, 1963, and the *Illustrated London News* for October 31, 1964, pp. 696–697. See now *Israel Exploration Journal*, XV (1965), pp. 79–81 and 103–104, as well as Plate 19.

[3] In the *Jerusalem* (Israel) *Post* for December 20, 1964, Yadin is reported from Beersheba to have discovered at Masada, only days earlier, a fragment $3\frac{1}{4}'' \times 4\frac{3}{4}''$ in size, containing Ps. 150:1–6.

Ps. 56:4	(6) 4QPs^{a}
57:1	(28) 1QpPs57
59:5–8	(26) 11QPs^{b}
62:13?	(6) 4QPs^{a}
63:2–4	(6) 4QPs^{a}
66:16–20	(6) 4QPs^{a}
67:1:7	(6) 4QPs^{a}
68:3	(27) 11QPs^{c}
68:13, 26, 27, 30, 31	(28) 1QpPs68
69:1–19	(6) 4QPs^{a}
71:1–14	(6) 4QPs^{a}
76:10–12	(10) 4QPs^{e}
77:1	(10) 4QPs^{e}
77:18–21	(26) 11QPs^{b}
78:1	(26) 11QPs^{b}
78:5–6, 8–11	(27) 11QPs^{c}
78:6–7, 31–33	(10) 4QPs^{e}
78:36–37(?)	(23) pap6QPs
81:2–3	(10) 4QPs^{e}
81:2–9	(27) 11QPs^{c}
81:3–17	(33) M1039–160
82:1–8	(33) M1039–160
83:1–19	(33) M1039–160
84:1–13	(33) M1039–160
85:1–6	(33) M1039–160
86:5–8	(1) 1QPs^{a}
86:10–11	(10) 4QPs^{e}
88:1–4	(10) 4QPs^{e}
88:12	(21a) 4QPs frag. 2
89:20–22, 26–28, 31	(21b) 4QPs89
89:44–46, 50–53	(10) 4QPs^{e}
91:1–16	(27b) 11QPsAp^{a}
91:5–8, 12–15	(7) 4QPs^{b}
92:4–8	(7) 4QPs^{b}
92:12–14	(1) 1QPs^{a}
92:13–15	(7) 4QPs^{b}
93:1–3	(25) 11QPs^{a}
93:3–5	(17) 4QPs^{m}
93:5	(7) 4QPs^{b}
94:1–4, 8–14	(7) 4QPs^{b}
94:16	(1) 1QPs^{a}
94:17–18, 21–22	(7) 4QPs^{b}
95:3–6	(17) 4QPs^{m}
95:11	(1) 1QPs^{a}
96:1–2	(1) 1QPs^{a}
96:2	(7) 4QPs^{b}
97:6–9	(17) 4QPs^{m}
98:4	(7) 4QPs^{b}
98:4–8	(17) 4QPs^{m}
99:1	(21a) 4QPs frag. 3

Ps. 99:5–6	(7) 4QPs^{b}
100:1–2	(7) 4QPs^{b}
101:1–8	(25) 11QPs^{a}
102:1–2	(25) 11QPs^{a}
?102:5	(7) 4QPs^{b}
102:10–29	(7) 4QPs^{b}
102:18–29	(25) 11QPs^{a}
103:1	(25) 11QPs^{a}
103:1–6	(7) 4QPs^{b}
103:2–11	(4) 2QPs
103:9–14, 20–21	(7) 4QPs^{b}
104:1–3	(10) 4QPs^{e}
104:1–5	(9) 4QPs^{d}
104:1–6	(25) 11QPs^{a}
104:3–5	(16) 4QPs^{l}
104:6–11	(4) 2QPs
104:8–11	(9) 4QPs^{d}
104:11–12	(16) 4QPs^{l}
104:14–15	(9) 4QPs^{d}
104:20, 21	(10) 4QPs^{e}
104:21–35	(25) 11QPs^{a}
104:22–25, 33–35	(9) 4QPs^{d}
105:1–12	(25) 11QPs^{a}
105:22–24	(10) 4QPs^{e}
105:25–45	(25) 11QPs^{a}
105:36–45	(10) 4QPs^{e}
107:2–14, 8–11, 13–15, 18–19, 22–30, 35–42	(11) 4QPs^{f}
109:4–6	(11) 4QPs^{f}
109:13	(10) 4QPs^{e}
109:21–31	(25) 11QPs^{a}
109:25–28	(11) 4QPs^{f}
112:4–5	(7) 4QPs^{b}
113:1	(7) 4QPs^{b}
114:7–8	(19) 4QPs^{o}
115:1–4	(19) 4QPs^{o}
115:2–3	(7) 4QPs^{b}
115:15–18	(10) 4QPs^{e}
116:1–3	(10) 4QPs^{e}
116:5–10	(19) 4QPs^{o}
116:17–19	(7) 4QPs^{b}
118:1	(25) 11QPs^{a}
118:1–3, 6–11	(7) 4QPs^{b}
118:8, 9	(25) 11QPs^{a}
118:15, 16	(25) 11QPs^{a}
118:18–20, 23–26	(7) 4QPs^{b}
118:25–29	(25) 11QPs^{a}
118:29	(7) 4QPs^{b}
118:29	(25) 11QPs^{a}

Ps. 119:1–6	(25) 11QPs[a]
119:10–21	(13) 4QPs[h]
119:15–28	(25) 11QPs[a]
119:31–34	(1) 1QPs[a]
119:37–43	(12) 4QPs[g]
119:37–49	(25) 11QPs[a]
119:43–48	(1) 1QPs[a]
119:44–46, 49–50	(12) 4QPs[g]
119:59–72	(25) 11QPs[a]
119:73	(12) 4QPs[g]
119:77–79	(1) 1QPs[a]
119:81–83	(12) 4QPs[g]
119:82–96	(25) 11QPs[a]
119:90–92	(12) 4QPs[g]
119:99–101, 104	(22) 5QPs
119:105–120	(25) 11QPs[a]
119:113–120	(22) 5QPs
119:128–142	(25) 11QPs[a]
119:138–142	(22) 5QPs
119:150–164, 171–176	(25) 11QPs[a]
120:6	(10) 4QPs[e]
121:1–8	(25) 11QPs[a]
122:1–9	(25) 11QPs[a]
123:1–2	(25) 11QPs[a]
124:7–8	(25) 11QPs[a]
125:1–5	(25) 11QPs[a]
125:2–5	(10) 4QPs[e]
126:1–5	(10) 4QPs[e]
126:1–6	(25) 11QPs[a]
126:6	(2) 1QPs[b]
127:1	(25) 11QPs[a]
127:1–5	(2) 1QPs[b]
128:3	(2) 1QPs[b]
128:3–6	(25) 11QPs[a]
129:1–8	(25) 11QPs[a]
129:8	(10) 4QPs[e]
130:1–3	(10) 4QPs[e]
130:1–8	(25) 11QPs[a]
131:1	(25) 11QPs[a]
132:8–18	(25) 11QPs[a]
133:1–3	(25) 11QPs[a]
133:1–3	(27a) 11QPs[d]
134:1–3	(25) 11QPs[a]
135:1–7	(25) 11QPs[a]
135:6–8, 11–12	(18) 4QPs[n]
Ps. 135:7–16	(15) 4QPs[k]
135:17–21	(25) 11QPs[a]
136:1–16	(25) 11QPs[a]
135:23	(18) 4QPs[n]
136:26	(25) 11QPs[a]
137:1–9	(25) 11QPs[a]
138:1–8	(25) 11QPs[a]
139:8–24	(25) 11QPs[a]
140:1–5	(25) 11QPs[a]
141:5–10	(25) 11QPs[a]
141:10	(27a) 11QPs[d]
142:4–8	(25) 11QPs[a]
143:1–8	(25) 11QPs[a]
143:6–8	(20) 4QPs[p]
144:1–7, 15	(25) 11QPs[a]
145:1–7, 13–21	(25) 11QPs[a]
146:9–10	(25) 11QPs[a]
146:10?	(9) 4QPs[d]
147:1–2	(25) 11QPs[a]
147:1–3, 13–17, 20	(9) 4QPs[d]
147:18–20	(25) 11QPs[a]
148:1–12	(25) 11QPs[a]
149:7–9	(25) 11QPs[a]
150:1–6	(25) 11QPs[a]
150:1–6	(34) M1103–1742

Another valuable source of Psalter textual readings is available in ancient nonbiblical manuscripts. Chaim Rabin, among others, has noted that "the non-biblical manuscripts can supply us with a great deal of information about the Bible text as read by the Qumran sect."[4] Whether or not they are "more valuable," as Professor Rabin thinks, is a moot question. This list is appended here because of the obvious value such a list, when completed, can have.[5] Some of the entries denote verbatim (or nearly so) quotations (*) of the MT Psalter; some indicate recognizable reflections (†) of Psalter readings, and others only tenuous influence (?).

Ps. ?1:4	1QH vii 23
*6:8	1QH v 34
?7:7	1QM xiv 16
?9:2	1QH iii 23

[4] Rabin, "The Dead Sea Scrolls and the Old Testament Text," *Journal of Theological Studies*, VI (1955), p. 179.

[5] The list is essentially an amalgam of similar lists drawn up by I. H. Eybers (in *New Light on Old Testament Problems* [University of Pretoria, South Africa, 1962], p. 3) and by Theodor H. Gaster (*The Dead Sea Scriptures* [1964], pp. 414–415); it varies only in the addition of one suggestion by Rabin (*op. cit.*), of four based on apocryphal portions of 11QPs[a], and in omissions and modifications resulting from verification.

Ps. ?10:10	1QH iii 25
†12:7	1QH v 16
†18:3	1QH ix 28–29
*18:5	1QH iii 28, 29
†18:6	1QH iii 9
?18:40	1QM i 13
?19:14	1QH iii 21
†20:9	1QH iv 22, 36
†21:14	1QM xiv 16
*22:14	1QH v 11
†22:15	1QH iv 33 vii 4
†24:8	1QM xii 9
?26:7	1QH iii 23
*26:12	1QH ii 29–30
†31:10	1QH v 35
†31:13	1QH iv 9
*31:19	1QH vii 11–12
*33:8	11QPs[a] ii 1–2
†33:15	CD i 10
†35:5	1QH vii 23
†35:7–8	1QH ii 29
?36:7	4Q DibHam[6] vii 7–8
?37:2	1QM xv ii
†37:23	1QH xv 13
?40:3	1QH vii 8
†41:10	1QH v 24
?42:6, 12	1QH viii 28
*42:7	1QH viii 32
†43:5	1QH viii 32
?45:5	1QS v 3–4
?46:7	1QH vi 7
?48:12	1QM xii 13 xix 5
†51:7	1QH iv 29–30
†51:10	1QH ii 5
†51:19	1QS viii 3
*54:5	1QH ii 21
?55:16	1QH viii 28
Ps. †56:14	1QS iii 7
†57:5	1QH v 6–7, 10
*57:6, 12	1QM xii 17
?58:5	1QH v 28
†58:7	1QH v 9–10
?59:4	1QH v 17
?59:8	1QH v 10
*64:4	1QH v 13
?65:4	1QH iv 37
?68:6	1QM xii 2
†69:22	1QH iv 11
?82:3	1QH ii 34
*86:14	1QH ii 21
†88:4–6	1QH viii 28–29
†89:8	1QH iv 25
†89:29–30	CD xiv 2 xix 1
†92:11	1QH vii 22
?102:6	1QH ix 4
†102:10	1QH v 34–35
?103:20	1QH viii 11 x 34–35
†105:15	CD ii 12
?106:6	CD xx 29
†106:25	CD iii 8
*107:16	1QH v 38
*107:27	1QH iii 14–15
†107:29	1QH v 18
*108:6	1QM xii 17
†116:3	1QH iii 28
?116:16	1QH xi 32
?119:1	1QM iv 22
*135:7	11QPs[a] xxvi 14–15
†137:6	1QH v 32
?138:3	1QH xii 1
†140:4	1QH v 13
*143:2	11QPs[a] xxiv 7
?LXX 145:7	1QS xi 14
†145:10–12	11QPs[a] ii 2–4

[6] A scroll of prayers published by M. Baillet in *Revue biblique*, LXVIII (1961), pp. 195–250.

APPENDIX III

Pre-Masoretic Psalter Bibliography

THE following bibliography lists the literature available to date on the Psalter as it was in pre-Masoretic times, that is, before about A.D. 100, after which time only the Psalter as we presently know it in our English Bibles (with very little exception) was used and copied in both Judaism and Christianity. In addition to reports on and publications of the recently discovered texts, and literature pertinent to the various apocryphal psalms, the bibliography also notes the most recent discussions of the problems in biblical textual criticism which arise out of the discoveries.

Publications of Texts

Qumran Psalter Texts

Discoveries in the Judaean Desert, Vols. I and III (1955, 1962) (for Qumran Caves 1–3 and 5–10).

J. T. Milik, "Deux documents inédits du désert de Juda," *Biblica*, XXXVIII (1957), pp. 245–255 (on 4QPs[q]).

P. W. Skehan, "A Psalm Manuscript from Qumran," *Catholic Biblical Quarterly*, XXVI (1964), pp. 313–322 (on 4QPs[b]).

J. A. Sanders, *The Psalms Scroll of Qumran Cave 11: Discoveries in the Judaean Desert of Jordan*, Vol. IV (1965) (on 11QPs[a]).

J. van der Ploeg, "Le Psaume xci dans une recension de Qumrân," *Revue biblique*, LXXII (1965), pp. 210–217 (on 4QPsAp[a]).

J. T. Milik, "Fragments d'une source du Psautier," *Revue biblique*, LXXIII (1966) pp. 94–104 (on 4QPs89).

J. Starcky, "Psaumes apocryphes de la grotte 4 de Qumran," *Revue biblique*, LXXIII (1966) (on 4QPs[f] columns VII to IX).

Y. Yadin, "Another Fragment (E) of the Psalms Scroll from Qumran Cave 11 (11QPs[a])," *Textus*, V (1966), pp. 1–10 (on 11QPs[a] frag. E).

Qumran Psalter Commentaries

J. M. Allegro, "A Newly-Discovered Fragment of a Commentary on Psalm xxxvii from Qumran," *Palestine Exploration Quarterly*, LXXXVI (1954), pp. 69–75 (on 4QpPs37).

J. M. Allegro, "Further Light on the History of the Qumran Sect," *Journal of Biblical Literature*, LXXV (1956), pp. 94–95 (on 4QpPs37).

J. M. Allegro, "Fragments of a Qumran Scroll of Eschatological Midrašim," *Journal of Biblical Literature*, LXXVII (1958), pp. 350–354 (on 4QFlorilegium).

H. Stegemann, "Der Pešer Psalm 37 aus Höhle 4 von Qumran," *Revue de Qumrân*, No. 14 (1963), pp. 235–270 (on 4QpPs37).

'En Gedi Psalter Text

Y. Yadin, "A Fragment of the Book of Psalms," *Israel Exploration Journal*, XI (1961), p. 40 and Plate 20 (on Nahal Hever fragment of Ps. 15:1–5 and Ps. 16:1).

Preliminary Reports

Qumran

"Le Travail d'éditions des fragments manuscrits de Qumrân," *Revue biblique*, LXIII (1956), pp. 49–67 (on Cave 4).

M. Baiet, "Psaumes, hymnes, cantiques et prières dans les manuscrits de Qumrân," *Le Psautier* (1962), pp. 389–405 (on Caves 1–10).

J. A. Sanders, "The Scroll of Psalms from Cave 11 (11QPss): A Preliminary Report," *Bulletin of the American Schools of Oriental Research*, No. 165 (February 1962), pp. 11–15 (on 11QPs[a]).

Masada

Y. Yadin, "Masada," *Illustrated London News,* October 31, 1964, pp. 693–697, esp. pp. 696–697 (on M1039–160: Psalms 81–85).

Jerusalem (Israel) *Post,* December 30, 1964 (on M1103–1742: Psalm 150:1–6).

Y. Yadin, "The Excavation of Masada—1963/64: Preliminary Report," *Israel Exploration Journal,* XV (1965), pp. 79–82, 103–104 (on M1039–160: Psalms 81:3–85:10).

The Five Syriac Apocryphal Psalms
(*before* 11QPs^a)

W. Wright, "Some Apocryphal Psalms in Syriac," *Proceedings of the Society of Biblical Archaeology,* IX (1887), pp. 257ff.

E. Sachau, *Verzeichniss der syrishchen Handschriften der königlichen Bibliothek zu Berlin,* Vol. I (1899), p. 209.

A. Mingana, "Woodbrooke Studies: (iii) Some Uncanonical Psalms," *Bulletin of the John Rylands Library,* XI (1927), pp. 492–498. Printed separately as *Woodbrooke Studies,* Vol. I (1927), pp. 288–294.

M. Noth, "Die fünf syrisch überlieferten apokryphen Psalmen," *Zeitschrift für die alttestamentliche Wissenschaft,* XLVIII (1930), pp. 1–23.

M. Delcor, "Cinq nouveaux psaumes esséniens?," *Revue de Qumrân,* No. 1 (1958), pp. 85–102. See now M. Delcor, *Les Hymnes de Qumrân* (1962), pp. 299–319.

M. Philonenko, "L'Origine essénienne des cinq psaumes syriaques de David," *Semitica,* IX (1959), pp. 35–48.

List of Old Testament Peshitta Manuscripts, Leiden (1961), p. 113.

Psalm 151

J. A. Sanders, "Ps 151 in 11QPs^a," *Zeitschrift für die alttestamentliche Wissenschaft,* LXXV (1963), pp. 73–86. Revised in *Discoveries in the Judaean Desert of Jordan,* Vol. IV (1965), pp. 53–64.

P. W. Skehan, "The Apocryphal Psalm 151," *Catholic Biblical Quarterly,* XXV (1963), pp. 407–409.

W. H. Brownlee, "The 11Q Counterpart to Psalm 151, 1–5," *Revue de Qumrân,* No. 15 (1963), pp. 379–387.

J. Carmignac, "La Forme poétique de Psaume 151 de la grotte 11," *Revue de Qumrân,* No. 15 (1963), pp. 371–378.

I. Rabinowitz, "The Alleged Orphism of 11QPss 28, 3–12," *Zeitschrift für die alttestamentliche Wissenschaft,* LXXVI (1964), pp. 193–200.

A. Dupont-Sommer, "Le Psaume cli dans 11QPs^a et le problème de son origine essénienne," *Semitica,* XIV (1964), pp. 25–62.

A. Dupont-Sommer, *David et Orphée,* Séance publique annuelle des Cinq Académies, lundi, 26 octobre 1964.

R. Weiss, in *Massa* (Hebrew), May 15, 1964, and January 29, 1965.

A. Hurvitz, in *Tarbitz* (Hebrew), 1965, pp. 224–227.

J. Carmignac, "Précisions sur la forme poétique de Psaume 151," *Revue de Qumrân,* No. 18 (1965), pp. 249–252.

M. Philonenko, "Une tradition essénienne dans le Coran," forthcoming in *Revue de l'histoire des religions.*

Psalms 154 and 155

J. A. Sanders, "Two Non-Canonical Psalms in 11QPs^a," *Zeitschrift für die alttestamentliche Wissenschaft,* LXXVI (1964), pp. 57–75. Revised in *Discoveries in the Judaean Desert of Jordan,* Vol. IV, 1965, pp. 64–76.

R. Weiss, in *Massa* (Hebrew) for August 7, 1964 (on Psalm 154).

P. W. Skehan, "A Broken Acrostic and Psalm 9," *Catholic Biblical Quarterly,* XXVII (1965), pp. 1ff. (on Psalm 155).

A. Hurvitz, "Observations on the Language of the Third Apocryphal Psalm from Qumran," *Revue de Qumrân,* No. 18 (1965), pp. 225–232 (on Psalm 155).

M. Delcor, "Zum Psalter von Qumran," *Biblische Zeitschrift,* X (1966), pp. 15–29 (on Pss. 151, 154, 155).

J. Strugnell, "Notes on the Text and Transmission of the Apocryphal Psalms 151, 154 and 155," forthcoming in the *Harvard Theological Review.*

Other Apocryphal Psalms

O. Braun, "Ein Brief des Katholikos Timotheus I über biblische Studien des 9 Jahrhunderts," *Oriens Christianus,* I (1901), pp. 299–313.

"Psaume de David quand il lutta avec Goliath," Codex xxxv in Jacques Vosté, *Catalogue de la Bibliothèque Syro-Chaldéenne du Couvent de Notre Dame des Semances près d'Alqoš (Iraq)* (1929), p. 16.

O. Eissfeldt, "Der Anlass zur Entdeckung der Höhle und ihr ähnliche Vorgänge aus älterer Zeit," *Theologische Literaturzeitung*, LXXIV (1949), cols. 597–600.

Pseudo-Philo's Liber Antiquitatum Biblicarum, edited by Guido Kisch (1949), paragraph lix, pp. 259–260; see also paragraph lxii:5.

M. Philonenko, "Remarques sur un hymne essénien de caractère gnostique," *Semitica*, XI (1961), pp. 43–54.

J. Strugnell, "More Psalms of 'David'," *Catholic Biblical Quarterly*, XXVII (1965), pp. 207–216 (a retroversion, Latin to Greek to Hebrew, of Pseudo-Philo paragraph lix).

A. Dupont-Sommer, "Notes qoumraniennes," *Semitica*, XV (1965), pp. 74–77.

Textual Criticism
(*pertinent titles only*)

P. W. Skehan, "The Qumran Manuscripts and Textual Criticism," *Vetus Testamentum*, Supplement IV (1957), pp. 148–158.

F. M. Cross, "The Old Testament at Qumran," *The Ancient Library of Qumran* (1961), pp. 163–194. Note also "A Catalogue of the Library of Qumran," pp. 30–47.

F. M. Cross, "The History of the Biblical Text in the Light of Discoveries in the Judaean Desert," *Harvard Theological Review*, LXII (1964), pp. 281–299.

S. Talmon, "Aspects of the Textual Transmission of the Bible in the Light of the Qumran Manuscripts," *Textus*, IV (1964), pp. 95–132.

J. A. Sanders, "Pre-Masoretic Psalter Texts," *Catholic Biblical Quarterly*, XXVII (1965), pp. 114–123. Revised in the present volume, above, pp. 143–149.

P. W. Skehan, "The Biblical Scrolls from Qumran and the Text of the Old Testament," *Biblical Archaeologist*, XXVIII (1965), pp. 87–100.

J. A. Sanders, "Variorum in the Psalms Scroll (11QPs[a])," *Harvard Theological Review*, LIX (1966), pp. 83–94. Revised in the present volume, above, pp. 9–14.

J. A. Sanders, "The Psalter at the Time of Christ," *The Bible Today*, XXII (1966), pp. 1462–1469.

S. Talmon, "Pisqah Be'emṣa' Pasuq and 11QPs[a]," *Textus*, V (1966), pp. 11–21. A longer version of the same article appeared (in Hebrew) in *Tarbitz* for March, 1966, pp. 214–234.

POSTSCRIPTUM

Fragment E of the Psalms Scroll

SOME time after the manuscript for this book had gone to the publisher I received the following telegram:

Jerusalem Israel   Dec 31 1965

Happy inform you prepress release Sunday my possession of fragment 11QPs containing chapters 118 104 147 beginning 105 in this order preceding your column one Stop Happy New Year

YIGAEL YADIN

Then on January 2, 1966, the *New York Times* carried the following item:

> Prof. Yigael Yadin, Israel's leading archeologist, announced tonight the acquisition of a fragment of a Dead Sea scroll containing portions of the Psalms.
>
> The Israeli fragment, Professor Yadin said, fits between several fragments and part of a larger scroll belonging to Jordan.
>
> The Jordanian manuscripts contain 38 of the Psalms of the Bible. The Israeli fragment contains parts of three additional Psalms and some missing verses of a Psalm in the larger scroll.
>
> Professor Yadin announced the acquisition at a meeting of a Bible study circle at the home of President Zalman Shazar. The fragment was purchased in 1960 from an anonymous American, who requested that publication be withheld for several years.

One can imagine the shock the news conveyed. I was totally unprepared for such a development as I had carefully checked all the materials that had been brought from Qumran Cave 11 into the Palestine Archaeological Museum in Jerusalem, Jordan, and knew that only four of those fragments belonged to the scroll. I knew also that all the Cave 11 yield had been under lock and key, by order of the trustees of the museum, since 1956 when the cave had been found until the fall of 1961 when I began the task of unrolling and editing the scroll. A number of essential questions remain unanswered, especially the crucial one of how the fragment got from the museum (or the cave) into the hands of the " anonymous American." Professor Yadin, who is not only one of the world's leading scholars but also a generous, thoughtful gentleman, informed me in subsequent correspondence of what he knew with the exception of the information which he was bound, by promise to the anonym, not to reveal. The pertinent facts of the affair are related in the following excerpt from Yadin's *editio princeps* of the fragment.[1]

> In a letter dated 16th September 1960, a citizen of the United States (who wishes to remain anonymous), offered me for sale at a high price, a fragment of a scroll. From a photograph attached to the letter I could ascertain that it was a genuine Qumran fragment, and that it contained several chapters from a Psalter, arranged in an order which differed from that of the MT. On the 27th of September of the same year, I countered Mr. Anonymous' offer with a price which I thought appropriate for the fragment. One can imagine my surprise when, on the 7th of October, I received a registered air mail manila envelope, mailed on the 3rd of October, which contained the fragment wrapped in an ordinary table napkin. The purchase price was promptly sent to the vendor.... I had a chance to meet Mr. Anonymous who—for his own reasons—insisted that I postpone the publication of the scroll for several years. Reluctantly I acceded to his request, and

---

[1] Yadin, "Another Fragment (E) of the Psalms Scroll from Qumran Cave 11 (11QPsᵃ)," *Textus*, V (1966). The quotation is taken from pre-paginated proofs supplied by Yadin.

left the deciphered MS to rest for a while. When I saw the first publication by Dr. J. A. Sanders of parts of 11QPsᵃ, I was struck by the identity of the script of my fragment with that of his. Since the complete publication of 11QPsᵃ was then imminent, I decided to wait a little longer before reaching a final conclusion. . . .

Yadin also informed me that the period of silence imposed on him by the agreement with the anonym was five years from December of 1960; hence he felt free to make the announcement on New Year's Day 1966 in the home of President Shazar after he had wired me the previous evening. Yadin is clearly a man of his word, and it is a joy for me to be associated with him in the publication of the fragment. Yadin readily supplied me with an infrared photograph of the fragment as well as with the first proofs of his article on it so that it could be included in this volume. It is too late to insert it above in its proper place between fragment D and column I of the scroll proper, since publication of this book is already well advanced at this writing. Setting it apart in this manner, however, as a *postscriptum* to the rest of the book, permits us not only to present the text of the fragment but also to tell the story about it and its rightful place in the scroll as a whole.

Fragment E raises the total number of compositions in the extant portions of the scroll to forty-nine: forty-one biblical psalms, seven nonbiblical psalms, and the prose composition in column XXVII. The three columns of the fragment contain parts of Pss. 118:25–29; 104:1–6, 21–35; 147:1–2, 18–20; and 105:1–12. Like the four other fragments, and the rest of the scroll in general, fragment E includes only approximately the top two-thirds of the columns it preserves; as stated in the introduction, the bottom third of the scroll's width was lost in antiquity by decomposition due to humidity. The fragment is designated by the letter 'E', indicating that it should follow fragments A to D, because column III of fragment E in its original length of twenty-five lines would have contained precisely the middle portion of Psalm 105 between verse 12 in the last line of the fragment and verse 25 at the top of column I of

the scroll proper. The presence in the fragment of Psalm 118 in its traditional guise indicates that the six or so verses which follow Psalm 136 at the top of column XVI are by no means a mutilated form of Psalm 118 but must be viewed as a coda to Psalm 136 made up of phrases familiar from Psalm 118. They should be viewed in the same manner as the incidence of a similar case in the apocryphal Hymn to the Creator in column XXVI, which contains verses known from Jeremiah 10 and Psalm 135; such floating bits of liturgical literature would have been familiar in more than one context. Psalm 118 is now available, therefore, in 4QPsᵇ and 11QPsᵃ (see Appendix II, p. 148) in its traditional guise.

The fact that Psalms 104 and 147 appear together in fragment E is significant in the light of the observation that the only other pre-Masoretic manuscript in which order is ascertainable they also appear together: in 4QPsᵈ Psalm 104 follows Psalm 147. Indeed, one of the most significant observations it is now possible to make about the pre-Masoretic Psalter texts is that there is no order of psalms in the Psalms Scroll contradicted by any order of the same psalms in any other Psalms manuscript from Qumran. The others are so fragmentary that there is no contradiction of order. On the contrary, the approximation of Psalms 104 and 147 in the scroll as well as in 4QPsᵈ is quite important in the light of the fact that the order of Psalm 141 followed by Psalm 133 is now attested both in 11QPsᵃ and 11QPsᵈ; 11QPsᵈ, like the Psalms Scroll (11QPsᵃ), also contains the apocryphal Plea for Deliverance of column XIX, though the fragments of the former do not indicate order. Manifestly, one must not view the order and contents of the Psalms Scroll as in any sense maverick.

In the summer of 1965 a reidentification of materials in the Cave 4 lot became possible when Professor John Strugnell, working with Abbé Jean Starcky, noted that a Cave 4 copy of some apocryphal psalms on which Starcky was working actually belonged to 4QPsᶠ, a Psalms manuscript assigned to Monsignor P. W. Skehan[2]. This is the first clear case of a Cave 4 Psalms manuscript

---

[2] Starcky, "Psaumes apocryphes de la grotte 4 de Qumran," *Revue biblique*, LXXIII (1966). Abbé Starcky generously mailed me a carbon copy of his article before publication, and a few of the variant readings in the "Apostrophe to Zion" of 4QPsᶠ have been noted above in Part III, pp. 124–127.

Fragment E of 11 QPs[a]. (Courtesy of Yigael Yadin, The Shrine of the Book, Jerusalem, Israel.)

containing apocryphal material. Other such re-identifications may become possible as time goes on, especially after all the mass of Cave 4 material has been published. It is sufficient for our purposes at the moment to note that one of the apocryphal psalms (now) belonging to 4QPs^f is the Apostrophe to Zion of column XXII of the Psalms Scroll! These converging bits of evidence clearly prohibit any cavalier treatment on our part of the significance of the Psalms Scroll, the one really imposing witness to the Hebrew Psalter in pre-Masoretic times.

If one has difficulty, as I do, conceiving of the Qumran sectarians as libertarian in their treatment of the Psalter, these observations take on considerable significance. The weight of authority attached to the name of David in the period from 100 B.C. to A.D. 100 would bring the Psalms the same respect which the Law and the Prophets commanded; as indeed Luke 24:44 indicates, the Psalms are cited by Jesus as having the same authority, for Christian purposes, as the Law and Prophets. If one may now speak of text families for the Pentateuch, the Former Prophets and Jeremiah, as Professor Frank Cross rightly does, we should probably think of the Qumran Psalter as representing, not so many textual aberrations, but a local Palestinian text with its own internal problems of limited fluidity.[3] It should be carefully noted, however, that we arrive at this hypothesis not because of data indicating textual *Vorlagen* of divergent Greek recensions of the 150 canonical psalms, but because of the unexpected and surprising order and content of the Qumran Psalms manuscripts. If the available Greek translations of the Psalter existed prior to the end of the first century A.D., and we cannot really be sure that the Greek Psalters we now have are the only ones ever made, then they presuppose a proto-Masoretic Hebrew Psalter dating well before the First Jewish Revolt of A.D. 66 to 69. Otherwise one must think of considerable recensional activity on the Psalter at the end of the first century,

at which time our present Greek Psalters came into being containing an amalgamated and edited Psalm 151, which was later dropped altogether from the Hebrew Psalter, which in turn became rigidly set at the long since time-honored figure of 150.[4]

Until the publication of the Psalms Scroll, Psalm 151, known only in Greek and derived translations, and Psalms 152 to 155, known only in Syriac, were largely overlooked in discussions of Psalter text and versions. There was no compelling need to bother with them, much less with psalms such as the one from Pseudo-Philo's *Liber Antiquitatum Biblicarum*, which John Strugnell last year retroverted from Latin to Greek to Hebrew, the original of which he dates from the time of Christ, a Davidic pseudepigraphon *ex persona David*.[5] As Strugnell rightly suggests, the presence in 11QPs^a of seven noncanonical psalms now lends importance to such heretofore overlooked "Davidic" literature. We are suddenly no longer satisfied to read the figure 150 back into Persian times as Frank Cross seemed willing to do when nine years ago he was writing his *Ancient Library of Qumran*.[6] On the contrary, we are now faced with an array of figures, all of which can be traced to at least the first century. Traditional Psalters contain 150 psalms; the Septuagint has 151; the oldest Syriac Psalter available (Mosul 1113) has 155; the Nestorian Patriarch Timotheus I, of the eighth century A.D., was told of manuscripts found in a cave south of Jericho containing over 200 psalms of David; and column XXVII of the Psalms Scroll gives the figure 4,050. Manifestly it is not a question of what the tenth-century King David wrote; that figure is unavailable. What is abundantly clear, however, is that even if there was a proto-Masoretic Psalter of 150 psalms *ne varientur* in hellenistic times, it did not particularly impress the sectarians at Qumran, who, it would appear, adhered to another Psalter tradition even as they adhered to another calendar tradition. Just as they did not devise their own

---

[3] Cf. Cross, "The History of the Biblical Text in the Light of Discoveries in the Judaean Desert," *Harvard Theological Review*, LXII (1964), pp. 281–299, which was based in part on D. Barthélemy's *Les Devanciers d'Aquila*, 1963 (an excellent review of which, by R. A. Kraft, is in *Gnomon*, XXXVII [1965], pp. 474–483). But see also P. W. Skehan, "The Biblical Scrolls from Qumran and the Text of the Old

Testament," *Biblical Archaeologist*, XXVIII (1965), pp. 87-100.

[4] Cf. S. Talmon, "Aspects of the Textual Transmission of the Bible in the Light of the Qumran Manuscripts," *Textus*, IV (1964), pp. 95–132.

[5] Strugnell, "More Psalms of 'David'," *Catholic Biblical Quarterly*, XXVII (1965), pp. 207–216.

[6] See above, p. 13.

calendar, neither did they devise their own Psalter out of a welter of traditional and nontraditional poems. They no more arranged their own private canon of Davidic literature than of Mosaic literature. We can be confident that they attributed to David what they collectively believed was Davidic. That their piety toward their Psalter tradition was sometimes superseded by their love and respect for David in not wanting to deny to him any psalm which he might have "spoken through prophecy," as the prose composition in the Psalms Scroll states, creates for us also the problem of the content of the Qumran Psalter, as distinct from the problem of the order of the canonical psalms in it. The last third of the Qumran Psalter indicates a still open-ended Psalter in the first century. It is safe to suggest that no Psalter text ever contained 4,050 psalms! What that and the other figures traceable to the first century indicate is what the similar statements at the end of the Gospel of John mean: the literature available and attributed to David carried with it the authority of his name, but beliefs about how much he wrote, just as beliefs about how many signs Jesus performed, prohibited, as yet, a rigidly closed canon.

What the Qumran Psalter literature indicates is that prior to the crisis of the First Jewish Revolt and the all-unifying conciliar decisions that it provoked, there was a Psalter textual tradition which exhibited the tension between a faithful piety toward the texts inherited and a pious faithfulness to the elastic memory of David, about whom it, too, could be said, "Were every one of them to be written, I suppose that the world itself could not contain the books that would be written" (John 21:25). The Psalter is distinct from the rest of the Hagiographa precisely because it bore the authority of the name David, comparable to the authority of the name Moses. But it is distinct from the Law and the Prophets, also, in that it was to a limited extent fluid and open-ended, at least in the text used at Qumran. The difference was perhaps somewhat the difference between the kinds of authority and loyalty which the names Moses and David elicited in the period in question: the one was the authority of Law, the other the authority of hope; the one represented God's theophany in the past, the other his theophany of the future, a future which in the Qumran period was believed imminent. David's name

both stabilized Psalter collections and prohibited a universal canon of Psalms *ne varietur*. The tragedy of the destruction of the Second Temple in the failure of the First Jewish Revolt put an end to the fluidity of the Psalter just as it eventually brought about a stabilization of the Hagiographa, the codification of Oral Law, the unification of Rabbinic Judaism, the writing of the Gospels, the eventual gathering and canonization of the New Testament, and the ultimate parting of the ways of Judaism and Christianity, the only two sects from Early Judaism to survive the tragedy.

Before A.D. 70, however, there was an open-ended Psalter tradition, independent of whatever proto-Masoretic Psalter existed before the end of the first century, which was both stable enough and fluid enough to satisfy the piety of those Jews who adhered to it. Such a state of affairs leaves wide open the question of the authority of variant readings. Each variant, as noted above in Part I, has to be carefully weighed on its own merits. The theory of the nineteenth-century scholar, Paul de Lagarde, is still valid: the route to the establishment of the best possible text of the Bible is eclectic, tedious, and difficult. It is in that mood that we turn now to consider the several substantive variants in fragment E (see above pp. 15–21).

The most interesting possibility of a variant in Psalm 118 occurs in verse 27 where the scroll appears to read, "The festal animals are bound with ropes, up to the horns of the altar" instead of "Bind the festal procession with branches, up to the horns of the altar." Medieval Rabbinic commentaries interpreted the verse to mean the binding of the festal victims, or sacrificial animals. Since, however, one cannot be absolutely certain that the scribe of our scroll always clearly distinguished between the Hebrew letters, *yod* and *waw*, the reading in the fragment is possibly Masoretic and not a variant at all.

The "Psalm of David" designation, which appears in the superscriptions of all other psalms where expected, fails in the scroll to appear at the beginning of Psalm 144 where the Masoretic text has it, but does appear at the top of Psalm 123 (see p. 20) and now on Psalm 104 in fragment E, where the Masoretic text does not include it.

The refrain familiar in Psalm 136 and reflected in 118 (see top of column XVI) is found also as a variant at the opening of Psalm 105 in fragment E: "O give thanks to the Lord, for he is good; for his steadfast love endures forever."

Other than those details which will interest scholars there are three variants in the fragment which exhibit substantive agreement with Septuagint readings. One of these we have already noted above: the "Psalm of David" superscription to Psalm 104 in the fragment is also in the Greek Psalter. Another occurs at the end of Psalm 147 where verse 20 reads, "He has not dealt thus with any other nation; he has not revealed any ordinances to them." The Masoretic text reads, "They do not know any ordinances." But the Septuagint reads, "He has not revealed his ordinances to them." The RSV translation as it now stands is only partially influenced by the Septuagint; any further revision should probably adopt the Greek reading in the light now of fragment E.

The third Septuagintal-type variant is perhaps the most interesting reading in the fragment. It supports the Septuagintal variant to the duplicate of Psalm 105 which occurs in I Chron. 16:10.

The Septuagint of Ps. 105:3 as it stands in the Psalter agrees with the Masoretic text, but the Septuagint of Ps. 105:3 as it stands in I Chron. 16:10 agrees with fragment E. The Masoretic text both in the Psalter and in Chronicles, as well as the Septuagint of the Psalter, read, "Let the hearts of those who seek the Lord rejoice." But the fragment and the Septuagint of Chronicles read, "Let the heart of him who seeks his favor rejoice." The meaning is not one whit changed. The importance of the variant lies not so much in how to read the text of Ps. 105:3, which should undoubtedly remain Masoretic, but rather in the emphasis such a reading brings to other Septuagintal interests in the scroll, especially to discussions of text traditions.

The introductory remarks at the beginning of Part II above are also pertinent here. The translation is that of the Revised Standard Version of the Bible except for the words and phrases in italics, which denote variants in the fragment and which are explained, in essence only, in the footnotes.

Fragment E i

Pss. 118:25–29; 104:1–6

Line

] (25)] הושיעה נא אנא 𐤉𐤄𐤅𐤄

] (26)]הבא בשם 𐤉𐤄𐤅𐤄 ברכנוכם ◦ ◦ ◦

]]𐤉𐤄𐤅𐤄 (27)אל 𐤉𐤄𐤅𐤄 ויאר לנו אסורי חג בעבותים

]]נות המזבח (28)אלי אתה ואודכה אלוהי ארוממכה

(29)]] ל֯𐤉𐤄𐤅𐤄 כי טוב כי לעולם חסדו

]] 104(1)לדויד ברכי נפשי

]]𐤉𐤄 אלוהינו גדלתה מואדה ה֯ו֯ד֯

] (2)]א֯ור כשלמה נוטה שמים כיריעה

(3)]] ה֯שם עבים רכובו המהלך על

] (4)]א[ ]ת֯יו אש לוהטת

(5)]]עד (6)ת֯ה֯ום

Fragment E 1

Pss. 118:25–29; 104:1–6

Line

[and be glad in it.] ⁽²⁵⁾Save us, [we beseech thee, O LORD!] O LORD, we beseech thee,   Ps. 118

[give us success! ⁽²⁶⁾Blessed be] he who enters in the name of the LORD! We bless you

[from the house of the L]ORD. ⁽²⁷⁾The LORD is God, and he has given us light.

ᵃThe festal animals are bound with ropes,ᵃ

[up to the hor]ns of the altar! ⁽²⁸⁾Thou art my God, and I will give thanks to thee; thou art my

God, I will extol thee

5   [⁽²⁹⁾O give thanks] to the LORD, for he is good; for his steadfast love endures for ever!

Of David.ᵇ Bless [the LORD,]   Ps. 104

O my soul! [O Lo]RD *ourᶜ* God, thou art very great! [Thou art

clothed with honor and majesty, ⁽²⁾who coverest thyself] with light as with a garment, who

stretched out the heavens like a tent,

[⁽³⁾who has laid the beams of *hisᵈ* chambers on the waters,] who makest the clouds *hisᵈ* chariot,

who ridest on

10   [the wings of the wind, ⁽⁴⁾who makest the winds *his* mess]en[gers,] *ᵉflaming fireᵉ hisᵈ* [ministe]rs.

[⁽⁵⁾Thou didst set the earth on its foundations, so that it should ne]ver [be shaken. ⁽⁶⁾Thou didst

cover it] with the deep

ᵃ⁻ᵃ Only in Q. RSV(MT) *Bind the festal procession with branches*
ᵇ Lacking in RSV(MT). Q = LXX, Lat
ᶜ Only in Q. RSV(MT) *my*
ᵈ RSV *thy*. Q = MT, LXX
ᵉ⁻ᵉ RSV *fire and flame*. Q = LXX, Lat (cf. MT)?

Fragment E II

Pss. 104:21–35, 147:1–2

(21)]]ף[ ] (22) [

השמש ויאספון ואל מעונותיהם [(23) [

לפועלו ולעבודתו עד ערב (24)מה רבו מעש[[

כולם בחוכמׄה עשיתה מלאה הארץ קנינכה (25)הים [ ]

ורחב ידים שמה רמש הרבה ואין למספר חיות קטנׄ[ ]

עם גדולות (26)שם אוניות יהלכון לויתן זה יצרתה לשחק

בו (27)כולם אליכה ישברו לתת להם אוכלם בעתו (28)תתן להם

וילקטון תפתח ידכה ישבעו טוב (29)תוסף רוחכה ויגועו

ואל עפרם ישובו (30)תשלח רוחכה ויבראון ותחדש פני

אדמה (31)ויהי כבוד 𐤉𐤄𐤅𐤄 לעולם ישמח 𐤉𐤄𐤅𐤄 במעשיו

(32)]בׄיט אל הארץ ותרעד יגע בהרים ויעשׁו (33)אשירה

[ ]𐤅𐤄 בחיי אזמרה לאלוהי בעודי (34)יערב עליו שיחי

[ ]𐤄𐤅𐤄 (35)כאשר יתמו חוטאים מארץ

[ ]רׄכׄיׄ נׄפׄשׄיׄ אׄת 𐤉𐤄𐤅𐤄 הללויה

vacat

147]]הלה (2)בונה ירושלים

Fragment E II

Pss. 104:21–35, 147:1–2

Line

[$^{(21)}$The young lions roar for their pre]y, [seeking their food from God.]   Ps. 104

$^{(22)a}$The sun [rises,] *and* they^a get them away and [lie down] in their dens. [$^{(23)}$Man goes forth]

to his work and to his labor until the evening. [$^{(24)}$O Lord,] how manifold are [thy] works!

In wisdom hast thou made them all; the earth is full of thy creatures. $^{(25)}$*The sea is* [*great*]^b

5   and wide, which teems with *many^c* things innumerable, living things both sma[ll]

and great. $^{(26)}$There go the ships, and Leviathan which thou didst form to sport

in it. $^{(27)}$These all look to thee, to give them^d their food in due season. $^{(28)e}$Thou givest to them,

and they^e gather it up; when thou openest thy hand, they are filled with good things. $^{(29)f}$ ^{g}Thou

takest away *thy^h* breath, *and* they^g die

and return to their dust. $^{(30)i}$Thou sendest forth thy spirit, *and* they^i are created; and thou renewest

the face

10   of the ground. $^{(31)}$*So* may the glory of the Lord endure for ever, may the Lord rejoice in his works,

[$^{(32)}$who looks] on the earth and it trembles, who touches the mountains and they smoke!

$^{(33)}$I will sing

[to the L]ord as long as I live; I will sing praise to my God while I have being. $^{(34)}$May my medi-

tation be pleasing to him,

[for I rejoice in the L]ord. $^{(35)}$ ^{j}*As* sinners *are^j* consumed from the earth,

[*so^j* let the wicked be no more! B]less the Lord, O my soul! Praise the Lord!

15   *vacat*

[Praise the Lord! For it is good to sing praises to our God; for he is gracious, and a   Ps. 147

s[ong of praise [is seemly.]

$^{(2)}$The Lord builds up Jerusalem;

$^{a-a}$ RSV (MT) *When the sun rises, they.* Q = LXX, Lat

^{b} Only in Q. RSV(MT) *Yonder is the sea, great*

^{c} Only in Q

^{d} Lacking in MT. Q = LXX^B, Lat (RSV)

$^{e-e}$ RSV(MT) *When thou givest to them, they.* Q = Syr

^{f} RSV(MT) *When thou hidest thy face, they are dismayed; when.* Lacking in Q

$^{g-g}$ RSV(MT) *when thou takest away their breath, they.* Q = LXX, Lat, Syr

^{h} Only in Q. RSV(MT) *their*

$^{i-i}$ RSV(MT) *When thou sendest forth thy spirit, they.* Q = LXX, Lat, Syr

$^{j-j}$ Only in Q. RSV(MT) *Let sinners be . . . , and*

Fragment E III

Pss. 147:18–20; 105: ?, 1–11

Line

(18)ישלח דברו]   (19)   [5

חוקיו ומשפטיו לֿ]   (20)   [

משפטים בל הודיעם]   [

105 הודו ל𐤉𐤄𐤅𐤄 כי טוב כי]   (1)   [

(2)   בשמו הודיעו בעמים עלי]   [

בכול נפלאותיו (3)התהללו בשם ק]   [10

רצונו (4)דרושו 𐤉𐤄𐤅𐤄 ועוזו בקשֿו]   (5)   [

נפלאותיו אשר עשה מופתיו ומשפט]   (6)   [

○○○○ עבדיו בני יעקוב בחירו (7)כי הוא]   [

משפטיו (8)זכר לעולם בריתו דבר צוה לאלף]   (9)   [

עם אברהם שבועתו לישחק (10)ויעמידה]   [15

לישראל ברית עולם (11)לאמור לכם אתן א]   [

ל] [[?

Fragment E III

Pss. 147:18–20, 105: ?, 1–11

Line

5 ⁽¹⁸⁾He sends forth his word, [and melts them; he makes his wind blow, and the waters Ps. 147
flow. ⁽¹⁹⁾He declares his word to Jacob,]

his statutes and ordinances to [Israel. ⁽²⁰⁾He has not dealt thus with any other nation;]

^a*he has not revealed any ordinances to them.*^a [Praise the Lord!]

^b*O give thanks to the* LORD, *for he is good; for* [*his steadfast love endures for ever!*^b ⁽¹⁾O   Ps. 105
give thanks to the LORD, call]

on his name, make known [his d]eeds among the peoples! [⁽²⁾Sing to him, sing praises to him, tell]

10 of all his wonderful works! ⁽³⁾Glory in [his h]oly name; [^c*let the heart of him who seeks*]

his favor^c rejoice! ⁽⁴⁾Seek the LORD and his strength, seek [his presence continually! ⁽⁵⁾Remember]

the wonderful works that he has done, his miracles, and the judgment[s he uttered, ⁽⁶⁾O offspring
of Abraham]

his servant*s*,^d sons of Jacob, his chosen one^e! ⁽⁷⁾*For*^f he is [our God^g;] his judgments are

[in all the earth.] ⁽⁸⁾He is mindful of his covenant for ever, of the word that he commanded, for a
thousand [generations, ⁽⁹⁾the covenant which he made]

15 with Abraham, his^h sworn promise to Isaac, ⁽¹⁰⁾which he confirmed [to Jacob as a statute,]

to Israel as an everlasting covenant, ⁽¹¹⁾saying, " To you I will give t[he land of Canaan as your
portion]

[for an inhe]ri[tance." . . .   ]

---

^{a–a} RSV *they do not know his ordinances.* MT *and they do not know any ordinances.* LXX *and he has not revealed his ordinances to them.* (Q approximates LXX)

^{b–b} Only in Q. See above xv 6, vi 1, 6 (Pss. 136:1; 118:1, 29)

^{c–c} Only in Q. RSV(MT) *let the hearts of those who seek the Lord.* Q = LXX I Chron. 16:10 (= Ps. 105:3)!

^d RSV(MT) *servant.* Q = LXX, Lat

^e RSV(MT) *chosen ones*

^f Only in Q

^g RSV(MT) *the* LORD *our God.* Q = MT? But see above, e.g., iii 6

^h MT, LXX, Lat, Syr *and his.* Q = RSV

INDEXES

GENERAL INDEX

INDEX TO THE SCROLL TEXT